An Ancient Rome Chronology, 264–27 B.C.

ALSO BY DAVID MATZ

Ancient World Lists and Numbers:
Numerical Phrases and Rosters in the Greco-Roman Civilizations
(McFarland, 1995)

Greek and Roman Sport: A Dictionary of Athletes and Events
from the Eighth Century B.C. to the Third Century A.D.
(McFarland, 1991)

An Ancient Rome Chronology, 264–27 B.C.

by DAVID MATZ

McFarland & Company, Inc., Publishers
Jefferson, North Carolina, and London

I would like to thank Professor James Ruebel, whose keen eye for historical detail saved me from several potentially embarrassing errors. Those flaws that may still lurk within these pages have survived only because my own ability to detect and correct them was insufficient.

British Library Cataloguing-in-Publication data are available

Library of Congress Cataloguing-in-Publication Data

Matz, David.
    An ancient Rome chronology, 264–27 B.C. / by David
Matz.
      p. cm.
    Includes bibliographical references and index.
    ISBN 0-7864-0161-3 (library binding : 50# alkaline paper) ∞
    1. Rome — History — 265–30 B.C. — Chronology. I. Title.
DG241.2.M38   1997
937'.04'0202 — dc21   96-46861
                                       CIP

Manufactured in the United States of America

McFarland & Company, Inc., Publishers
  Box 611, Jefferson, North Carolina 28640

To Betsy, Mike and my parents

Table of Contents

Introduction

If "history is just one damned thing after another," then the key to understanding history can be found in knowing the proper sequence of all those damned things. The purpose of this book is to provide a practical chronological survey of the final 237 years of the Roman republic.

The years 264 and 27 B.C. are two of the signal dates of Roman republican history, and it is partially for that reason that they have been selected as the *termini post et ante quem.* In many ways, 264 marked the emergence of Rome as a player on the international stage, with the eruption in that year of the first of three terrible conflicts which the Romans fought with Carthage. Also, the beginnings of reliable Roman history and historiography may be traced from 264; the further to the left one retreats on the time line, the murkier Roman history becomes.

The precise date of the collapse of the Roman republic is difficult to pinpoint; indeed, it was probably more a process or an evolution than a specific event occurring at an easily identifiable point in time. For the purposes of this book, however, 27 B.C. has been selected as the republic's endpoint, since that was the year in which Gaius Julius Caesar Octavianus solidified his hold on the government both practically and symbolically. In that year, his offer to resign his offices was rejected by the Roman senate; he therefore maintained his consular authority, and also his tribunician power, which theoretically gave him the right to veto the proposals of other officials in the government.

And on January 16 of that year, a military officer and former provincial governor named Lucius Munatius Plancus proposed that Octavianus be given the cognomen Augustus (the revered one). The Latin word *augustus* had a multiplicity of religious connotations, so its conferral upon Octavianus brought with it an aura of sanctity, if not near deification.

In any event, 264 and 27 seemed to be convenient starting and ending points for a chronological survey of the later Roman republic.

1

Organization of Material

Two formats (at least) are possible for a book of this nature: a strictly chronological presentation, in which all the principle events in a given year are listed. Or, a topical format, in which events are grouped into various categories, and then listed. The second of these has been employed in the book; the material has been divided into the following six categories:

Politics. Dates of political activities and proposals of individuals and groups (*e.g.,* the Roman senate) appear in this section of the book. Also, nonmilitary foreign affairs (*e.g.,* the founding of colonies) have been placed here.

Laws, Decrees, Speeches. This category includes the dates of the proposing and passing of specific legislation, and also senatorial decrees. Speeches made by noted politicians, and dates of celebrated court cases also may be found here.

Military Events. Included in this grouping are the dates of major battles, military maneuverings and deeds of individual commanders.

Literary Milestones. Significant dates in the lives and professional careers of Rome's *literati* are included in this category.

Art and Architecture. The dates of the construction of roads, bridges, aqueducts, temples and similar structures appear in this section, as well as the sculptures and paintings that adorned them.

Miscellaneous. As the heading implies, material which is not readily subsumed into any of the five previous categories has been included in the miscellaneous section. Dates of marriages, floods and fires, religious matters, sporting events and many other items may be found here.

An obvious problem with a topical format arises when one is confronted with deciding on the placement of an entry that might logically fall under two or even three of the categories listed above. For example, this entry —

81   Conveyed in Sulla's triumphal processions were 29,000 pounds of gold and 121,000 pounds of silver, the bounty from his various military victories.

— might logically be placed in the military category, since it contains information related to Sulla's battlefield exploits. Or, since triumphal processions were often used to make political statements, the entry could justifiably appear in the section pertaining to politics. However, because the content of the entry is only tangentially pertinent to either military affairs or politics, it has found its place among the miscellaneous listings.

These sorts of overlaps occur fairly often. In each such case, an effort has been made to assign a particular entry to the most logical category (in the author's opinion). In any case, the index assures access to all of the information herein regardless of its categorical assignment.

Some would undoubtedly argue that entries pertaining to speeches — especially those of Cicero — would more appropriately be placed under literature or politics rather than in a different category. The literary and political aspects of Ciceronian oratory are evident; however, the legal tone and content of the speeches more compellingly allies them with the *Laws, Decrees, Speeches* category.

Inclusion Criteria

Certain celebrated milestones — *e.g.,* the Battle of Cannae; Cato the Elder's consulship; Tiberius Gracchus' tribunate; Cicero's consulship; Caesar's crossing of the Rubicon; Caesar's assassination; the Battle of Actium, *etc.* — were obvious candidates for inclusion. Many of the other entries pertain to the activities of the leading figures of the later republic, or to the events for which they served as the catalysts. Still other entries will undoubtedly appear to be idiosyncratic. They were selected primarily because of their intrinsic appeal, even if (in some cases) their impact on the long course of Roman republican history is not immediately apparent.

Some categories (*e.g., Politics* and *Military Events*) contain far more entries than others (*e.g., Literary Milestones*). There was no conscious effort to create such an imbalance; it is merely reflective of the apparently greater fondness of the Romans for campaigning, both military and political, than for producing works of literature.

Similarly, the preponderance of entries pertaining to events of the first century B.C. exists because that time period is more fully and reliably documented than earlier centuries. Hence, the complex political and military situation of the final decades of the republic inevitably produced far more grist for the chronological mill than did the preceding time periods.

A Note on the Accuracy of Dates

The chronology of the later Roman republic is fairly well established; nevertheless, the passage of two millennia inevitably raises difficulties in the matter of exact dating. Even a presumably obvious point on the timeline like the birthdate of Julius Caesar arouses scholarly debate, with some favoring 102 B.C., others 100. In all controversial or uncertain cases, the consensus view, as closely as it can be determined, has been recorded in this book. These dates have been gathered primarily from the modern annotations of ancient texts, from reference works of high repute, notably the *Oxford Classical Dictionary*, and from the books highlighted in the following bibliographical survey.

An attempt has been made to eschew the *circa* designation wherever possible; for some entries it has, however, been employed, albeit reluctantly.

Bibliographical Survey

As mentioned above, the *Oxford Classical Dictionary* is an indispensable source for dates and other information. The relevant volumes of the *Cambridge Ancient History* offer almost equally useful material. Broughton's *The Magistrates of the Roman Republic* is another invaluable resource.

The Loeb series of translations of classical authors once again proved to be a superb resource, a *sine qua non* for anyone wishing to acquire an understanding of ancient history and literature. The introductory essays and annotations to be found within the pages of a typical Loeb volume are nearly as essential as the translation itself. The most frequently consulted authors in the Loeb series include Appian, Cicero, Dio Cassius, Livy, Pliny the Elder, Plutarch and Velleius Paterculus.

Several works of contemporary scholars should be noted for their contributions to the present book. H. H. Scullard's *From the Gracchi to Nero* offers a sober, sophisticated and yet highly readable survey of the tumultuous final years of the Roman republic. M. Cary's *History of Rome*, while perhaps somewhat outdated, remains an erudite, exhaustive and informative resource. *Life and Leisure in Ancient Rome*, by J.P.V.D. Balsdon, is an excellent social history, particularly valuable for its copious endnotes. For analytical brilliance, coupled with meticulous attention to factual detail, it would be difficult to name a more impressive volume than Erich Gruen's *The Last Generation of the Roman Republic*.

Some Notes on Names

Augustus: Prior to Julius Caesar's official (though posthumous) adoption of his grandnephew, the young man's name was Gaius Octavius. By the terms of that adoption (in 44) he acquired the full name of his adoptive father, with his original *nomen* retained, in slightly altered form, as an *agnomen*: Gaius Julius Caesar Octavianus, or Octavian. In 27, he was given the honorary title Augustus, by which he is probably best known to the contemporary world. If historical exactitude is a desideratum, then all references to this individual prior to his adoption should be under the name "Octavius"; between 44 and 27, he should be called "Octavian"; after 27, the name "Augustus" should be employed.

However, clarity often has an equal or greater claim on an author's selection of terminology, and such is the case here, where the name "Octavian" has been used throughout this book.

Antony/Antonius: All holders of the nomen Antonius are so identified, except for the triumvir; he is referred to as Mark Antony (Roman name: Marcus Antonius).

Pompey/Pompeius: References to Gnaeus Pompeius Magnus — Pompey the Great — display the anglicized form of the name: Pompey. His son, however, is identified as Sextus Pompeius.

Orthographic Considerations

Spelling used in the current volume	Variant spelling, employed in some other sources
Aquillius	Aquilius
Dyrrhachium	Dyrrachium
Mithridates	Mithradates
Messalla	Messala
Paullus	Paulus
Pompillius	Pompilius
Vergil	Virgil

A Note on Abbreviations

Source citations are to author's names only (both ancient and modern). The one exception is GN, which refers to *From the Gracchi to Nero*, by H. H. Scullard. Full listings for modern authors may be found in the bibliography. Abbreviations employed include the following:

CAH = Cambridge Ancient History
LCL = Loeb Classical Library
MRR = The Magistrates of the Roman Republic
OCD = Oxford Classical Dictionary (second edition)

In cases where information was drawn from an essay or an annotation in the Loeb series, the citation appears as in this example:

Rolfe LCL Suetonius *Augustus* 250

where Rolfe is the last name of the translator, followed by LCL, the ancient author's name and title of work (if necessary), and finally the Loeb volume page number.

References to the *Cambridge Ancient History* utilize this format:

CAH IX 251

where the Roman numeral refers to the volume number, and the Arabic numeral to the page number.

The locution "*s.v.*" means "(see) under the word —."

1. Politics

253   Tiberius Coruncanius was elected pontifex maximus, the first plebeian to hold that office. (OCD *s.v.* Coruncanius [1])

245   According to Velleius Paterculus (1.14), a Roman colony was established in Brundisium in this year.

242   A new office was created, that of praetor peregrinus. The praetor peregrinus was responsible for mediating lawsuits in which one or both litigants were foreigners. (OCD *s.v.* praetor)

241   The number of Roman tribes (traditional groupings of the populace for voting and public policy decisions) was set at 35. (OCD *s.v.* Tribus)

231   The Romans sent envoys to Massilia, to negotiate with the Carthaginian leader Hamilcar, and to determine the intentions of the Carthaginians stationed in Spain. Hamilcar told the delegation that the Carthaginians were merely attempting to raise money to pay the indemnity that the Romans demanded of them after the First Punic War. (CAH VIII 27)

227   Sicily and Sardinia became Roman provinces. Gaius Flaminius became the first Roman governor of Sicily. (OCD *s.v.* Flaminius [2]; *s.v.* Sicily)

227   The number of praetors was increased from two to four. In 197, two more were added, bringing the total to six. (OCD *s.v.* praetor)

226   The Romans sent a diplomatic delegation to the Carthaginian commander Hasdrubal, then in Spain. He agreed not to extend the Carthaginian sphere of influence beyond the Ebro River, in southeastern Spain. (OCD *s.v.* Hasdrubal [1])

218   Cremona, a prosperous Latin colony in northern Italy, was founded. (OCD *s.v.* Cremona)

217   Quintus Fabius Maximus was appointed dictator; his prime responsibility was to develop a strategy to thwart Hannibal's movements in Italy. (OCD *s.v.* Fabius [5])

216   The consul Marcus Terentius Varro appointed Marcus Fabius Buteo dictator, an unusual move in that Quintus Fabius Maximus already held the office. A dual dictatorship was unprecedented; Buteo's appointment, however, was apparently ad hoc, for the sole purpose of co-opting new senators. After he completed that task, he resigned. (Livy 23.23)

216   The Roman senate's numbers had been decreased by natural deaths and by Punic War casualties. Several proposals were offered for remedying the situation. The solution of choice: the dictator Marcus Fabius Buteo chose men who had held public offices but had not yet been appointed to the senate; and then, men who had never held office, but who had distinguished themselves in battle by taking spoils from the enemy or by earning the civic crown. In this way, 170 new members were enrolled in the senate. (Livy 23.23)

215   Tiberius Sempronius Gracchus and Lucius Postumius Albinus had been elected consuls for this year; Postumius, however, lost his life in battle early in the year, so a special election was held to select his replacement. The successful candidate, Marcus Claudius Marcellus, was not permitted to enter office, because of unpropitious omens: had Marcellus become consul, it would have marked the first time in Roman history that two plebeians held the office.

    Marcellus resigned, and was superseded by Quintus Fabius Maximus Cunctator. (Livy 23.31)

214   Quintus Fabius Maximus became consul for the second consecutive year, an occurrence apparently without precedent. His colleague, Marcus Claudius Marcellus, would also have been serving his second consecutive term, except that he had resigned the consulship to which he had been elected in 215. (See entry above; Livy 24.9)

214   Publius Cornelius Scipio was elected aedile, although he was only

22 years old at the time. The tribunes opposed his candidacy (because of his age); however, he appealed directly to the voters, who supported him so enthusiastically that the tribunes withdrew their objections. (Livy 25.2)

214   The censors Marcus Atilius Regulus and Publius Furius Philus prosecuted and degraded in rank numerous men who had plotted to abandon Rome after the Battle of Cannae. Similar action was taken against those of draft age who had not served in the army. (Livy 24.18)

213   Rarely in Roman history did brothers hold the same magistracy concurrently, but such a coincidence reputedly happened in 213, when Publius and Marcus Cornelius Scipio both served as aediles. (Shipley LCL Velleius Paterculus 66)

212   An electoral upset: Publius Licinius Crassus defeated two older and more distinguished candidates for the office of pontifex maximus. Crassus' two opponents — Quintus Fulvius Flaccus and Titus Manlius Torquatus — had both held the consulship and the censorship. According to Livy (25.5), over the course of the next 120 years, only one other man would be elected pontifex maximus who had never held any important prior office.

206   Publius Cornelius Scipio returned to Rome from Spain in this year; the numerous soldiers whom he left in Spain founded the town of Italica, future hometown of the emperors Trajan and Hadrian. (Balsdon 240)

204   One of Cato the Elder's first public conflicts with the Scipio family occurred in this year, when he was sent to Sicily to serve as Publius Cornelius Scipio's (later Africanus) quaestor. Cato objected to the lavish way in which Scipio spent money, both on himself and on the soldiers. (Plutarch *Cato the Elder* 3)

203   King Syphax of Numidia was imprisoned in an underground chamber in the Roman colony of Alba Fucens (about 50 miles east of Rome). Other noted prisoners held here: King Perseus in 167, and the Gallic chieftain Bituitus in 121. (MacKendrick 101)

199   Titus Quinctius Flamininus announced his candidacy for the consulship, a move opposed by the tribunes Marcus Fulvius and Manius Curius, on the grounds that Flamininus had not held

the customarily prerequisite offices of aedile and praetor. The matter was ultimately referred to the senate, which ruled in Flamininus' favor. Hence, he proceeded with his candidacy, and gained election to the consulship for 198. (Livy 32.7)

198   Cato the Elder governed Sardinia in an honest and parsimonious manner, thus earning the gratitude of the local populace. (Plutarch *Cato the Elder* 6)

197   Two new Spanish provinces were created: Hispania Citerior (nearer Spain), and Hispania Ulterior (farther Spain). (OCD *s.v.* Spain)

197   The establishment of a number of new colonies was authorized: five on the Italian seacoast; two at the mouths of the Vulturnus and Liternus Rivers; one at Puteoli; another at Castrum Salerni; and one at Buxentum. Three hundred families were sent to each of these colonies. (Livy 32.29)

196   The northern Italian city of Comum — birthplace of both Plinys — came under Roman control. (OCD *s.v.* Comum)

196   Hannibal assumed control of the Carthaginian government, charged with the responsibility of putting an end to the widespread corruption prevalent in Carthaginian politics directly after the close of the Second Punic War. (OCD *s.v.* Hannibal)

195   Cato the Elder held the consulship. As a portent of his actions as censor (in 184), he opposed a repeal of the Oppian Law (a sumptuary measure). (OCD *s.v.* Cato [1])

195   The residents of the Italian town of Ferentinum, a Roman colony, applied for Roman citizenship, on the ground that their tenancy of a Roman colony should validate their request. However, the senate refused to grant approval to their application. (Livy 34.42)

194   The town of Puteoli (near Naples) became a Roman colony. In later times, it acquired a reputation as an upscale retreat for wealthy Romans, including Sulla and Cicero. (OCD *s.v.* Puteoli)

193   Lucius Aemilius Paullus was elected aedile over a strong field of 12 other candidates, all of whom eventually held the consulship. This was Paullus' first elective office. (Plutarch *Aemilius Paullus* 3)

190   Manius Acilius Glabrio declined to run for the censorship, after

his credibility was hurt by a charge of financial dishonesty brought against him by Cato the Elder. (CAH VIII 370–371)

189   The political influence of the Aetolian Confederacy came to an end, when the Romans absorbed confederation members as subject allies. (OCD *s.v.* Aetolian Confederacy)

189   Cato the Elder denigrated one of the consuls for 189, Marcus Fulvius Nobilior, for awarding honorary crowns to soldiers for performing even the most mundane tasks, such as building walls or digging wells. (Aulus Gellius 5.6)

189   Publius Cornelius Scipio Africanus was selected as princeps senatus for the third time. (Livy 38.28)

188   Residents of the towns of Fundi, Formiae and Arpinum (the latter the birthplace of Marius and Cicero) were all granted Roman citizenship. (CAH VIII 354)

187   Two tribunes requested Lucius Cornelius Scipio (Asiagenus) to explain his disposition of 500 talents which he had received from King Antiochus III after the Battle of Magnesia. Scipio defied the request. (CAH VIII 371)

185   Patrician candidates for the consulship included Lucius Aemilius, Quintus Fabius and Servius Sulpicius Galba. All were (in Livy's words) *veteres candidati*, "veteran candidates," *i.e.* all had lost in previous tries for the office. Their track record remained intact in 185: Publius Claudius Pulcher won, in his first consular campaign. (Livy 39.32)

184   Cato the Elder held the office of censor, in which he promulgated a number of unpopular reforms, including crackdowns on citizens who stole water from the aqueducts, significantly higher taxes on luxury goods, and higher rental rates for public lands. During his campaign for the office (in the previous year), the senatorial establishment was so concerned over the prospect of Cato's election that they recruited seven candidates to run against him. However, he defeated them all; he and his mentor Lucius Valerius Flaccus were elected. (Plutarch *Cato the Elder* 16; OCD *s.v.* Cato [1])

184   As censor, Cato expelled from the senate a man of high repute named Manilius, merely because Manilius had embraced his wife

during the day, with their daughter looking on. (While this public display of affection seems innocuous enough, the Greek verb *periplakenai*— rendered as "embrace" by most translators — can also refer to a more intimate spousal activity.) (Plutarch *Cato the Elder* 17)

184   The censors Cato the Elder and Lucius Valerius Flaccus removed seven men from the senate, including Lucius Quinctius Flamininus, an ex-consul (192) and older brother of the prestigious Titus Quinctius Flamininus. (Livy 39.42)

183   The Romans established a colony at Mutina (in Cisalpine Gaul), a town of some commercial and strategic importance. (OCD *s.v.* Mutina)

179   This was the only year in Roman history in which brothers held the consulship concurrently: the sons of Quintus Fulvius Flaccus and Lucius Manlius Acidinus Fulvianus. (Velleius Paterculus 2.8)

179   Marcus Aemilius Lepidus assumed concurrently the censorship and the post of princeps senatus. He held the latter until his death in 152. (OCD *s.v.* Lepidus [1])

178   The senate sent a letter to the Rhodians, who were then abusing and harassing the people of Lycia, that they should relent or face the unpleasant prospect of Roman intervention. (Livy 41.6)

177   It had become customary by this time for the Romans to share war spoils equally with their Latin allies. However, this practice was not observed in the distributions of booty following the Istrian and Ligurian campaigns of 177. The allies' resentment was obvious as they paraded in the triumphal procession: *taciti ut iratos esse sentires*, "They were quiet; you could tell that they were annoyed." (Livy 41.13)

174   The harsh censorship of Quintus Fulvius Flaccus and Aulus Postumius Albinus occurred in this year. Among other deeds, they expelled from the senate nine men, including two of praetorian rank: Marcus Cornelius Maluginensis and Lucius Cornelius Scipio. Lucius (or Gnaeus, according to Velleius Paterculus) Fulvius Flaccus, Quintus' brother, was also expelled. (Livy 41.27)

173   The consul Lucius Postumius Albinus visited the town of Praeneste,

where he created a scandal by demanding free lodging, entertainment and other perquisites. (Magistrates normally received per diem allowances from the senate to cover such costs; "double-dipping" à la Postumius was considered unethical.) (Livy 42.1)

173   The senate displayed nearly boundless generosity to Apollonius, an ambassador representing King Antiochus IV (Epiphanes), when he visited Rome in this year. He was given a gift of 100,000 *asses*, a house to use while in Rome, and an unlimited expense account. (Livy 47.6)

172   The consuls Gaius Popillius Laenas and Publius Aelius Ligus took office. This was apparently the first year in which both consuls were plebeians. (Livy 42.9; Sage/Schlesinger LCL Livy [Vol. XII] 317)

172   Measures were taken to ensure that public lands in Campania were accurately surveyed and zoned, and that appropriately legal leases were issued. (Livy 42.19)

172   An embassy of Carthaginians appeared before the senate, to request a resolution of boundary disputes between Carthage and the Numidians. The Carthaginians were prohibited (by the terms of the treaty ending the Second Punic War) from waging war beyond their boundaries, or against Roman allies. (Livy 42.23)

171   The consul Publius Licinius Crassus and the praetor Gaius Lucretius Gallus used their power to expropriate 150,000 bushels of corn from Athens. Lucretius was later tried and convicted for his treatment of the Athenians. (CAH VIII 293)

169   Marcus Aemilius Lepidus was selected as princeps senatus for the third time, a signal honor. (Livy 43.15)

169   The severely anti-equestrian measures of the censors Tiberius Sempronius Gracchus and Gaius Claudius Pulcher resulted in an effort to overturn their enactments regarding public works and tax farming. The tribune Publius Rutilius was the leader of the opposition. The censors, however, prevailed. (Livy 43.16) After Rutilius left office, the censors avenged themselves by degrading him from equestrian status and disenfranchising him. (Livy 44.16)

168   When the censors Gracchus and Claudius proposed a lengthening of their terms of office (so that they could complete various public works projects which they had begun), a tribune named Gnaeus Tremellius vetoed their initiative, apparently at least partially out of spite; these censors had failed to enroll him in the senate. (Livy 45.15)

A few years later, in 159, Tremellius (as praetor) opposed the pontifex maximus Marcus Aemilius Lepidus on some unspecified matter; he was unsuccessful, and suffered the imposition of a fine.

167   Direct taxation (*tributum*) of Roman citizens was permanently ended. (OCD *s.v.* tributum)

167   Prusias II, king of Bithynia, won for himself the disrespect of the Romans, by his obsequious behavior. When he met with the senators in Rome in this year, he referred to them as gods and saviors. He then delivered a speech characterized by servility and flattery. (Diodorus Siculus 31.3)

167   A warmongering praetor named Manius Juventius Thalna tried to persuade the Comitia Centuriata to declare war on Rhodes without consulting the senate. The effort was vetoed by two tribunes, and hence quashed. (Cary 295)

164   The censorship of Lucius Aemilius Paullus, in which 337,452 Roman citizens were registered. (Plutarch *Aemilius Paullus* 38)

162   Gnaeus Octavius (praetor 168; consul 165), according to Cicero the first man in the Octavian gens to attain high office, was murdered in Laodicea; he had traveled there on an embassy whose mission was to enforce treaty agreements with the Syrian King Antiochus Eupater. (OCD *s.v.* Octavius [1])

159   Marcus Aemilius Lepidus was selected for a fifth five-year term as princeps senatus. He was chosen for a sixth term in 154, but died (152) before completing it. (Livy *Epitome* 47; OCD *s.v.* Lepidus [1])

155   When the noted Greek philosophers Carneades, Diogenes and Critolaus addressed the Roman senate, Gaius Acilius served as their interpreter. Acilius was also the author of a history of Rome, now lost. (OCD *s.v.* Acilius [4])

c.152   Corduba, a city in central Spain, was reconstituted as a Roman colony, an important initial step in the Romanization of Spain. (OCD *s.v.* Corduba)

c.150   The octogenarian Cato the Elder, still active in politics, visited Carthage. He was astonished at the comeback which the city had made from its disastrous defeat at the hands of the Romans, some 50 years before. When Cato returned to Rome, he urged the complete destruction of Carthage, a deed which was carried out in 146. (Plutarch *Cato the Elder* 26, 27)

149   Servius Sulpicius Galba, an ex-praetor, was prosecuted for provincial rapacity while serving in Spain. He managed to gain an acquittal by parading his weeping family members before the tribunal at his trial. (OCD *s.v.* Galba [3])

148   Publius Cornelius Scipio Aemilianus divided Numidia, the kingdom of Masinissa (d. 148) among his three sons, Micipsa, Gulussa and Mastanabal. (Livy *Epitome* 50)

148   Scipio Aemilianus ran for the aedileship, but instead was elected consul, although he was too young and had not held any prerequisite office. After much debate over the propriety of his assuming the consulship, his election was ultimately sanctioned. (OCD *s.v.* Scipio [11])

146   Macedonia became a Roman province. (OCD *s.v.* Macedonia)

146   A difficult year for the praetor Gaius Plautius; he was soundly defeated in battle by Viriathus in Spain, and then, upon his return to Rome, he was prosecuted for dereliction of duty. He subsequently went into exile. (Diodorus Siculus 33.2)

146   Ten respected senators arrived in Africa to aid Scipio Aemilianus in his efforts at organizing the province. (MRR I 468)

144   The third try for the consulship was a charm for Quintus Caecilius Metellus Macedonicus. He won the office on his third attempt, after having lost in two previous elections. (Livy *Epitome* 51; OCD *s.v.* Metellus [3])

142   According to Aulus Gellius (2.7), three prime examples of corrupt and avaricious public officials would be Clodius, Catiline, and one of the praetors in 142: Lucius Hostilius Tubulus, a bribe-taker.

141   The consulship of Quintus Pompeius, a distant relative of Pompey the Great, and the first of his family to hold the office of consul. (Velleius Paterculus 2.1)

c.140   Publius Cornelius Scipio Aemilianus and a group of Roman ambassadors arrived in Alexandria, where they were lavishly entertained by King Ptolemy VIII. The ambassadors later visited Cyprus and Syria, where they also received warm welcomes. (Diodorus Siculus 33.28b)

137   As quaestor, Tiberius Sempronius Gracchus was assigned to serve in Spain, under the consul Hostilius Mancinus. While en route to his post, he observed that slave labor had displaced small-scale free landholders. This experience reputedly motivated him to propose some controversial land reform measures a few years later, during his tribunate (133). (Plutarch *Tiberius Gracchus* 5, 8)

133   The tribunate of Tiberius Sempronius Gracchus, in which he promulgated some highly controversial land reform proposals, including the enforcement of an old law limiting landholders to 500 *iugera* (about 310 acres).

133   The tribune Marcus Octavius was impeached by a vote of the Tribal Assembly, for refusing to withdraw his veto of Tiberius Gracchus' land reform legislation. (Plutarch *Tiberius Gracchus* 12)

133   King Attalus III of Pergamum died, having willed his kingdom to the Roman people; Pergamum subsequently became Rome's first Asian province. (OCD *s.v.* Attalus III)

133   The pontifex maximus, Publius Cornelius Scipio Nasica Serapio, headed a band of senators who commenced the fatal attack on Tiberius Gracchus. Ironically, Scipio Nasica and Gracchus were cousins. (Plutarch *Tiberius Gracchus* 19)

131   A turbulent year for the censor Quintus Metellus Macedonicus (who had led the Romans to victory in the Fourth Macedonian War): he attempted to pare from the senate's rolls a tribune named Gaius Atinius Labeo Macerio. So incensed was Atinius that he dragged Metellus toward the Tarpeian Rock, intending to hurl him over the edge. Fortunately for Metellus, several other tribunes intervened to save his life.

    He also made a speech in this year, *De Prole Augenda* (*On*

Increasing Offspring), in which he touted enforced marriages as a necessary albeit unpleasant means for stimulating the birth rate. (OCD *s.v.* Metellus [3])

131   The tribunate of Gaius Papirius Carbo, who carried a measure authorizing the use of secret ballots at legislative assemblies. (OCD *s.v.* Carbo [1])

131   The censorship was held by two plebeians for the first time: Quintus Pompeius and Quintus Caecilius Metellus Macedonicus. (OCD *s.v.* Pompeius [1])

*c.*128   The colony of Auximum (south central Italy) was founded, and soon became a flourishing community. (OCD *s.v.* Auximum)

125   Marcus Fulvius Flaccus proposed the extension of Roman citizenship to the northern Italians. In 122, he held the tribunate, with a view toward collaborating with Gaius Gracchus on the enfranchisement scheme. (OCD *s.v.* Flaccus [3])

125   Flaccus (see above) was conveniently removed from the political scene when the Roman senate packed him off to Massilia (MRR I 510), to assist in quelling some disturbances in the area.

125   One of the augurs, Marcus Aemilius Lepidus Porcina, was publicly censured for renting a house for 1,500 denarii per year, a sum apparently considered extravagant, and not in keeping with priestly dignity. (Velleius Paterculus 2.10)

124   When Gaius Sextius Calvinus, consul in this year, was in the process of selling some defeated Gauls as slaves, a certain captive named Crato approached him and told him that he had always supported the Roman cause. His arguments persuaded Calvinus to release him and 900 others. (Diodorus Siculus 34.23)

123–   The tribunates of Gaius Sempronius Gracchus (the brother of
122   Tiberius), who proposed a number of land, legal and foreign policy reforms. The unrest which these proposals engendered resulted in the Roman senate's first-ever proclamation of the *senatus consultum ultimum*, a declaration of martial law. These events culminated in the violent death of Gracchus in 121. (OCD *s.v.* senatus consultum ultimum)

122   The Romans founded the colony of Aquae Sextiae (in Gaul). The place was noted for its mineral waters (hence the name "Aquae";

Sextiae derived from the founder's name, Gaius Sextius). Aquae Sextiae was also the site of Gaius Marius' victory over the Teutones in 102. (Livy *Epitome* 61; Harper's *s.v.* Aquae Sextiae)

122   The tribune Marcus Livius Drusus prevented the implementation of Gaius Gracchus' plan to confer citizenship on Rome's Italian allies. He also proposed the founding of colonies, and the granting of some minor privileges to the allies, to assuage their anticipated resentment over his opposition to their enfranchisement bid. (OCD *s.v.* Drusus [1])

121   The ex-consul (125) Marcus Fulvius Flaccus, a supporter of Gaius Gracchus, was killed in the rioting that erupted in Rome in this year. Flaccus' 18-year-old son was also executed, by a decree of the consuls. (OCD *s.v.* Flaccus [3])

c.119 The formal dissolution of the commission created during the Gracchan period to oversee land reform and redistribution occurred around this time. (CAH IX 99)

118   The Romans founded Narbo (southern Gaul) as a colony, one of their first colonies outside Italy. While this sort of colonization (*i.e.* extra–Italian) was relatively common by Caesar's time, it was rare in the second century. (CAH IX 463)

118   Micipsa, king of Numidia, died; he left his kingdom to his two sons Adherbal and Hiempsal, and his adopted son, the protracted nemesis of the Romans, Jugurtha. (Livy *Epitome* 62)

115   Gaius Marius won the praetorship for this year, despite having gained the fewest votes of the elected candidates. He was charged with electoral bribery and barely acquitted. (OCD *s.v.* Marius [1])

115   The censors Lucius Caecilius Metellus Delmaticus and Gnaeus Domitius Ahenobarbus expelled from the Roman senate 32 of its members. (Livy *Epitome* 62)

115   The consulship of Marcus Aemilius Scaurus, who rose to the post despite his family's heretofore undistinguished background. He also served as princeps senatus. (OCD *s.v.* Scaurus [1])

109   One of the tribunes, Gaius Mamilius Limetanus, was instrumental in establishing a commission to investigate official misconduct in Roman dealings with Jugurtha. He was also associated

with regulations on property lines; hence, the name *Limetanus*, "Boundary-man." (OCD *s.v.* Mamilius [3])

107   Quintus Lutatius Catulus made his first unsuccessful try for the consulship. He was defeated again in 106 and in 105, before finally succeeding on his fourth attempt, in 103. (MacDonald LCL *Pro Murena* 234; OCD *s.v.* Catulus [1])

104   In this year, Gaius Marius held the first of his five consecutive consulships (seven in all). He was re-elected for 103 *in absentia*. (MRR I 558; Plutarch *Marius* 14)

103   Lucius Appuleius Saturninus, a Gracchan-style social reformer, became tribune for the first time. He held the office again in 100, when he was killed in a riot. (OCD *s.v.* Saturninus [1])

102   The censor Quintus Caecilius Metellus Numidicus attempted to forbid the former tribunes Saturninus and Gaius Servilius Glaucia from enrollment in the senate. His efforts resulted in a riot, which forced him to abandon the plan. (Scullard GN 57.)

102   The ever-persistent Quintus Lutatius Catulus finally assumed the consulship. He had been defeated in three prior attempts to gain election to the office. (OCD *s.v.* Catulus)

c.102   Cilicia was annexed as a province. (OCD *s.v.* Cilicia)

100   Quintus Caecilius Metellus Numidicus (consul in 109, censor in 102) was banished from Rome because he refused to swear an oath in support of the land redistribution laws promulgated by the tribune Saturninus. He was the only senator who would not take the oath. He subsequently went into voluntary exile to Rhodes, where he attended lectures and studied philosophy. (Livy *Epitome* 69; OCD *s.v.* Metellus [6])

100   The Romans established a colony at Eporedia, in northwestern Cisalpine Gaul. (OCD *s.v.* Eporedia)

97   The censor Marcus Antonius (grandfather of Mark Antony) conferred citizenship upon a number of Italians, a controversial precedent which was negated two years later by the consuls for 95. (OCD *s.v.* Antonius [1])

96   King Ptolemy Apion bequeathed Cyrenaica (in north Africa) to Rome. The Romans accepted the bequest, but allowed the city

of Cyrene to retain its independence. (Livy *Epitome* 70; OCD *s.v.* Cyrene)

95   Ariobarzanes I, a Cappadocian king whose career, in the words of the *Oxford Classical Dictionary* "consist[ed] almost entirely of a series of expulsions and restorations":

    95   Became king of Cappadocia with Sulla's assistance.
    93   Expelled, by Tigranes of Armenia.
    89   Restored, by Manius Aquillius.
    88   Expelled.
    85   Restored, by Gaius Scribonius Curio.
    78   Expelled, again by Tigranes.
    66   Restored, by Pompey.

*c.*95   Gaius Norbanus (tribune 103) was tried for treason in this year. He was successfully defended by Mark Antony's grandfather, Marcus Antonius. (OCD *s.v.* Norbanus)

94   Gaius Coelius Caldus, a *novus homo*, was elected consul for this year, although he ran against two opponents whose wealth and connections were far superior to his own. (Q. Cicero [?] *Handbook of Electioneering* 11)

94   A major upset occurred in the consular elections for 93: Marcus Herennius, a relative unknown, defeated the far more prominent Lucius Marcius Philippus. (Philippus was successful in a bid two years later.) (Cicero *Pro Murena* 36; OCD *s.v.* Philippus [4])

*c.*94   Publius Rutilius Rufus assisted the consul Quintus Mucius Scaevola in organizing the province of Asia. Although effective and conscientious in the discharge of his duties, he was later accused of extortion, convicted, and exiled to Smyrna, in 92. (OCD *s.v.* Rutilius [1])

92–
88   The unusually long governorship of Macedonia, by Gaius Sentius. Most governors held their posts for two years at most. A century earlier, Titus Quinctius Flamininus had done a four-year stint as the governor of Macedonia, from 197 to 194. (MRR I 18ff; 334ff)

91   The tribune Marcus Livius Drusus attempted — unsuccessfully — to secure citizenship for Rome's Italian allies. He also proposed adding 300 equestrian members to the senate, thus doubling its size. Additionally, he suggested resettling poor citizens in colonies. (OCD *s.v.* Drusus [2])

91   *Similem mei civem habebit res publica?* "Will the republic [ever again] have a citizen like me?" According to Velleius Paterculus, these were the last words spoken by Marcus Livius Drusus, the tribune, who was assassinated while walking home from the forum.

90   The south central Italian city of Corfinium was selected by rebellious Italians as the capital of their confederacy. (OCD *s.v.* Corfinium)

89   The praetor Aulus Sempronius Asellio was murdered by disgruntled creditors, because of his failure to assist them in recovering their loans with the interest which was due. He was killed in the midst of a religious ceremony, while offering sacrifices to Castor and Pollux. (Appian *Civil Wars* 1.54; Livy *Epitome* 74)

88   Gaius Julius Caesar Strabo ran for the consulship, later called an illegal candidacy by Cicero, since Strabo had not yet held the prerequisite office of praetor. (Cicero *On the Response of the Soothsayers* 43; Watts LCL Cicero *Soothsayers* 374)

88   The tribune Publius Sulpicius Rufus sponsored several controversial measures, including the expulsion from the Roman senate of any member who was more than 2,000 denarii in debt. He also proposed transferring the command against King Mithridates from Sulla to Marius. (OCD *s.v.* Sulpicius [1])

88   When Sulla took possession of Rome, one of his first acts was to pass a formal declaration of exile against his leading opponents, including Gaius Marius and Publius Sulpicius Rufus. The latter was slain as he fled Rome; his severed head was then displayed in Rome, a portent of the Sullan proscription. (Velleius Paterculus 2.19)

*c.*88   Quintus Sertorius was defeated in an election bid for the tribunate. His failure was due in some measure to Sulla's opposition, one of the factors leading to Sertorius' Marian sympathies, and ultimately his insurrection in Spain. (Plutarch *Sertorius* 4; Gruen 17)

87   Lucius Cornelius Merula, flamen Dialis (priest of Jupiter), was granted a titular consulship to replace the deposed Lucius Cornelius Cinna. When Cinna returned to reclaim the post, Merula committed suicide. (OCD *s.v.* Merula)

87–   The years of the *dominatio Cinnae*, in which Cornelius Cinna held
84   successive, self-appointed consulships, and ruled Rome as a mil-
      itary dictator. (OCD *s.v.* Cinna [1])

86   On the very first day (January 1) of Marius' consulship, he ordered
      a senator named Sextus Licinius (or Lucinus) to be cast from the
      Tarpeian Rock. (Livy *Epitome* 80; Plutarch *Marius* 45)

86   Gaius Marius entered upon his seventh and final consulship; he
      died only a few days after taking office. (He also held the post
      in 107 and 104–100.) Marius was replaced by Lucius Valerius
      Flaccus. Flaccus was chiefly noted as the author of a law per-
      mitting debtors to repay only one-fourth of the money which
      they owed. (OCD *s.v.* Marius [1]; *s.v.* Flaccus [6])

82   Quintus Lucretius Ofella, who captured Praeneste for Sulla, ran
      for the consulship in this year, contrary to Sulla's wishes. The
      dictator subsequently ordered Ofella's execution. (OCD *s.v.*
      Ofella)

82   A reflection of the times: in answer to the Sicilian Mamertine's
      complaints about high-handed Roman behavior in Sicily, Pom-
      pey said: "Do not bother quoting laws to those who carry
      swords." (Plutarch *Pompey* 10)

82–   The dictatorship of Lucius Cornelius Sulla, in which he proposed
79   numerous reforms; the most enduring of these was his restruc-
      turing of the criminal court system. Sulla's dictatorship marked
      the first time which that office had been held since the year after
      Hannibal departed from Italy (203).

81   The senator Marcus Fidustius survived the Sullan proscriptions,
      only to be prosecuted again by the triumvirs, more than 30 years
      later. According to Pliny the Elder, Fidustius' name appeared on
      the second list merely on a whim of Mark Antony.

79   Pompey was a strong supporter of Marcus Aemilius Lepidus' can-
      didacy for the consulship, much to Sulla's dismay; he called Lep-
      idus the "worst of all men." Sulla's opinion notwithstanding,
      Lepidus was elected, along with Quintus Lutatius Catulus, a Sul-
      lan favorite. Pompey's attitude apparently caused Sulla to omit
      him from his will. (Plutarch *Pompey* 15)

78   Marcus Aemilius Lepidus, one of the consuls for 78, introduced a wide-ranging program of change and reform: 1. the restitution of the powers of the tribunate (emasculated a few years earlier by Sullan legislation); 2. the reinstatement of exiled citizens; 3. a renewed availability of low-priced corn. (OCD *s.v.* Lepidus [2])

77   Lucius Marcius Philippus (consul in 91) proposed granting Pompey the command in Spain against Sertorius. The senate approved, and Pompey traveled to Spain in the following year to take up his new duties. (Plutarch *Pompey* 17, 18)

77   The *senatus consultum ultimum* was passed against Marcus Aemilius Lepidus. (Gruen 15)

76   The tribune Gnaeus Sicinius initiated a movement to restore the tribunician powers nullified by Sulla's legislation. In his speeches, he often sarcastically ridiculed the consuls Gnaeus Octavius and Gaius Scribonius Curio. (Cicero *Brutus* 216–217; Gruen 24)

75   The tribune Quintus Opimius spoke out against the Sullan restrictions on the tribunate; his speeches were characterized by sarcastic jabs at conservative politicians like Quintus Hortensius and Quintus Lutatius Catulus. The following year, he was prosecuted by Hortensius et al., for overstepping his authority. His subsequent conviction ruined him both politically and financially. (Gruen 24–25)

75   Cicero held the office of quaestor.

74   Bithynia, and parts of Pontus and Cyrenaica became provinces. Bithynia came into Roman hands as a legacy of its recently deceased king, Nicomedes IV. (OCD *s.v.* Bithynia)

74   Marcus Cornelius Cethegus, a savvy Machiavellian political operator, assisted: Marcus Antonius in gaining a command against the pirates; Marcus Aurelius Cotta in obtaining the governorship of Bithynia; Lucius Licinius Lucullus in acquiring the command against King Mithridates. (OCD *s.v.* Cethegus)

73–71 The years of Gaius Verres' governorship in Sicily. Other three- or four-year governorships (a relatively long period in such a post):

    78–75   Publius Servilius Vatia, in Cilicia.
    61–59   Quintus Tullius Cicero, in Asia.
    57–55   Aulus Gabinius, in Syria.
    56–53   Publius Cornelius Lentulus Spinther, in Cilicia.

73   The noted annalist Gaius Licinius Macer, tribune in this year, agitated strongly for the full restoration of tribunician privileges. (Gruen 25; OCD *s.v.* Macer)

71   Lucullus, Pompey, Crassus and Metellus Pius all celebrated triumphal processions in this year. (Payne 102)

71   The tribune Marcus Lollius Palicanus — although a second-rate orator — took up the cause of full restoration of tribunician powers. He was aided in this effort by the influential backing of Pompey. (Gruen 25; OCD *s.v.* Lollius)

71–70 Lucullus spent the winter of 71–70 in the province of Asia, dealing with a financial crisis: in 84, Sulla had levied a fine of 20,000 talents on the cities of Asia, a fine which they had tried to pay by borrowing money from Roman businessmen, at inflated interest rates. Thus, their debt had mushroomed to 120,000 talents by 71. Lucullus solved the problem by reducing the amount owed to 40,000 talents, and arranging for a series of installments for the repayment. (Plutarch *Lucullus* 4, 20)

70   Pompey and Crassus held the consulship; the two of them shared this office again in 55.

70   The censors Gnaeus Cornelius Lentulus Clodianus and Lucius Gellius Publicola removed some 64 senators from the Roman senate. One of the 64 was Gaius Antonius Hybrida, consul in 63, and brother of Mark Antony. (OCD *s.v.* Antony [3])

70   Pompey and Lollius Palicanus reinvested the tribunate with all its traditional powers and prerogatives. (The office had been emasculated by Sulla about a decade earlier.) (OCD *s.v.* Pompeius [4])

69   Cicero held the office of aedile.

69   The consul Quintus Hortensius was assigned the post-consular task of conducting a war against Crete. However, because of his affinity for life in Rome and especially for his legal career, he declined. Quintus Caecilius Metellus Creticus, his colleague in office, assumed the command. (Dio 36.1)

68   Quintus Marcius Rex was virtually the sole consul in this year: his duly elected colleague died in office, as did the suffect. (OCD *s.v.* Rex [2])

*c.*67   Crete was subdued by Quintus Caecilius Metellus Creticus, and subsequently annexed as a province. (Velleius Paterculus 2.38)

67   A disturbance arose when several Roman senators attempted to assassinate the tribune Gabinius (for proposing Pompey's extraordinary command against the pirates). This, in turn, nearly cost the conspiratorial senators their lives, when they themselves were set upon by an angry mob. (Dio 36.24)

66   Cicero's praetorship. According to Plutarch (*Cicero* 9), there were many distinguished candidates who had vied with Cicero in the election for this post, but he gained more votes than any of his rivals (eight were elected in all).

66   Catiline's candidacy for the consulship was disallowed because he was the defendant in an (as yet unresolved) case involving a charge of bribery. (OCD *s.v.* Catiline)

66   The consuls-elect, Publius Autronius Paetus and Publius Cornelius Sulla, were both prosecuted for electoral bribery. Both were convicted, and hence required to forfeit their claims to the consulship. During his trial, Autronius tried to break up the proceedings by employing a crowd of slaves and gladiators to create a disturbance. The ploy backfired, serving only to render his conviction all the more certain. (OCD *s.v.* Autronius)

65   Marcus Licinius Crassus held the censorship. He attempted to implement various self-aggrandizement schemes in Spain and Egypt, as well as in domestic politics. However, his machinations came to nothing, and he left Rome soon after his term expired. (Plutarch *Crassus* 13; OCD *s.v.* Crassus)

65   (Summer.) Catiline was acquitted of all extortion charges. (Gardner LCL Cicero *Pro Caelio*, etc. 417)

65   Caesar held the aedileship in this year. Among other deeds, he attempted to rehabilitate Gaius Marius' reputation by restoring certain of Marius' monuments. (Velleius Paterculus 2.43)

64   Catiline's first legitimate campaign for the consulship ended in failure when he was defeated by Cicero and Gaius Antonius Hybrida. Antonius, the uncle of Mark Antony, was elected despite his checkered past, including expulsion from the senate in 70. (OCD *s.v.* Antonius [3])

64   During his campaign for the consulship, Cicero delivered a speech entitled *Oratio in Toga Candida* (*Oration in a White Toga*, *i.e.* a campaign speech). Although only fragments of the speech are extant, Cicero apparently attacked the activities of his rival candidates so effectively that his election was virtually assured. (CAH IX 484)

*c.*64   Pompey annexed Syria as a Roman province. (OCD *s.v.* Syria)

63   Cicero's consulship, the zenith of his political career.

63   Cicero conceived of his grand plan for ending the civil strife besetting Rome: a *concordia ordinum*, a sort of political alliance of the senatorial and equestrian classes. (Cary 374)

63   (March.) Julius Caesar was elected pontifex maximus, an office which placed him in charge of the religious bureaucracy. The well known conservative politician Quintus Lutatius Catulus was Caesar's chief opponent. Caesar was also elected praetor (for 62) in this year. (Suetonius *Julius Caesar* 13)

63   (December.) A certain Lucius Tarquinius accused Marcus Licinius Crassus of complicity in the Catilinarian conspiracy. Tarquinius' testimony, however, was subsequently discredited. (Sallust *War Against Catiline* 48.3–4; Gruen 285–286)

63   The discredited consul for 71, Publius Cornelius Lentulus Sura, joined the Catilinarian conspiracy in part to fulfill a corrupt prophecy that three Cornelii would be absolute rulers in Rome. Two had already achieved the distinction: Lucius Cornelius Sulla and Lucius Cornelius Cinna. Lentulus hoped to be the third. (Plutarch *Cicero* 17; OCD *s.v.* Lentulus Sura)

63   Catiline's chief issue in his second run at the consulship was his debt cancellation plan (*novae tabulae*, literally "new tablets"). His electoral failure prompted him to engage in conspiratorial violence to attempt to gain power. (Cary 371–372)

63   The Catilinarian conspiracy was exposed (November and December), and quashed in January of the following year.

63   This year marked the emergence of Cato the Younger as a major player in Roman politics; he gave a fiery, anti–Catilinarian speech in the senate, virtually single-handedly motivating his fellow senators to act against Catiline's conspiracy. (Suetonius *Julius Caesar* 14)

63   Cato the Younger cancelled a journey to Lucania upon hearing the news that his enemy Quintus Caecilius Metellus Nepos planned to run for the tribunate. Cato himself stood for the office, and gained election to it (as did Metellus). (Plutarch *Cato the Younger* 20)

63   (December 5). A band of armed Roman knights, seized and guarded the approaches to the Capitoline Hill, to protect the senators who were debating the fate of the Catilinarian conspirators. (Cicero *Pro Sestio* 28; Gardner LCL Cicero *Pro Sestio* and *In Vatinium* 70)

63   (December 19). Plutarch (*Cicero* 18) indicates that this date was targeted by the Catilinarian conspirators for their desperate (and unrealized) attempts at killing as many senators as possible, and burning Rome to the ground.

63   The father of the senator Aulus Fulvius killed his own son because of the son's involvement in the Catilinarian conspiracy. (Dio 37.36)

62   The tribune Quintus Caecilius Metellus Nepos attacked Cicero for the latter's disregard of proper legal procedure in the execution of the Catilinarian conspirators; he also proposed that Pompey be recalled from the east to deal with the civil unrest in Rome. Metellus Nepos held the offices of praetor (60) and consul (57). (OCD *s.v.* Metellus [10])

62   Violence erupted in the senate when the tribunes, led by Cato the Younger and Quintus Minucius Thermus, attempted to veto the senate's refusal to permit Pompey to return to Italy with his army. According to Dio (37.43), a rock-throwing, sword-brandishing skirmish ensued, until cooler heads restored order.

62   Gaius Julius Caesar and Marcus Calpurnius Bibulus both held the praetorship in this year, a foreshadowing of their stormy joint consulship in 59. (MRR II 173)

62   Lucius Vettius, a former devotee of Catiline turned informer, divulged the names of a number of men who had participated in the conspiracy. (Dio 37.41)

62   (December.) Pompey celebrated a triumphant return to Rome from the eastern provinces.

61   Julius Caesar embarked upon a governorship in Spain.

61   The trial of Publius Clodius, for committing sacrilege (in late 62) by crashing the Bona Dea festival, a religious ceremony restricted to women. He was acquitted in the subsequent trial, which occurred in the spring of 61. (OCD *s.v.* Clodius [1])

61   Pompey engineered the election of Lucius Afranius and Quintus Caecilius Metellus Celer to the consulship for 60, in the hope that both would be effective political allies for him. Afranius, however, proved inept — Dio calls him a better dancer than administrator — while Metellus was openly hostile to Pompey for having divorced his sister Mucia. (Dio 37.49)

61–59 Cicero's brother Quintus served as the governor of Asia. Marcus sent two lengthy and detailed letters to him during his tenure there; the letters were filled with admonitions and advice.

60   Lucius Lucceius (praetor in 67) ran for the consulship, competing against Julius Caesar and Marcus Calpurnius Bibulus. Although Lucceius bankrolled both his own campaign and Caesar's, the two successful candidates were Caesar and Bibulus. (OCD *s.v.* Lucceius)

60   Julius Caesar's political enemies, conspiring to deprive him of an influential provincial governorship after his consulship in 59, invented a meaningless appointment for him: "woods and mountain pastures." (Suetonius *Julius Caesar* 19)

60   (Summer.) Caesar hastened to Rome from Spain, where he had been serving as governor, to run for the consulship. (MRR II 185)

60   Formation of the First Triumvirate, an informal political alliance consisting of Pompey, Caesar and Crassus.

60   One of the consuls for the year, Quintus Caecilius Metellus Celer, was briefly imprisoned by order of the tribune Lucius Flavius. Metellus had obstinately opposed Flavius' land distribution proposals. The defiant consul demanded that the senate convene in the prison. When Flavius took a seat at the entrance to Metellus' cell to prevent senators from entering, Metellus ordered that a hole be cut in the wall to afford access to the senators. Flavius ultimately relented. (Dio 37.50)

60   Publius Clodius attempted to gain plebeian status, so as to qual-
      ify for election to the tribunate. One of the consuls, Quintus
      Caecilius Metellus Celer, blocked Clodius' effort. Ironically, the
      two were brothers-in-law, Metellus having married Clodius' sis-
      ter Clodia. In the following year, however, Clodius obtained the
      desired status, with Julius Caesar's assistance.
          Metellus died in the following year, a death widely rumored
      to have been caused by poisoning, at Clodia's hand. (Gardner
      LCL Cicero *Pro Sestio* 214; OCD *s.v.* Clodius [1])

60–   Octavian's father, Gaius Octavius, served as the provincial gover-
59   nor of Macedonia. (OCD *s.v.* Octavius)

59   Julius Caesar's consulship, in which he so thoroughly dominated
      the political scene that his colleague in the office, Marcus Calpur-
      nius Bibulus, spent most of the year at home, declaring that
      unfavorable omens precluded his participation in public life.
      (Suetonius *Julius Caesar* 20)

59   Bibulus (see above) suffered rude treatment on a number of occa-
      sions. In one of these instances a crowd of malefactors dispersed
      Bibulus' lictors and dumped a basket of manure on his head.
      (Plutarch *Cato the Younger* 32)

59   (March.) The ratification of Publius Clodius' petition to be trans-
      ferred from patrician to plebeian status, thus enabling him to
      run for the tribunate. (OCD *s.v.* Clodius [1])

59   Julius Caesar's daughter Julia married Pompey, thus cementing the
      political alliance between father and son-in-law. Their ties were
      weakened considerably some five years later, with Julia's death
      in 54. (OCD *s.v.* Julia [1])

59   (July.) The death of Gaius Cosconius, a land commissioner, cre-
      ated a vacancy offered to Cicero. He refused it, however, declar-
      ing that the commission's unpopularity with the senatorial class
      would taint him as well. (Cicero *Letters to Atticus* 2.19)

59   Cato the Younger so vigorously denounced the political marriages
      of the year (Caesar's daughter to Pompey [as above], and Cae-
      sar to Calpurnia, daughter of the consul for 58), and so angrily
      criticized the extraordinary provincial command granted to Cae-
      sar, that Caesar briefly imprisoned him. However, Caesar soon
      relented, and ordered Cato to be released. (Plutarch *Caesar* 14)

59   Most Roman senators so hated or feared Julius Caesar that they seldom appeared at senate meetings over which he presided in this year. However, one aged member, a certain Considius, had an exemplary record of attendance. When Caesar questioned him about this matter, he replied that he was too old to be afraid, given that he probably had little time to live in any case. (Plutarch *Caesar* 14)

59   The first date of publication of the *Acta Diurna* (*Daily Proceedings*) of political and social events; this record was virtually the Roman equivalent of a daily newspaper. (Suetonius *Julius Caesar* 20)

59   Lucius Vettius, an unscrupulous political agent, claimed to have knowledge about a plot to assassinate Pompey. In the official inquiry that followed, Vettius accused several prominent senators of complicity in the alleged scheme. The matter was never resolved; Vettius himself died under mysterious circumstances. (OCD *s.v.* Vettius)

59   In a letter to Atticus (2.17), Cicero expressed his fear that Julius Caesar was aiming for a tyranny, given certain premonitory events of the year: the marriage of Caesar's daughter to Pompey; Caesar's land redistribution proposals; and his *effusio pecuniae*, "outpouring of money."

59   In another letter to Atticus (2.20), Cicero made a particularly doleful comment on the state of the republic: *Certi sumus perisse omnia.* "I am certain that everything has perished."

58   The praetors Gaius Memmius and Lucius Domitius Ahenobarbus proposed to launch an inquiry into Caesar's acts as consul. However, nothing came of this, and so Caesar left Rome for his provincial command in Gaul. (Suetonius *Julius Caesar* 23)

58   The newly elected tribune (for 57) Publius Sestius visited Julius Caesar in Gaul, in an effort to solicit his support in recalling Cicero from exile. (OCD *s.v.* Sestius)

58   Cicero enlisted the aid of a tribune named Lucius Ninnius Quadratus to veto any measures proposed by Publius Clodius, Cicero's archenemy. Clodius learned of the arrangement and tricked Cicero and Quadratus into remaining silent by promising not to introduce legislation hostile to Cicero's interests, a pledge which he subsequently broke. (Dio 38.14)

58   Publius Clodius' tribunate; he engineered the exile of Cicero, who
      was recalled in the following year. (OCD *s.v.* Clodius [1])

58   (June 1.) A proposal to recall Cicero from exile was vetoed by the
      tribune Aelius Ligus, whom Cicero termed a "nonentity," and
      an "excrescence from the ranks of my enemies" (tr. Sabben-Clare;
      MRR II 195)).

58   The aedile Marcus Aemilius Scaurus minted coins commemorat-
      ing his military victory over the (decidedly inferior) forces of the
      Nabataeans, in 65. This Scaurus owned a Palatine mansion with
      an atrium featuring 38-foot-tall marble columns. (OCD *s.v.*
      Scaurus [1])

58   Ptolemy XII, Egyptian king since 80, was expelled by the Alexan-
      drians in this year. He fled to Rome, where he solicited assis-
      tance in regaining his position. He was ultimately reinstated in
      55, with the aid of Aulus Gabinius, whose involvement in the
      case was assured by the offer of a large bribe (10,000 talents).
      (OCD *s.v.* Ptolemy XII; Gabinius [2])

58–   If Cicero is to be believed, Sextus Cloelius, an agent of Clodius,
56   engaged in a vast array of nefarious activities in these years: arson
      (including the burning of temples and public buildings), van-
      dalism and the fomenting of violence.(Cicero *Pro Caelio* 78)

57   (January 23.) A fracas broke out when a tribune named Quintus
      Fabricius announced that he would offer a proposal to the sen-
      ate for Cicero's recall from exile. Cicero later claimed that Rome
      had not seen such a civil disturbance since Sulla's march into Italy
      some 30 years before. (Gardner LCL Cicero *Pro Sestio* and *In
      Vatinium* 19; MRR II 202)

57   At a senate meeting, Pompey read a statement praising Cicero for
      saving the Roman state, and proposing his recall from exile. Four
      hundred and sixteen senators approved the statement. The lone
      dissenter: Publius Clodius. Even Cicero's longtime political
      enemy, Quintus Caecilius Metellus Nepos, did not object to the
      recall motion. (Gardner LCL Cicero *Pro Sestio* 21)

57   The tribune Titus Annius Milo supported Cicero's recall from
      exile, and also began his tumultuous rivalry with Publius Clodius,
      whom he twice attempted to prosecute in 57 for inciting vio-
      lence. Both prosecutions (in February and November) were

thwarted by one of the consuls for 57, Quintus Caecilius Metellus Nepos. (OCD *s.v.* Milo)

57   (August 5.) Cicero arrived in Brundisium from Greece, thus ending his brief period of exile. On September 5 of this year, he addressed the Roman senate, thanking that august body for its assistance in his return to Italy and Rome. (OCD *s.v.* Cicero [1])

57   An Alexandrian ambassador, Dio, was assassinated in Rome. The incident had political overtones, as Dio had traveled to Rome to plead with the senate not to restore the exiled Ptolemy XII to power in Egypt. (Gardner LCL Cicero *Pro Caelio*, etc. 427)

57   Violence erupted during the vote on Cicero's recall from exile, when Publius Clodius disrupted the proceedings with a contingent of gladiators whom he had obtained to perform at funeral games for a recently deceased relative. The measure, accordingly, failed to pass (at this time). (Dio 39.7)

57   (December.) Cicero noted with surprise the number of senators (about 200) attending a senate meeting so close in time to the celebration of the Saturnalian festival. (Cicero *Letters to His Brother Quintus* 2.1)

56   (May 15.) The senate refused to authorize a public thanksgiving (*supplicatio*) for Aulus Gabinius, for his administration of Syria. (Cicero *On the Consular Provinces* 14)

56   The Conference at Luca, in northern Italy, to renew the triumvirate. In addition to the triumvirs, some 200 Roman senators also attended the meeting. (Suetonius *Julius Caesar* 24)

56   Lucius Domitius Ahenobarbus, a candidate for the consulship, promised if elected to require Caesar to resign his Gallic command and disband his army. (Domitius withdrew from the race when one of his torchbearers was murdered before his eyes.) (Dio 39.31)

56   Lightning struck a statue of Jupiter early in the year. The augurs interpreted this as a sign that the Romans should not press on with the campaign to restore Ptolemy XII to the Egyptian throne. Also, soothsayers were consulted to explain the meaning of some unusual sounds heard on the edge of the city. They interpreted the noises as representations of the gods' anger over the desecration of sacred sites and the violation of solemn vows. Clodius

attempted to put a political spin on this analysis by claiming that Cicero's reoccupation of his Palatine home constituted a sacrilege, since Clodius had previously dedicated a shrine to Liberty on the site. (Watts LCL Cicero *Pro Archia Poeta* [etc.] 45)

56   (April 5). The senate voted to grant to Pompey 40,000,000 sesterces to administer the corn distribution program. (Gardner LCL Cicero *Pro Sestio* and *In Vatinium* xix)

56   Publius Clodius assumed the office of aedile, and immediately began using the post as a springboard for political attacks on Titus Annius Milo, and by implication, Cicero and Pompey. (Dio 39.18)

56   The friendship between Cicero and Cato the Younger cooled somewhat, when Cicero successfully urged the senate to invalidate Clodius' official acts as tribune. Cato was particularly dismayed at Cicero's action because among the abrogated decrees was the ratification of Cato's administration of the province of Cyprus. (Plutarch *Cicero* 34)

56   A lively discussion took place in the senate regarding the possible candidacies of Pompey and Crassus for the consulship. In the manner of a true politician, Pompey stated that he might or might not seek the office; Crassus said that if his candidacy would benefit Rome, he would run. (Both, of course, were ultimately elected.) (Plutarch *Crassus* 15)

55   Crassus and Pompey held a joint consulship, as they had in 70. According to Velleius Paterculus, they won office unfairly, apparently by prevailing upon the tribunes to delay by veto the election day until after the terms of the consuls for 56 had elapsed. (Both of those consuls — Gnaeus Cornelius Lentulus Marcellinus and Lucius Marcius Philippus — were political opponents of Pompey and Crassus.)

55   A year of limited political influence for Cato the Younger, as he was never on friendly terms with Pompey or Crassus (the two consuls). Their armed guards made it difficult for Cato to give public speeches or participate at all in politics. (Plutarch *Crassus* 15)

c.55   During a senatorial debate over the allocation of provincial governorships, Marcus Licinius Crassus became so incensed with a speech of one Lucius Annalius that he punched him in the face.

The bloodied Annalius was compelled by his injuries to leave the forum. (Plutarch *Comparison of Nicias and Crassus* 2)

54   Crassus was so eager to travel to his proconsular province, Syria, that he set sail from Brundisium in a heavy storm, with a resultant loss of many of his ships. (Plutarch *Crassus* 17)

54   Titus Annius Milo initiated his campaign for the consulship of 52 by sponsoring public entertainments costing 1,000,000 sesterces. (OCD *s.v.* Milo)

54   Gnaeus Domitius Calvinus gained election to the consulship (for 53) under suspicious circumstances; his formal entry into office was delayed until July. (OCD *s.v.* Calvinus [2]) The mercurial Calvinus had held the tribunate in 59; the praetorship in 56 (in this capacity he presided over the celebrated trial of Caelius); and the consulship again in 40.

54   Cato the Younger held the praetorship in this year. To show his contempt for the laws passed during Julius Caesar's consulship in 59, he spitefully refused to refer to them by their titles or names. (Dio 38.7)

54   In a letter to Publius Cornelius Lentulus, Cicero recalled that in 59 (Caesar's consular year), the republic did not have consuls, but merely *mercatores provinciarum et seditionum servos ac ministros*: "province salesmen and facilitators of rebellions." (Cicero *Letters to His Friends* 1.9)

52   In an unusual move for a conservative Roman politician, Marcus Calpurnius Bibulus (consul 59) proposed the conferring of a sole consulship upon Pompey for this year. (OCD *s.v.* Bibulus)

52   The consular elections of 53 had been continually postponed because of civil violence. Early in 52, the supporters of two of the candidates, Publius Plautius Hypsaeus and Quintus Caecilius Metellus Pius, attacked the interrex Marcus Aemilius Lepidus, in an effort to compel his to establish a date for the elections. (OCD *s.v.* Plautius [2])

52   Pompey was selected *consul solus*, the only consul to (initially) hold office in this year. However, Pompey's marriage this same year to Cornelia, the daughter of Quintus Caecilius Metellus Pius Scipio, was consummated partially to allow Pompey to offer her

father the vacant consulship; he thus hoped to blunt the criticism leveled at him for ruling Rome without a consular colleague. He also wanted to deprive Caesar of an opportunity to demand the consulship. (OCD *s.v.* Pompeius [4])

52   Publius Clodius was murdered in a gang-related street brawl.

51   Servius Sulpicius Rufus finally held the office of consul, eleven years after his first try for the post. He apparently resisted the extreme anti–Caesarian stance of his colleague Marcus Claudius Marcellus. (OCD *s.v.* Sulpicius [2])

51   Cicero departed from Rome for a one-year provincial governorship of Cilicia, a post which he reportedly undertook with no great enthusiasm. (OCD *s.v.* Cicero [1]

51   The consul Marcus Claudius Marcellus, an aggressive opponent of Julius Caesar, proposed that Caesar be recalled from his Gallic province. The anti–Caesarian stance was also adopted by his cousin Gaius (consul 50), and his brother Gaius (consul 49). (OCD *s.v.* Marcellus [4])

50   In this turbulent year, the tribune Gaius Scribonius Curio represented Caesar's interests in Rome by opposing measures designed to require Caesar to return to the city from Gaul. Instead, he offered a compromise: that Caesar would disband his legions, should Pompey agree to do likewise. The proposal was not adopted. Pliny the Elder notes sarcastically that Curio derived his wealth from the *discordiam principum,* "dissension among the leaders," one of whom (Caesar) paid him a large bribe for his support. According to Velleius Paterculus (2.48), the bribe amounted to 10,000,000 sesterces.

50   One of the consuls, Lucius Aemilius Paullus, accepted a bribe of 1,500 talents from Julius Caesar, presumably to hold in check the other — aggressively anti–Caesarian — consul Gaius Claudius Marcellus. Paullus wanted the cash to further his renovations of the Basilica Aemilia. (OCD *s.v.* Paullus [3])

49   (January 1). Quintus Caecilius Metellus Pius Scipio proposed that Caesar be declared a public enemy, should he refuse to disband his army. (OCD *s.v.* Metellus [11])

49   (Early January.) Titus Labienus, Julius Caesar's longtime Gallic legate, deserted to the Pompeians, at the same time divulging a good deal of information about Caesar's plans. (Dio 41.4)

49   Julius Caesar granted Roman citizenship to all the residents of the Spanish town of Gades. He had a particular affection for Gades, because it was there that he had had a dream which indicated that he would one day enjoy a one-man rule. (Dio 41.24)

49   Caesar received his first dictatorship; he was granted a second, third and fourth dictatorship in 48, 46 and 44, respectively. His fourth was awarded for life. (OCD *s.v.* Caesar [1])

49   Upon assuming his first dictatorship, Julius Caesar allowed all exiled Romans to return to the city, with the exception of Titus Annius Milo. (Dio 41.36)

49   Julius Caesar expropriated the funds stored in the *aerarium* (state treasury) for his private use. (OCD *s.v.* aerarium)

48   Pompey appealed to the Dacian king Burebistas for assistance in the continuing battles with Caesar's legions. (OCD *s.v.* Burebistas)

48   The praetor Marcus Caelius Rufus was evicted from his office for opposing the implementation of Julius Caesar's debt reform law; riots had broken out because of Caelius' actions. (Scullard GN 144)

48   A tangled year for politicians, as four consuls-elect all claimed the post. Two were elected in Rome: Julius Caesar and Publius Servilius Isauricus. But the citizens (including some 200 senators) who had fled from Rome to Greece felt that they, too, had elective rights, and they retained the previous year's consuls, simply giving them new job titles. But none of this mattered, since it was evident that Caesar and Pompey had abrogated all authority onto themselves. (Dio 41.43)

48   Shortly after the Battle of Pharsalus, numerous powers were voted to Julius Caesar, including the right to mete out whatever punishment he wished to Pompey's sympathizers; the right to decide matters of war and peace without consulting the senate or the people; the right to hold the consulship for five consecutive one-year terms. (Dio 42.20)

48   The behavior of Mark Antony, newly appointed magister equitum, caused many observers to believe that he was aiming for a monarchy. Among other things, he walked about the streets of

Rome armed with a sword, and he was attended by a large body of soldiers. (Dio 42.27)

48   Mark Antony appointed his uncle, Lucius Julius Caesar, to the post of praefectus urbi, because he (Antony) had decided to leave Rome to supervise the legions that Caesar had sent back to Italy after the Battle of Pharsalus. (Dio 42.30)

47   Angry public quarrels broke out between two of the tribunes, Lucius Trebellius and Publius Cornelius Dolabella. They argued over debt reform; their squabbling instigated unrest and violence among the populace. (Dio 42.29; MRR II 287)

47   Julius Caesar set up Cleopatra as the ruler of Egypt. Fearing, however, that the Egyptians might not accept a woman in such a position of authority, he arranged for her a sham marriage with her brother, Ptolemy XIII, that they both might nominally share power. In reality, Cleopatra ruled alone, since her brother/husband was only about 16 years of age at the time. (Dio 42.44)

47   During Caesar's journey from the east to Italy, he collected large amounts of money from all the towns along his route. He justified this virtual extortion by stating that empires depended upon two elements for prosperity — money and soldiers — and that soldiers could not be maintained without money, nor could money be obtained without soldiers. (Dio 42.49)

47   In order to reward his political supporters, Julius Caesar increased the numbers of magistrates and priests, and then appointed his cronies to these offices. In particular, he raised the number of praetors from six to ten. (Dio 42.51)

47   This year almost passed without consuls, until Quintus Fufius Calenus and Publius Vatinius were selected in September and December, respectively. (OCD s.v. Fufius Calenus; Vatinius)

46   When encamped in Africa, Caesar dreamt that he saw an army weeping; he interpreted this to mean that Carthage should be repeopled with Roman colonists. Hence, just before his assassination in 44, he made arrangements to have 3000 landless Romans sent as colonists to the site of Carthage. (Appian Punic Wars 136)

46   (Summer.) Caesar pardoned 300 wealthy Roman businessmen in

Utica (north Africa), but at a price: an indemnity of 200,000,000 sesterces, to be remitted in six payments over three years. (*De Bello Africo* 90, author uncertain.)

46   One of Julius Caesar's acts as dictator involved reviewing the rolls of those receiving free corn from the government. He ultimately pared the list from 320,000 recipients to 150,000. (Suetonius *Julius Caesar* 41)

46   Julius Caesar created the province of Numidia, in Africa. (Velleius Paterculus 2.39)

45   (May.) Marcus Claudius Marcellus (consul in 51) was stabbed to death in Greece by a certain Marcus Magius Cibo, a close friend. The details of the murder are contained in a letter from Servius Sulpicius to Cicero (*Letters to His Friends* 4.12)

45   Roman magistrates were expected to take an oath of loyalty to a dictator's (and later, an emperor's) enactments, *acta*. The first instance of this oath-taking occurred in 45, when all office holders pledged to support Caesar's *acta*. (OCD *s.v.* Acta)

45   In an uncharacteristically audacious move, Cicero drafted a letter (not extant) to Julius Caesar, apparently lecturing him on the excessive power which he was usurping. The letter, however, never reached Caesar's hands. (Duff 266–267)

45   Gaius Caninius Rebilus probably holds the record for the shortest consulship in Roman history. When one of the consuls — Quintus Fabius Maximus — suddenly died on the last day in 45, Julius Caesar appointed Caninius as the replacement; he held the office for only a few hours. Cicero joked that Caninius was probably the most conscientious consul in Roman history, since never once did he sleep during his term of office. (OCD *s.v.* Caninius)

45   Julius Caesar appointed his ex–Gallic legatus Gaius Trebonius as suffect consul. The next year, however, Trebonius turned against his benefactor by participating in the Ides of March assassination. (OCD *s.v.* Trebonius)

44   The death of Publius Servilius Vatia Isauricus, a distinguished public servant. Career highlights:

79   consul
78   governor of Cilicia
74   granted a triumph for his victories over the pirates in and around Cilicia
63   strongly supported Cicero in his attacks on the Catilinarian conspirators
55   censor
(OCD *s.v.* Servilius [1])

44   Caesar increased the number of praetors, quaestors and aediles. The additional aediles were principally responsible for supervising grain distributions. (Suetonius *Julius Caesar* 41)

44   Shortly after Caesar's assassination, Marcus Aemilius Lepidus allied himself to Mark Antony, a move strongly opposed by Juventius Laterensis, one of Lepidus' aides. When Lepidus failed to heed his advice, Juventius committed suicide. (Velleius Paterculus 2.63)

44   In May of this year, Mark Antony acquired the governorship of portions of Gaul, instead of Macedonia (which had been previously allotted to him). He believed that these more strategic and prestigious provinces would afford him a stronger base of operations against any future hostilities initiated by Octavian. (OCD *s.v.* Antony [4])

44   In July, the Caesarian conspirators Brutus and Cassius — to whom the senate had assigned provincial governorships in Crete and Cyrene, respectively — sought for themselves more influential commands. Their request was met with vague threats from Mark Antony, whereupon Brutus fled to Greece, Cassius to Asia. (OCD *s.v.* Brutus [5]; Cassius [6])

44   Two energetic tribunes, Lucius Epidius Marullus and Lucius Caesetius Flavus, denounced Octavian's perceived designs on kingship. Showing great restraint, Octavian contented himself with publicly stigmatizing them. (Velleius Paterculus 2.68)

44   Marcus Aemilius Lepidus was (irregularly) elected to the office of pontifex maximus. His path to the office was smoothed by Mark Antony, whom he supported militarily immediately after Caesar's death. Lepidus held the post until his own death, in 12 BC. (OCD *s.v.* Lepidus [3])

44   (March 15.) On the evening of Caesar's fateful day, Mark Antony confiscated 4,000 talents formerly belonging to the dictator, as well as certain papers and documents. He recalled certain exiles and released prisoners, supposedly on Caesar's posthumous authority. (Plutarch *Antony* 15)

44   (March 18.) The terms of Julius Caesar's will were revealed to the public. His funeral followed. (KER LCL Cicero *Philippics* 9)

44   (April.) Julius Caesar's 18-year old grandnephew Octavian arrived in Italy from Greece, where he had been studying and writing, to attempt to assume the mantle of leadership and power. (Plutarch *Antony* 16)

44   (April 18.) Cicero and Octavian met at Puteoli, where Octavian treated the orator with deference and respect. (KER LCL Cicero *Philippics* 13)

44   (May.) Mark Antony's return to Rome was greeted by a request from Octavian for Julius Caesar's fortune, which Antony had confiscated. Antony curtly replied that the money had been spent. (KER LCL Cicero *Philippics* 14)

44   (June 3.) By a special vote of the citizens, Octavian received a five-year command in Cisalpine and Transalpine Gaul. The suffect consul, Publius Cornelius Dolabella, was simultaneously granted a provincial governorship in Syria. (MRR II 316; OCD *s.v.* Dolabella [3])

44   (August.) The Caesarian conspirators Brutus and Cassius left Italy, after having first issued a proclamation stating that they were willing to live in permanent exile, if such an act would promote harmony and prevent the recurrence of a civil war. (Velleius Paterculus 2.62; KER LCL Cicero *Philippics* 13)

44   (October.) Mark Antony detained several members of Octavian's bodyguard at Suessa Aurunca (in Latium, south of Rome, noteworthy as the birthplace of the satirist Lucilius), and later executed them on the pretext that they had plotted to assassinate him. The event caused something of a scandal. (CAH X 11)

44   (December 20.) For the first time, Cicero publicly (in the *Third Philippic*) referred to Octavian as "Caesar," thus implying his support for Octavian's political and military status. (CAH X 13)

44–   During these years, one of Mark Antony's most outspoken defend-
43   ers was Quintus Fufius Calenus (tribune 61; praetor 59; consul
       47). Calenus therefore found himself frequently pitted against
       Cicero during this period. Dio (45.1–28) records a lengthy speech
       made by Calenus in 43, in which he vigorously defended Antony.

43   The Second Triumvirate was organized; it consisted of Octavian,
       Mark Antony and Marcus Aemilius Lepidus. One of their first
       enactments was the publication of a proscription list, which
       included the name of Cicero. The famous orator was killed as a
       result, in December of 43. However, Cicero's close friend and
       confidant Titus Pomponius Atticus was spared, possibly because
       of past financial benefactions to Mark Antony. (Boren 150)

43   A certain tribune named Marcus Terentius Varro, whose name was
       similar to a Varro who had been proscribed, issued a public state-
       ment differentiating himself from the other. The ploy, although
       evidently effective, was widely ridiculed. (Dio 47.11)

43   Publius Cornelius Dolabella assassinated Gaius Trebonius, gover-
       nor of Asia, and one of the tyrannicides. (Velleius Paterculus
       2.69)

43   (January 2.) The senate enacted some extraordinary measures on
       Octavian's behalf, including the right to hold offices ten years
       before he was eligible to do so, and to be reimbursed by the state
       for money which he had spent to train and equip his soldiers.
       (Dio 46.29) He was also granted consular status in senate meet-
       ings, and the right to command an army. (Augustus Res Gestae
       1.1)

43   Octavian and Quintus Pedius were elected consuls, to finish the
       terms of Quintus Vibius Pansa and Aulus Hirtius, who had died
       at the Battle of Mutina. Pedius, grandnephew and heir of Julius
       Caesar (as, of course, was Octavian) was clearly the subordinate
       consul. (Dio 46.46)

43   The tribune Publius Titius successfully impeached his colleague
       Publius Servilius Casca (a Caesarian assassin) for dereliction of
       duty. Dio remarks (46.49) that when Titius died soon there-
       after, he suffered the fate that befell Brutus, Tiberius Gracchus
       and Cinna, all of whom died shortly after removing colleagues
       from office.

43   A senator by the name of Silicius Corona voted to acquit Marcus
      Junius Brutus of murdering Caesar, and afterwards, he loudly
      boasted about his vote. The fact that Octavian took no imme-
      diate action against him earned for the former a reputation for
      tolerance. Later, however, Silicius's name was placed on the pro-
      scription list and he was executed. (Dio 46.49)

43   The important Gallic town of Lugdunum (modern Lyon) was
      refounded as a Roman colony by Lucius Munatius Plancus.
      (OCD s.v. Plancus)

43   (December 7.) Cicero was murdered in the proscriptions, by a cer-
      tain Gaius Popillius Laenas, whom he had once defended in
      court. Not content with (merely!) the deed itself, Popillius erected
      an inscribed statue depicting himself sitting near Cicero's sev-
      ered head. (Dio 47.11)

43   The triumvirs declared that they would permit widows of pro-
      scribed men to retain their dowries, and children their inheri-
      tances, but these promises were soon disregarded. (Dio 47.14)

43   The proscriptions in this year showed little regard for family ties:
      Mark Antony placed on the list the name of his uncle, Lucius
      Julius Caesar; Marcus Aemilius Lepidus proscribed his brother,
      Lucius Aemilius Paullus, as did Lucius Munatius Plancus his
      own brother Lucius Plotius Plancus. Caesar and Paullus escaped
      execution; Plotius did not. (Velleius Paterculus 2.67; MRR II
      339; OCD s.v. Paullus [3]; Caesar [4])

42   Even after the proscriptions, the triumvirs found themselves short
      of money. So in this year, they drew up a list of citizens who
      were expected to provide a tithe to the government. Dio (47.16)
      states that, far from contributing one-tenth of their property to
      the official coffers, they had scarcely one-tenth left over for them-
      selves after the triumvir's extractions.

42   Immediately after the Battle of Philippi, Octavian and Mark
      Antony assigned themselves provinces; Octavian took Spain and
      Numidia, while Antony received Gaul and Africa. The third
      member of the triumvirate, Lepidus, was not present during
      these deliberations. Octavian and Antony decided to assign him
      Africa, should he demand a share of the provincial commands.
      (Dio 48.1)

41 Fulvia, Mark Antony's wife, was very influential in this year, so much so that Dio (48.4) suggests that she and Antony were running the government, while the consuls (Lucius Antonius and Publius Servilius Isauricus) held office in name only.

41 A difficult year for Octavian: senators and other wealthy men wished to retain the property and possessions that Octavian needed to distribute to his soldiers. By seizing those assets, Octavian would naturally incur the wrath of the dispossessed; but by not doing so, the army would be restless. He found it difficult to please either faction, and was nearly assassinated by a group of disgruntled military veterans. (Dio 48.8–9)

40 Lucius Cornelius Balbus, a native of Spain, became consul, the first foreign-born holder of the office. (OCD s.v. Balbus [3])

40 Octavian's sister Octavia married Mark Antony; it was a union bred more by politics than by love, designed to seal the rapprochement that husband and brother reached at Brundisium in this year. (OCD s.v. Octavia [2])

40 Herod visited Mark Antony and Octavian in Rome to seek their support for his efforts to gain the kingship of Judaea. (OCD s.v. Herod [1])

40 As one of the consuls in 40, Gaius Asinius Pollio helped to arrange the Peace of Brundisium, a reconciliation of Octavian and Mark Antony. (OCD s.v. Brundisium; s.v. Pollio)

40 "Nothing in the life of man is lasting" were the words used by Dio (48.33) to describe the sudden downfall of Quintus Salvidienus Rufus. Octavian had given Salvidienus a governorship in Gaul in early 40, even though Salvidienus had not yet held the consulship. Later in the year, however, Octavian suspected Salvidienus of plotting against him; he was accused before the senate, and executed.

40 Gnaeus Domitius Calvinus and Gaius Asinius Pollio both resigned their consulships, probably around December 1. Their terms were completed by Publius Canidius Crassus and Lucius Cornelius Balbus. (MRR II 378)

39 Negotiations were held between Sextus Pompeius and Octavian/Mark Antony (which ultimately led to the Treaty of Misenum), on one of Pompey's ships —in carinis suis, "on his own keels," as

he put it, a word play on Carinae. The Carinae was a residential section of Rome where Sextus' late father (Pompey the Great) had owned a home; ironically, in 39, the owner of the property was Mark Antony. (Velleius Paterculus 2.77)

39   The signing of the short-lived Treaty of Misenum, in which Octavian and Mark Antony agreed to grant to Sextus Pompeius a five-year command in Sicily, Sardinia, Corsica and Achaea. (OCD s.v. Misenum)

39   The measures carried out by the triumvirs since the formation of their alliance in 43 were formally ratified by the senate. (Dio 48.34)

39   An unnamed slave had somehow contrived to ascend to the praetorship. When the irregularity was discovered, the unfortunate man was granted his freedom and then thrown from the Tarpeian Rock (a form of execution reserved for free citizens). (Dio 48.34)

37   Mark Antony and Octavian met in Tarentum, to renew the Second Triumvirate for an additional five years, to 33. (OCD s.v. Tarentum)

37   An aedile named Marcus Oppius announced his plans to resign his office because of his poverty. So highly esteemed was he, however, that the citizenry took up a collection to provide him with sufficient funds to retain his aedileship, an act that irritated the senate. (Dio 48.54)

37   Gaius Sosius, governor of Syria and Cilicia, installed Herod the Great as king of Judaea, a post he held until his death in 4. (OCD s.v. Sosius)

36   Marcus Aemilius Lepidus, one of the triumvirs, tried to expropriate Sicily as his domain. His soldiers, however, soon deserted to Octavian, who expelled Lepidus from the triumvirate. Lepidus spent the remainder of his life (d. 12 B.C.) in exile.

36   Octavian enrolled Marcus Valerius Messalla Corvinus as an augur, even though there were no vacancies at the time. Ironically, Messalla's name had been entered on Octavian's proscription list in 43, but he apparently became reconciled to Octavian later, and fought on his side against Sextus Pompeius. (Dio 49.16; OCD s.v. Messalla [3])

36   Octavian received a lifetime grant of tribunician power. (Shipley LCL Augustus *Res Gestae* 361)

c.36   In return for Capua's permission to settle his soldiers in their territory, Octavian granted to the Capuans large tracts of land in and around Cnossos, in Crete. (Dio 49.14)

35   Octavian celebrated the execution of Sextus Pompeius by organizing circus games, and by granting to Mark Antony statues in the temple of Concord, a ceremonial chariot and the right to sponsor banquets. (Dio 49.18)

34   (January 1.) Mark Antony resigned his consulship on his first day in office; he was replaced by Lucius Sempronius Atratinus. (Dio 49.39)

34   (Autumn.) Mark Antony celebrated a magnificent triumph in Alexandria, to commemorate his victories in Armenia. He also allocated various lands in Egypt and elsewhere to his children and to Cleopatra. These so-called Donations of Alexandria stirred up a good deal of suspicion against Antony in Rome. (Scullard GN 173–174)

34   Caesarion, son of Cleopatra and (allegedly) Julius Caesar, was given the title "King of Kings." As such, he became a potential rival to Octavian's designs on power. (Dio 49.41)

33   Marcus Agrippa agreed to hold the office of aedile (a distinctly downward career move for a man who had been consul) so that he could supervise various building programs and shows, at the behest of Octavian. (Dio 49.43)

33   With all major foreign disturbances settled, Octavian and Mark Antony set in motion a series of mutually hostile actions that culminated in the Battle of Actium. (Dio 50.1)

33   When an (unnamed) praetor died on his last day in office, Octavian appointed a replacement to serve out the few remaining hours on the term. (Dio 49.43)

32   The consulship of Gaius Sosius and Gnaeus Domitius Ahenobarbus, both partisans of Mark Antony. They refused to make public the messages Mark Antony sent to them from Egypt detailing his arrangements and distributions for the eastern provinces, and also his benefactions to Cleopatra and their children. (Sosius

and Ahenobarbus apparently feared an adverse reaction from the citizenry.) (Dio 49.41)

32   In a senate meeting, the consul Gaius Sosius proposed a censure vote directed against Octavian, a move vetoed by one of the tribunes. When Octavian defended himself at a subsequent meeting, Sosius (his consular colleague), Lucius Domitius Ahenobarbus, and some 300 senators deserted the city and joined themselves to Mark Antony. (Scullard GN 174)

32   A scandal erupted in Rome when Octavian seized Mark Antony's will from the guardianship of the Vestal Virgins, and made public its contents. *Inter alia*, the will specified that Antony was to be buried at Cleopatra's side in Alexandria, a clause that was widely interpreted to signify Antony's intent to transfer the capital to the Egyptian city. (Dio 50.3)

32   Lucius Munatius Plancus and his nephew Marcus Titius deserted Mark Antony to join forces with Octavian. Dio (50.3) speculates that their disgust over Antony's infatuation with Cleopatra caused the split. The two revealed much valuable information to Octavian.

32   So great was Cleopatra's sway over Mark Antony that she persuaded him to assume the office and title of gymnasiarch to the citizens of Alexandria. (A gymnasiarch was the activities director for a gymnasium; Antony's acceptance of the position was viewed by many in Rome as yet additional evidence of his growing attachment to Cleopatra and Egyptian affairs.) (Dio 50.5)

32   Mark Antony promised his soldiers that within two months of their putative victory over the forces of Octavian, he would lead a drive to restore to the Roman people and senate their former authority. (He later amended the time frame to six months.) (Dio 50.7)

32   Antony attempted to bribe Octavian's adherents — especially those in Rome and in Italy — to desert to his cause. For his part, Octavian donated money to his soldiers to ensure their continued loyalty. (Dio 50.7)

30   A plot to assassinate Octavian on his return to Rome from Greece failed, when the perpetrator, Marcus Aemilius Lepidus (son of

the triumvir) was captured and executed. (OCD *s.v.* Lepidus [4])

*c.*30   Gaius Cornelius Gallus became the first prefect of the newly created province of Egypt. Three years later, he committed suicide, possibly for incurring Octavian's displeasure at an inscription Gallus had erected, in which he boasted that he had penetrated farther into Egypt than any previous Roman commander. (OCD *s.v.* Gallus [3])

29   Octavian celebrated a three-day triumph to commemorate his military victories against the northern tribes; Antony and Cleopatra; and Egypt, respectively. Although he had not been able to capture Cleopatra alive, he ordered an effigy of her to be included in the procession. (Dio 51.21)

29   The consul Marcus Valerius Messalla Potitus presided over public sacrifices in honor of Octavian's return from the east. According to Dio, no person had ever before received such an honor.

29   According to Dio (52.42), Octavian issued a decree prohibiting senators from leaving Italy without his permission or by his command.

29   Dio (52.42) reported that Octavian removed from office a tribune named Quintus Statilius, for reasons unknown.

29   Octavian began to use the word *Imperator* (commander) as an official title, and as a praenomen. (Dio 52.41)

28   Octavian became princeps senatus, a title which he retained to the end of his life. (Augustus *Res Gestae* 1.7)

28   Octavian and Agrippa, as consuls for the year, reduced the number of senators from almost 1,000 to 800. According to Dio (52.42), he first tried "friendly persuasion"; about 50 senators thus voluntarily resigned. Another 140 he compelled to leave. The year 28 B.C. was the first in over two decades when both consuls remained in Rome for the entire twelve months of their terms of office.

27   (January 13). Octavian made a surprise announcement at a senate meeting: that he intended to surrender all his powers and all claims to any provinces. (Dio 53.8–9)

27   A separate province of Achaea was founded; it had formerly been a part of Macedonia. (OCD *s.v.* Achaea)

27   Octavian received the title Augustus by an act of the Roman senate. (OCD *s.v.* Augustus)

27   As an indication of the high esteem in which Octavian held Titus Statilius Taurus, he granted to him the power to select one praetor. (CAH X 133)

2. Laws, Decrees, Speeches

232   The passage of the *Lex Flaminia*, which authorized the distribution of certain lands in Gaul for the use of Roman colonists, occurred in this year. (OCD *s.v.* Flaminius [2])

215   The tribune Gaius Oppius proposed and passed the *Lex Oppia*, which placed restrictions on women's rights to own gold, wear expensive clothing, and ride in elaborate carriages. The law was repealed some 20 years later. (OCD *s.v.* Oppius)

204   The enactment of the *Lex Cincia*, which forbade courtroom orators (*advocati*) from accepting fees for their services; it also restricted certain kinds of donatives that might influence the administration of justice. Cicero accepted a gift of books from his friend Lucius Papirius Paetus (in 60) only after ascertaining that in so doing, he would not be violating the *Lex Cincia*. (OCD *s.v.* lex; Cicero *Letters to Atticus* 1.20)

199   During the tribunate of Publius Porcius Laeca, a *Lex Porcia* was passed; this law granted to Roman citizens in Italy and the provinces the right of appeal (*provocatio*) in capital cases. (OCD *s.v.* lex)

198   The consulship of Sextus Aelius Paetus Catus, who wrote an important historical interpretation of the law of the Twelve Tables. His treatise, entitled *Tripertita*, does not survive. (OCD *s.v.* Aelius [1])

197   A measure was passed requiring candidates for the consulship to have previously held the office of praetor. (OCD *s.v.* cursus honorum)

195   A vigorous effort was undertaken to repeal the *Lex Oppia* (of 213

B.C., a sumptuary law directed at women). Many Roman women took to the streets, accosting their husbands and others and begging them to support the repeal drive. The effort was successful; the Oppian law was removed from the books. (Livy 34.1; OCD *s.v.* Oppius [1])

191   The consul Manius Acilius Glabrio sponsored a law which required regular intercalations in the lunar calendar then in use, so that it would better correspond to the civic year. (OCD *s.v.* Glabrio [1])

189   The aediles Publius Claudius Pulcher and Servius Sulpicius Galba successfully prosecuted the grain dealers for withholding their inventory. To commemorate the event, they set up 12 golden shields on the Capitol. (Livy 38.35)

187   Latins living in Rome illegally (*i.e.* without citizenship) were banished by the consuls. A similar expulsion occurred in 177. (Cicero *Pro Sestio* 30; Gardner LCL Cicero *Pro Sestio* and *In Vatinium* 72–73)

186   The Roman senate passed an edict regulating Bacchic rites, sometimes rowdy celebrations associated with the worship of the god Bacchus. (OCD *s.v.* Bacchanalia)

184   Scipio Africanus endured a number of prosecutions in his later years. In 185, a tribune named Marcus Naevius accused him of granting King Antiochus (defeated at Magnesia in 189) generous terms of peace in return for a healthy bribe. Scipio deflected the charge by reviewing his distinguished record of service to the state. (Aulus Gellius 4.18; MRR I 376)

184   Cato the Censor made a speech in which he condemned the practice of setting up statues of women in the provinces. While apparently successful in that matter, he could not prevent the placement of such statues in Rome. (Pliny 34.31)

181   The passage of the short-lived *Lex Baebia*, which specified that four and six praetors should be chosen in alternate years. (Livy 40.44)

181   The consuls for the year, Publius Cornelius Cethegus and Marcus Baebius Tamphilus, proposed an anti-bribery law. The last such measure had been enacted in 358. (Livy 40.19; Sage/Schlesinger LCL Livy [Vol. XII] 62–63)

180 The *Lex Villia Annalis*, a term-limit measure, prohibited an office holder from running for reelection to the same office for a second consecutive term. (OCD *s.v.* Villius)

179 Quintus Caecilius Metellus made a speech in which he lectured the two new censors, Marcus Aemilius Lepidus and Marcus Fulvius Nobilior, on interpersonal relationships. These two censors had a history of feuding with one another, but both promised to cooperate in the future, for the good of Rome. (Livy 40.46)

177 Ambassadors from several allied towns complained to the Roman senate that many of their leading citizens had immigrated to Rome or to other large towns, thus depriving the allies of needed manpower. The senate responded by introducing legislation requiring the immigrants to return to their native towns and to surrender their Roman citizenship, if fraudulently acquired. (Livy 41.8)

171 When recruitment for the Second Macedonian War was underway, 23 former chief centurions presented themselves for reenlistment, hoping to be reinstated at their previous rank. One of these, a certain Spurius Ligustinus, made an impassioned speech before the assembly, in which he stated his case for a chief centurionship. The assembly and senate both approved his request. (Livy 42.34)

171 An unusual delegation arrived in Rome: Spanish-born children of Roman soldiers, with a request for a town in which they could reside. The senate decreed that they be settled in Carteia, in southern Spain. (Livy 43.3)

169 The passage of the *Lex Voconia* restricted the amount of money which women could receive in inheritances. The law was proposed by the tribune Quintus Voconius Saxa; Cato the Elder expressed his support for it in a contemporaneous speech. (Livy *Epitome* 46)

168 Prior to embarking upon the campaign against Perseus, the consul Lucius Aemilius Paullus made a speech before the people in which he assured them that he would discharge his responsibilities vigorously. He also leveled an attack upon noncombatants who might attempt to criticize his policies or strategies. (Livy 44.22)

167   Cato the Elder made a speech on behalf of the Rhodians, whom the Romans were planning to attack. His words were of no avail. About a century later, Cicero's educated secretary Tiro, in a letter to one of Cicero's friends, criticized the text of Cato's speech. (Aulus Gellius 6.3; OCD *s.v.* Cato [1])

161   The *Lex Fannia* was enacted; this law attempted to restrict the amount of money which could be spent on entertainments. Specifically, an expenditure limit of 120 *asses* was imposed upon dinner parties. (Aulus Gellius 2.24)

161   The praetor Marcus Pomponius proposed, and the Roman senate passed, a decree banishing all philosophers and rhetoricians from the city. (Suetonius *On Rhetoricians* I)

c.161   Cato the Elder made a speech in which he sarcastically remarked that prostitutes and pickled fish commanded higher purchase prices than farmland and oxen, a telling indictment of the degraded conditions of the times (in Cato's opinion). (Diodorus Siculus 36.24)

154   The ex-consul Lucius Cornelius Lentulus Lupus was found guilty of embezzlement, as were several praetors. (Livy *Epitome* 47; MRR I 450)

c.150   Gaius Laelius proposed a land redistribution scheme, but withdrew it in the face of intense opposition from wealthy landowners. (He subsequently earned the cognomen *Sapiens*, "wise," for his prudence in abandoning the plan.) (Plutarch *Tiberius Gracchus* 8)

c.150   The passage of the *Lex Aebutia* permitted praetors a certain degree of procedural flexibility in presiding over court cases. (Scullard GN 210)

c.150   The passage of the *Lex Atinia* gave tribunes the right to become members of the senate. (Aulus Gellius 14.8; Livy *Epitome* 50)

c.150   Gaius Cornelius Cethegus was fined 600 sesterces for allegedly raping a free woman in the employ of Publius Decius Subulo. (Livy *Epitome* 48)

c.150   Two Roman noblewomen, Publilia and Licinia, were tried for murdering their husbands, both ex-consuls. The two women were ultimately dispatched not by the state, but by the order of their own relatives. (Livy *Epitome* 48)

149   The passage of the *Lex Calpurnia* gave to provincials access to Roman courts, in matters of alleged extortion by governors or other officials. (OCD *s.v.* lex)

149   The tribune Lucius Calpurnius Piso Frugi authored the *Lex de pecuniis repetundis*, which established a special court (*quaestio*) to try extortion cases. Other *quaestiones* were added later, notably by Sulla. (OCD *s.v.* Piso [1])

149   The last prosecution of Cato's long career occurred in 149, when he unsuccessfully impeached Servius Sulpicius Galba for treachery and mismanagement in Spain. More specifically, Galba was accused of ordering the slaughter of some Lusitanians who had surrendered. (Livy *Epitome* 49; OCD *s.v.* Galba [3])

*c.*140 Decimus Junius Silanus was accused by the Macedonians of provincial mismanagement. Presiding over the inquiry was Silanus' father, Titus Manlius Torquatus; the father found his own son guilty, and banished him. Silanus subsequently committed suicide. (Livy *Epitome* 54)

139   The tribune Aulus Gabinius proposed the use of secret ballots in elections, to replace the public declaration method. (OCD *s.v.* Gabinius [1])

132   The consuls Publius Rupilius and Publius Popillius Laenas presided over a special court established to investigate and punish the surviving adherents of Tiberius Gracchus. (OCD *s.v.* Rupilius)

131   The tribune Gaius Papirius Carbo offered a bill which would have legalized reelection to the tribunate; the measure was not enacted. He was more successful with another initiative: the ratification of his proposal to extend the secret ballot to legislative assemblies. (OCD *s.v.* Carbo [1])

131   Several *leges Rupiliae*, dealing with Sicilian affairs, were passed. Their chief promulgator was Publius Rupilius (consul in 132). (OCD *s.v.* lex; *s.v.* Rupilius)

131   Scipio Aemilianus delivered a lengthy speech in which he remarked that his kinsman Tiberius Sempronius Gracchus had been justly killed. (Livy *Epitome* 59)

126   The *Lex Junia* became law; it restricted non-citizen access to Rome,

and provided for the expulsion of those currently residing in the city. (OCD *s.v.* lex)

123– Gaius Sempronius Gracchus proposed numerous legislative ini-
122   tiatives during these two years. The most noteworthy:

1. *Lex frumentaria*, to regulate the supply and price of corn.

2. *Lex militaris*, a prohibition against enrolling young men — perhaps below the age of 17 — into the army.

3. *Lex Sempronia de provinciis consularibus*, which provided that provincial governorships should be assigned before — not after — consular elections.

4. *Lex de provincia Asia*, which dealt with tax collection policies in Asia.

5. *Lex agraria*, to continue his brother's earlier efforts at land redistribution.

6. *Lex de coloniis deducendis*, on the founding of colonies.

7. *Lex ne quis judicio circumveniatur*, which provided for punitive consequences for corrupt jurors.

8. *Lex Acilia de rebus repetundis*, (a law sponsored by Grac-chus' fellow tribune Manius Acilius Glabrio) which directed that members of the equestrian class supersede senators on juries in extortion cases. Gracchus later expanded the scope of this initiative by proposing the abolition of all senatorial juries.

9. *Lex de sociis et nomine Latino*, which addressed the prob-lem of citizenship for Rome's Italian allies.

10. *Lex Rubria*, which sanctioned the founding of a colony at Carthage. Debates over its proposed repeal in the following year (121) ultimately led to the rioting in which Gracchus was killed. (MRR II 513–514; 517–518; Scullard GN 34–36)

122   Marcus Livius Drusus (consul 112) suggested the establishment of 12 colonies, consisting of 3,000 people apiece. The colonists, mostly poor people, would be allowed to live on the land rent-free. (MRR II 517)

121   The senatus consultum ultimum, "final decree of the senate," was a declaration of martial law. It was first employed in 121 against Gaius Gracchus and his partisans. (OCD *s.v.* senatus consultum ultimum)

120   Lucius Opimius, a leading opponent of Gaius Gracchus, was tried for his role in the riots of 121, which led to the violent deaths of

3,000 Roman citizens. He was also accused of jailing citizens without a trial. Ultimately, however, he was acquitted. (Livy *Epitome* 61; OCD *s.v.* Opimius)

120   The tribune Publius Decius prosecuted Lucius Opimius (consul 121) for unjustly punishing Roman citizens. (MRR II 524)

119   Lucius Licinius Crassus — at the age of 21— prosecuted Gaius Papirius Carbo, an estranged supporter of Gaius Gracchus. Crassus later held the offices of consul (95) and censor (92). (OCD *s.v.* Crassus [3])

119   As tribune, Gaius Marius sponsored the *Lex Maria*, a measure narrowing the bridges which voters traversed before casting their ballots. This law rendered voter intimidation more difficult. (OCD *s.v.* lex)

114   Three Vestal Virgins, Aemilia, Licinia and Marcia, were tried for unchastity. When two (Licinia and Marcia) were acquitted by a religious tribunal, a new trial took place, under the auspices of a secular court. A hostile ex-consul, Lucius Cassius Longinus Ravilla, presided and gained convictions for all three in 113. (Livy *Epitome* 63; Scullard GN 47–48)

114   The tribune Gnaeus Aufidius proposed and passed a law repealing the ban on the importation of elephants into Italy. (Pliny 8.64)

c.113 Gaius Porcius Cato (grandson of Cato the Elder) was tried and convicted of extortion for his proconsular administration of Macedonia. According to Velleius Paterculus (2.8), the sum involved was a relatively paltry 4000 sesterces. However, the judges based their decision on the intentions and character of the perpetrator, not on the amount of money.

109   The tribune Gaius Mamilius Limetanus prosecuted several aristocrats for various kinds of corruption. The court under which the trials were conducted was called the *quaestio Mamilia* (after Mamilius). (OCD *s.v.* Mamilius)

107   The tribune Gaius Coelius Caldus prosecuted the military commander Gaius Popillius Laenas for treason (for assenting to unworthy terms of surrender after a battle in Gaul). Also in 107, Coelius introduced the secret ballot for jurors hearing treason cases. (OCD *s.v.* Coelius)

104   Prior to the passage of the *Lex Domitia* in 104, members of the various priestly colleges were chosen by a nominations process; this law required that they be elected. Lucius Domitius Ahenobarbus, promulgator of this law, was elected pontifex maximus in consequence. (OCD *s.v.* Domitius [3]; *s.v.* lex)

*c.*103   The passage of the *Lex Licinia* resulted in the imposition of limits of 100 *asses* for dinner parties held during specified holidays, 200 for weddings, and 30 for dinners on other days. (Aulus Gellius 2.24; Rolfe LCL Aulus Gellius [Vol. I] 204)

103   The propraetor Titus Albucius was convicted of provincial extortion in Sardinia. A man whose obsessive philhellenism made him the butt of many a joke, he spent his exile studying philosophy in Athens. (OCD *s.v.* Albucius)

99   A senatorial decree declared that sacrifices of full-grown victims should be offered whenever an earthquake occurred with sufficient force to shake the sacred spears of Mars in the Regia. (Aulus Gellius 4.6)

*c.*99   Manius Aquillius (consul in 101) was tried for extortion and, although clearly guilty, acquitted. As the trial was concluding, Marcus Antonius, Aquillius' lawyer, bared his client's chest to display the battle scars he had received from his action in a recent servile war. This dramatic flourish swayed the jury in Aquillius' favor. (Cicero *Pro Flacco* 98; Livy *Epitome* 70)

98   The terms of the *Lex Caecilia et Didia*, passed in this year, specified that a proposed law must be promulgated at least three weeks prior to a vote on it. (OCD *s.v.* Didius [1])

97   The Roman senate outlawed human sacrifice in religious observances. (Cary 316)

95   Due to the servile uprisings in Sicily (135–132; 102–99), Roman officials passed laws forbidding the natives to carry weapons. On one occasion in 95, a huge boar was brought to the praetor Lucius Domitius Ahenobarbus. When its slayer appeared before him, he admitted to having killed it with a spear. Domitius immediately ordered the unfortunate hunter to be crucified, for violating the weapons ban. (Cicero *In Verrem* 2.5.7)

95   The enactment of the *Lex Licinia Mucia* empowered the consuls to expel any non-citizen Italians who were residing in Rome. (Scullard GN 63–64)

95   Gaius Norbanus was charged with treason, and defended by Marcus Antonius (grandfather of the triumvir). Norbanus was acquitted. (OCD *s.v.* Norbanus)

95   Quintus Servilius Caepio (quaestor in 100) was tried for treason. He was defended by one of the outstanding advocates of the day, Lucius Licinius Crassus, who gained his acquittal. (OCD *s.v.* Caepio [2])

92   The censors Gnaeus Domitius Ahenobarbus and Lucius Licinius Crassus stated in a public proclamation that they did not view favorably the activities of rhetoric teachers in Rome. The two felt that these teachers were purveying unwelcome innovations in pedagogical method and content. (OCD *s.v.* Domitius [3])

90   The passage of the *Lex Julia*, which conferred citizenship on Rome's (loyal) Italian allies. The law's chief sponsor was one of the consuls for 90, Lucius Julius Caesar. (OCD *s.v.* Caesar [2]; *s.v.* lex)

90   The tribune Quintus Varius Severus Hybrida passed a measure (*Lex Varia*) establishing a special equestrian court to deal with cases of inciting violence. Ironically, Varius was convicted in 89 of violating his own law, and was exiled. Cicero held a high opinion of Varius' oratorical ability, calling him *disertus* ("eloquent"). (Cicero *Brutus* 305; OCD *s.v.* Varius [1])

89   The censors Publius Licinius Crassus and Lucius Julius Caesar placed legal limits on trafficking in imported wine and perfume. (MRR II 33)

89   The tribunes Marcus Plautius Silvanus and Gaius Papirius Carbo secured passage of the *Lex Plautia Papiria*, which conferred citizenship on rebel Italians willing to lay down their arms. (OCD *s.v.* Plautius)

*c.*88   Cicero began attending the lectures and speeches of Philo of Larissa, a philosopher who immigrated to Rome at about this time. Philo was highly respected generally, and became of one Cicero's most influential teachers. (Plutarch *Cicero* 2; OCD *s.v.* Philon)

86   The passage of the *Lex de aere alieno*, on debt relief. The law was proposed by Lucius Valerius Flaccus, who became consul suffectus upon the death of Gaius Marius in this year. (OCD *s.v.* Flaccus [6])

86   Lucius Marcius Philippus (consul in 91) defended Pompey on a charge of *peculatus* (embezzlement). During the trial, he referred to his high regard for Alexander (as Pompey was occasionally called), stating that it should hardly be surprising for Philip to love Alexander. (Plutarch *Pompey* 2)

82   Lucius Valerius Flaccus, interrex in this year, proposed the law conferring a dictatorship on Sulla. Flaccus then became Sulla's magister equitum. Flaccus had held the consulship in 100, the censorship in 97; at the time of his legislative initiative, he was princeps senatus. (OCD *s.v.* Flaccus [5])

81   Cicero delivered his *Pro Quinctio*, his earliest extant speech. (OCD *s.v.* Cicero [1])

80   Cicero delivered his *Pro Roscio Amerino*, a case involving a charge of parricide; he successfully defended Amerinus. (CAH IX 756)

78   The *Lex Lutatia* was enacted, under the sponsorship of the consul Quintus Lutatius Catulus. It was the first law drafted to deal specifically with violence, especially in connection with elections and other political matters. (OCD *s.v.* lex; *s.v.* vis)

78   While presiding over a court case, the praetor Lucius Licinius Lucullus failed to rise from his chair when a fellow politician, one Manius Acilius Glabrio, passed by. Incensed by the perceived insult, Glabrio broke Lucullus' chair. The latter's only response: to stand while he finished hearing the case. (Dio 36.41)

78   While studying rhetoric in Rhodes under the famed Apollonius, Cicero delivered a speech in Greek. Everyone who heard it, except Apollonius, praised him; the latter remained pensively silent. When Cicero asked for feedback, Apollonius replied that Greece would lose to Rome through Cicero its only two distinctions: learning and eloquence. (Plutarch *Cicero* 4)

78   The consul Marcus Aemilius Lepidus made a speech (preserved in Sallust *Histories* 1.55) in which he denounced Sulla's actions.

77   Julius Caesar's initial foray into public life occurred in this year, with his unsuccessful prosecution of Gnaeus Cornelius Dolabella (consul in 81), for extortion. (OCD *s.v.* Caesar [1])

77   (January.) Lucius Marcius Philippus (consul in 91) delivered a speech in which he denounced the plans of Marcus Aemilius

Lepidus to run for a second consecutive consulship. (Sallust *Histories* 1.77)

c.77 A certain Quintus Calidius, on being found guilty of extortion, remarked that a man of praetorian rank could not be found guilty for less than 300,000 sesterces. (Gruen 31)

76 Julius Caesar prosecuted Mark Antony's brother Gaius, on a charge of provincial extortion. (Ker LCL Cicero *Philippics* 4)

75 The consul Gaius Aurelius Cotta carried legislation which nullified a Sullan measure prohibiting tribunes from seeking higher office. He also addressed the Roman in a speech in which he attempted to assuage their anxieties over events in Spain (especially Sertorius' activities), and the designs of King Mithridates. (Sallust *Histories* 2.47)

75– An otherwise unknown official named Terentius Varro stood trial
74 in both years for extortion. Defended by the influential Quintus Hortensius, he was acquitted, although judicial improprieties were alleged. (Gruen 31, 38)

74 The trial of Albius Oppianicus *et al.*, on a charge of poisoning. After the trial, Oppianicus' advocate, Lucius Quinctius, successfully prosecuted the presiding judge (Gaius Junius) on a charge of bribery. (Gruen 32; Scullard GN 94)

73 The *Lex Terentia Cassia* was passed in response to a grain shortage in Rome; its chief provisions: increase the amount of corn imported from Sicily, and subsidize its distribution to the neediest citizens. (OCD *s.v.* Lucullus [3])

73 The tribune Gaius Licinius Macer gave a speech to the people in which he urged them to demand their rights in the face of increasing patrician power. (Sallust *Histories* 3.48)

72 The passage of the *Lex Gellia Cornelia* ratified Pompey's bestowal of citizenships in Spain. (OCD *s.v.* lex)

70 Cicero wrote two speeches against the corrupt ex-governor Gaius Verres. He spoke only the first; Verres fled before his trial was completed. Verres was defended by several noted pleaders, including Quintus Hortensius, the leading orator of the day, and Lucius Cornelius Sisenna, a statesman and historian. (OCD *s.v.* Verres)

70   The orator Hortensius habitually carried a statuette of the sphinx, a gift which Verres gave to him during the latter's trial in this year. During the trial, Cicero was making a complicated point when Hortenius objected that he could not understand Cicero's riddles. Cicero replied: "You ought to. You've got the sphinx right there with you!" (Pliny 34.48)

c.70   The *Lex Pompeia de parricidiis* was passed; it dealt with the murder of near relations. (OCD *s.v.* parricidium)

c.70   Passage of the *Lex Plotia*, which restored Romans who were exiled after the conspiracy of Lepidus. Included in the group of returnees was Julius Caesar's brother-in-law, Lucius Cornelius Cinna. (Suetonius *Julius Caesar* 5)

70   Near the end of this year, an uneducated Roman knight named Onatius Aurelius made a brief speech before the assembly in which he described a dream he had had, in which Jupiter appeared; the god ordered him to relay the message to the two (often feuding) consuls Pompey and Crassus that they should put aside their enmity. They outwardly complied, by shaking hands. (Plutarch *Crassus* 12)

69   Cicero defended Aulus Caecina in an inheritance case.

c.69   The ex-quaestor Publius Oppius was tried for sedition and murder, while serving under the proconsul Marcus Aurelius Cotta in Bithynia. He apparently was attempting to blame Oppius for his own bungled operations against King Mithridates. (Gruen 269)

67   Pompey made a self-deprecating speech in which he claimed that he did not desire the extraordinary command against the pirates. According to Dio (36.24), however, Pompey was skilled at dissembling in such a manner, and thus often obtaining the very offices and honors which he publicly professed to disdain.

67   During the senatorial debate over the proposed command for Pompey against the pirates, the highly regarded Quintus Lutatius Catulus (consul in 78) spoke in opposition. When he posed a rhetorical question to his listeners about whom they would choose should they lose Pompey, they all replied: "You, of course!" Thereupon, Catulus resumed his seat; he could make no retort. (Plutarch *Pompey* 25; Velleius Paterculus 2.32)

67   The passage of the *Lex Gabinia* (under the sponsorship of the tribune Aulus Gabinius), giving Pompey wide powers to clear the Mediterranean Sea of pirates. The optimates attempted to persuade the other tribunes to veto the measure, but only two of the nine — Lucius Trebellius and Lucius Roscius Otho — were amenable. And even these two, cowed by popular sentiment, remained silent when the proposal was debated. (Dio 36.24)

67–   Quintus Hortensius and Quintus Lutatius Catulus, two of the most
66   eminent orators of the day, spoke in opposition to special military commands (*e.g.* as granted by the *Lex Gabinia*) proposed for Pompey. (OCD *s.v.* Hortensius [2]; Catulus [3])

67   The *Lex Roscia* was enacted, a measure which restored the right of the equestrian class to have reserved for them the first fourteen rows of seats in theaters. (OCD *s.v.* Roscius [2])

67   The tribune Gaius Cornelius proposed and or carried several legislative initiatives, including: prohibitions on electoral bribery; restrictions on provincials' ability to borrow money when in Rome. When the senate attempted to delay consideration of Cornelius' proposals, the people accosted the consul Gaius Calpurnius Piso (an opponent of Cornelius), broke his fasces, and nearly killed him. Cornelius was later prosecuted for treason; Cicero defended him (in 65). (MRR II 144; OCD *s.v.* Cornelius [1])

66   Cicero defended Aulus Cluentius Habitus (*Pro Cluentio*) against charges of poisoning and bribery. (OCD *s.v.* Cicero [1])

66   The *Lex Manilia*, passed in this year, conferred wide powers upon Pompey to organize and supervise Roman hegemony in the eastern Mediterranean region. (OCD *s.v.* Manilius [2])

66   Lucius Licinius Lucullus was prosecuted for embezzling money during his Asian campaigns. He fought the charge vigorously, and with the help of many of his influential friends, managed to escape conviction. (Plutarch *Lucullus* 37)

66   Plutarch (*Cicero* 9) relates the case of a certain Licinius Macer, who was tried for fraud, before Cicero, one of the praetors for the year. Confident that he would be acquitted, because of his influential contacts, Macer went home before the case was decided, to celebrate his anticipated victory. So great was his shock upon being informed of his conviction that he died the very same day.

Plutarch also recounts the case of Gaius Manilius, Pompey's operative, who was accused of embezzlement; Cicero presided at this trial, also. He granted Manilius only one day to prepare his defense (instead of the usual ten days). Manilius and his friends were initially outraged, until Cicero explained that his term as praetor had only two or three days remaining, and that Manilius would likely receive a fairer hearing from him than from his successor.

66   Faustus Cornelius Sulla (son of the dictator) was tried for illegally possessing property confiscated during his father's proscriptions in the 80s. He was acquitted. (Gruen 276)

65   In a letter to Atticus (1.2), Cicero confided that he was considering defending Catiline against a charge of provincial mismanagement.

65   Both consuls-elect for 65 — Publius Cornelius Sulla and Publius Autronius Paetus — resigned because of electoral bribery. (MRR II 157)

64   The senate passed a ban on all *collegia* ("clubs," or "associations") except those of certain craftsmen. Some of these *collegia* functioned as political action groups; hence, the senate's concern over their activities. (Scullard GN 120–121)

64   Catiline was prosecuted for murder by Cicero's wealthy friend, Lucius Lucceius. Catiline was acquitted. (OCD *s.v.* Lucceius)

64   Julius Caesar instigated prosecutions (and gained convictions of) Lucius Annius Bellienus and Lucius Luscius, two men who had been involved in carrying out the Sullan proscriptions. (Dio 37.10)

c.64   (Possibly earlier.) The passage of the *Lex Fabia* restricted the size of the official coterie accompanying political candidates. (Cicero *Pro Murena* 71)

63   Cicero's three speeches *Contra Rullum* (*Against Rullus*) in which he opposed a land redistribution bill offered by the tribune Publius Servilius Rullus. (MRR II 168)

63   Cicero's *Lex Tullia* prohibited political candidates from sponsoring shows in any biennium before they ran for office. The law

also specified a 10-year exile for those convicted of violating it. (Gruen 222–223)

63   The tribune Titus Labienus initiated a prosecution (for treason) of the aged senator Gaius Rabirius, in connection with his alleged complicity in the death of Saturninus, some 37 years earlier. (MRR II 167; OCD s.v. Rabirius [1])

63   The tribune Lucius Caecilius Rufus proposed a measure restoring the civil rights of the discredited consuls-elect for 65, Publius Autronius Paetus and Publius Cornelius Sulla. The proposal never came to a vote. (Cicero *Pro Sulla* 62)

63   Cicero twice defended a certain Aulus Thermus, described by the orator as *innocens et bonus vir*, "a harmless and good man." The particulars of the trials are unknown, however. (Cicero *Pro Flacco* 98; MacDonald LCL Cicero *In Catilinam*, etc. 549)

63   The tribunes Titus Labienus and Titus Ampius proposed a measure permitting Pompey to wear a golden crown and other triumphal garb at circus games, and that he should also be allowed to wear the crown and distinctive clothing to the theater. (Velleius Paterculus 2.40)

63   In November and December of this year, Cicero presented four scathing speeches against Catiline, a bankrupt aristocrat who was fomenting a revolution against the government of Rome.

63   During the senatorial debates over the fate of the captured Catilinarian conspirators, the first speaker, the consul-elect Decimus Junius Silanus, suggested the "extreme penalty"; in the face of Julius Caesar's opposition to their execution, Silanus later clarified his statement, explaining that he referred merely to incarceration. (Plutarch *Cicero* 20–21)

63   Cicero presented a speech (not extant) in which he reportedly implicated both Crassus and Caesar in the Catilinarian conspiracy. (Plutarch *Crassus* 13)

63   (December 31.) On the last day of his consulship, Cicero attempted to make a speech reviewing his accomplishments in office. However, his audience refused to allow him to speak, so great was the resentment they felt toward him for his role in the execution of the Catilinarian conspirators. (Dio 37.38)

62   (January 1.) Julius Caesar proposed a measure depriving Quintus Lutatius Catulus of his oversight of the restorations of the Capitol, and transferring the job to Pompey. He subsequently withdrew the proposal, in the face of stiff aristocratic opposition. (Suetonius *Julius Caesar* 15)

62   Early in the year, the tribune Quintus Caecilius Metellus Nepos proposed a bill authorizing Pompey to rescue the Roman republic from Cicero's alleged autocracy. (OCD *s.v.* Metellus [10])

62   Cicero successfully defended Publius Cornelius Sulla (*Pro Sulla*) against a charge of complicity in the second Catilinarian conspiracy. Cicero's reputation suffered somewhat, as it came to light that the wealthy Sulla had loaned him the immense sum of 2,000,000 sesterces to purchase a house on the Palatine Hill. (Aulus Gellius 12.12; OCD s.v Sulla [2])

62   Cicero delivered his oration *Pro Archia*, a plea for citizenship for the Greek poet Archias. (OCD *s.v.* Cicero [1]) The speech is noteworthy for its lengthy section on literary criticism.

62   The consulship of Lucius Licinius Murena. Cato the Younger (*et al.*) had prosecuted him in 63, while consul-elect, for electoral bribery. According to Plutarch (*Cato the Younger* 21), Cato would also have brought suit against the other consul, Decimus Junius Silanus, except that Silanus was his brother-in-law. Murena was defended by Cicero *et al.* Cicero's speech (*Pro Murena*) is extant.

59   The passage of the *Lex Vatinia*, which granted to Julius Caesar a five-year Gallic command, occurred in this year. (OCD *s.v.* Vatinius)

59   Marcus Caelius Rufus prosecuted Gaius Antonius Hybrida (consul in 63) for provincial mismanagement in Macedonia. Although Cicero defended him at the trial, he was convicted. In the course of this trial, Cicero made some critical remarks about Julius Caesar. Caesar's countermove: approve Publius Clodius' application for transfer to plebeian rank, thus rendering him eligible to run for the tribunate, and begin his formal harassment of Cicero. (OCD *s.v.* Antonius [3]; Suetonius *Julius Caesar* 20)

59   Lucius Valerius Flaccus was successfully defended by Cicero (*Pro Flacco*), against a charge of extortion. (OCD *s.v.* Flaccus [7])

59   A law enacted at the urging of Julius Caesar specified that victorious generals could not demand the traditional *aurum coronarium*

(gold crown) until a formal triumph had been sanctioned. (OCD *s.v.* aurum coronarium)

59   The passage of the *Lex Julia de agro Campano* made available public land near Capua for the resettlement of military veterans, and also some civilians. (Gardner LCL *Pro Caelio*, etc. 383)

59   A far-ranging law — the *Lex Julia repetundarum*— passed by Julius Caesar severely restricted the prerogatives of provincial governors. The law contained no fewer than 101 clauses, and continued to be observed into the next century. (CAH IX 459) The measure was well regarded; even Cicero (*Pro Sestio* 135), usually no admirer of Caesar, referred to it as an *optima lex*, an "excellent law." (Gruen 242–243)

59   Cato the Younger opposed a particular piece of legislation favored by Caesar, and so Cato engaged in a day-long one man filibuster to prevent the measure from coming to a vote. Caesar was so annoyed by this tactic that he ordered Cato to be imprisoned, a directive shortly thereafter rescinded. (Aulus Gellius 4.10)

59   Quintus Fufius Calenus, praetor in this year, sponsored a law requiring each of the three jury classes — senators, knights and treasury tribunes — to record their votes on legislative matters separately. The intent of this measure seemed to have been to force each class to assume responsibility for its legislative actions, instead of assigning blame for poor legislation to one of the other classes. (Dio 38.8)

59   Cicero publicly lamented the condition of the republic; his words so offended Julius Caesar that Caesar immediately approved Publius Clodius' petition for a transfer to plebeian rank. (Suetonius *Julius Caesar* 20)

59   A speech which Caesar was presenting in the forum was disrupted by the other consul, Marcus Calpurnius Bibulus. A scuffle ensued, and Bibulus was escorted from the scene. At that point, Cato the Younger attempted to resume the hostilities, but Caesar's adherents forcibly removed him. (Appian *Civil Wars* 2.11)

59   Many senators, including Cato, refused to swear allegiance to the new laws passed by Caesar. He brought them all into line, however, by threatening them with capital punishment if they continued to oppose his enactments. (Appian *Civil Wars* 2.12)

58   The tribune Publius Clodius proposed a law which would prescribe exile for any Roman who had executed citizens without a trial, a measure generally (and later specifically) aimed at Cicero, for his role in the demise of the Catiliniarian conspirators. (Scullard GN 121)

58   The *Lex Clodia* conferred provincial commands upon Aulus Gabinius (in Syria) and Lucius Calpurnius Piso Caesoninus (in Macedonia). (CAH IX 456)

58   The tribune Lucius Antistius launched an abortive prosecution against Julius Caesar, for Caesar's various actions as consul in the previous year. (Suetonius *Julius Caesar* 23)

57   During the tumultuous debate over Cicero's recall from exile, his brother Quintus spoke on his behalf. Violence erupted, and Quintus was able to save himself only by lying among the dead and wounded, and feigning death. (Cicero *Pro Sestio* 76; Plutarch *Cicero* 33)

57   (December.) Publius Rutilius Lupus delivered a detailed address before the Roman senate in opposition to Caesar's law (of 59) pertaining to the distribution of lands in Campania. Cicero noted that the senate listened to him in deep silence. (Cicero *Letters to His Brother Quintus* 2.1)

57   (December.) Cicero made a strident speech in the senate decrying the actions of Publius Clodius. Clodius responded in an equally vituperative manner; the meeting adjourned with many acrimonious sentiments bandied about by the adherents of the two rivals. (Cicero *Letters to His Brother Quintus* 2.1)

57   Cicero presented a speech entitled *De Domo Sua* (*Concerning His Own House*), in which he attacked Clodius for seizing and destroying his Palatine home, during his (Cicero's) period of exile. The house was valued at 2,000,000 sesterces by the consuls for the year. (Cicero *Letters to Atticus* 4.2)

57   The consul Publius Cornelius Lentulus Spinther made his son an augur, although a law forbade two members of the same family from being augurs concurrently. (A member of the Cornelian gens, Sulla's son Faustus, was enrolled at the time.) So Spinther evaded the law by transferring his son to the Manlian gens. (Dio 39.17)

56   (February 10.) The senate issued a decree disbanding all political clubs and similar gatherings, apparently to curb violence and bribery. (Cicero *Letters to His Brother Quintus* 2.3)

56   Cicero's speech *Pro Balbo*, in which he successfully defended Lucius Cornelius Balbus against a charge of illegally gaining Roman citizenship. (OCD *s.v.* Balbus [3])

56   Cicero's *In Vatinium*, a vituperative attack on one of Julius Caesar's cronies. Ironically, Cicero defended Vatinius two years later, against a charge of bribery. (OCD *s.v.* Vatinius)

56   Marcus Caelius Rufus prosecuted Lucius Calpurnius Bestia for bribery. As in the case against Gaius Antonius in 59, Caelius found himself opposing Cicero. In this instance, Cicero prevailed. (OCD *s.v.* Caelius)

56   Cicero delivered his *De Provinciis Consularibus* (*On Consular Provinces*), in which he argued in favor of an extension of Julius Caesar's Gallic command. (Gardner LCL Cicero *Pro Caelio*, etc. 525ff)

56   In his speech *In Pisonem*, Cicero attacked Lucius Calpurnius Piso Caesoninus, Julius Caesar's father-in-law, charging him with mismanagement during his tenure as the governor of Macedonia.

56   Cicero defended Publius Asicius (in a speech now lost) against a charge of murdering Dio, an Alexandrian ambassador who had traveled to Rome to register his fellow citizens' disapproval of Ptolemy XII's reinstatement to the Egyptian throne. (Gardner LCL Cicero *Pro Caelio*, etc. 402–403)

56   In his defense of Marcus Caelius Rufus in this year, Cicero excoriated the anomalous behavior of Clodia, who sprang from a distinguished consular family: her father, uncle, grandfather, great-grandfather, great-great-grandfather and his father had all held consulships, in 79, 92, 143, 177, 212 and 249 respectively. (Gardner LCL Cicero *Pro Caelio*, etc. 447)

56   Cicero *et al.* defended Publius Sestius against a charge of civil violence. He won a unanimous acquittal for his client (March 11 of this year.) (Cicero *Letters to His Brother Quintus* 2.4; OCD *s.v.* Sestius)

56   Cicero remarked that it was possible to observe the true mindset of the Roman people in three settings: 1. at public meetings

(*contiones*); 2. in Assembly meetings (*comitia*); 3. at plays and gladiatorial shows (*ludorum gladiatorumque consessu*). (Cicero *Pro Sestio* 106)

55   A law sponsored by five tribunes — Mamilius, Lucius Roscius Fabatus, Aulus Allienus, Sextus Peducaeus and Gaius Fabius — was enacted; the law apparently pertained to land distribution matters. (MRR II 217)

55   The passage of the *Lex Trebonia*, which conferred five-year military commands on Crassus (in Syria) and Pompey (in Spain). (OCD *s.v.* Trebonius)

55   As consuls, Pompey and Crassus proposed sumptuary legislation (even though they both enjoyed luxurious lifestyles). But the orator Quintus Hortensius so eloquently defended the concept of conspicuous consumption that the consuls abandoned their effort. (Dio 39.37)

54   (March 1.) The date on which Julius Caesar's five-year command in Gaul was supposed to expire. He had successfully conspired, with Crassus and Pompey, for an extension to 50 B.C. The arrangement was formalized by the passage of the *Lex Licinia Pompeia* (in 55). (OCD *s.v.* Lex)

54   Three separate prosecutions were launched against Aulus Gabinius (consul in 58): for treason, extortion and bribery. He was acquitted of treason, much to the chagrin of Cicero, who nonetheless defended him against the extortion charge. This time, Gabinius was convicted and exiled; the third charge was dropped. Cicero suggests that even with the active support of Pompey, Gabinius was nearly convicted on the treason charge, with 32 of 70 jurors voting against him. (Cicero *Letters to His Brother Quintus* 3.4; OCD *s.v.* Gabinius [2])

54   The trial of Marcus Aemilius Scaurus. He lined up a most unlikely defense team, including Cicero and Cicero's longtime nemesis Publius Clodius; Clodius' bitter rival Titus Annius Milo; and Quintus Hortensius, whom Cicero had opposed in 70, in the celebrated Verres trial. With all this firepower engaged on his behalf, it is little wonder that Scaurus was acquitted. Cicero's speech (*Pro Scauro*) survives. (Gruen 333–336)

54   Cicero and Quintus Hortensius successfully defended Gnaeus

Plancius (quaestor in 58, tribune in 56) against a charge of electoral bribery. (OCD *s.v.* Plancius)

52   Titus Annius Milo made a speech in the forum; he defended his role in the riot in which Clodius was killed. He also delivered a withering posthumous attack on Clodius. The audience — many of whom had been partisans of Clodius — did not respond favorably. A disturbance broke out, and Milo escaped the subsequent violence only by disguising himself as a slave. (Appian *Civil Wars* 2.22)

52   Cicero wrote his speech in defense of Titus Annius Milo, the *Pro Milone*; Milo had been implicated in the murder of Clodius. However, when Cicero entered the courtroom and observed the presence of armed guards, he was so intimidated that his usual eloquence deserted him, and he departed without delivering his speech. Milo soon after fled to Massilia, where he enjoyed a life of ease ironically made possible in part by Cicero's failure to secure an acquittal for him. (OCD *s.v.* Milo)

52   Cato the Younger gave a speech in which he declared his support for Milo's acquittal (for the murder of Clodius). (Velleius Paterculus 2.47)

52   As a result of the civil disturbances occurring in Rome at the death of Publius Clodius, Pompey issued an edict forbidding any unauthorized person to carry a weapon. (Pliny 34.139)

52   Legislation promulgated by Pompey required that candidates for office could not run *in absentia*; and that a period of five years must be observed before an ex-magistrate could assume a provincial governorship. (Scullard GN 125)

51   At the age of 12, Octavian eulogized his recently deceased grandmother, Julia. (Suetonius *Augustus* 8)

50   In the last case of his celebrated 45-year legal career, the orator Quintus Hortensius assisted in the defense of Appius Claudius Pulcher, against charges of provincial mismanagement and electoral corruption. Claudius was acquitted of all charges. (Cicero *Brutus* 324; OCD *s.v.* Claudius Pulcher [12])

49   After Pompey's forces had fled Italy for Greece, Julius Caesar delivered a speech to the senate, in which he attempted to assure the senators that his aims were noble and that they should face the

future optimistically. He also spoke to the people, promising them grain and a grant of 300 sesterces apiece. (Dio 41.16)

46   Cicero delivered his *Pro Marcello* (on behalf of the consul for 51); it was a speech filled with praise for Julius Caesar, for permitting Marcellus to return to Italy from exile in Mytilene. The *Pro Marcello* was also Cicero's first speech in six years. (OCD *s.v.* Marcellus [4])

46   The date of Cicero's *Pro Ligario*, in which he successfully argued in favor of the recall of Quintus Ligarius from Africa. (OCD *s.v.* Ligarius)

46   Upon his triumphant return to Rome, Julius Caesar addressed the senate, attempting to reassure the members that they had nothing to fear from him. The speech was received with a mixture of optimism and skepticism. (Dio 43.15–18)

46   In his *Brutus* (261), composed in this year, Cicero stated that Julius Caesar was the preeminent orator of his time.

45   Cicero defended the client-king Deiotarus (*Pro Rege Deiotaro*) of Galatia, against charges that he had attempted to murder Julius Caesar. (OCD *s.v.* Deiotarus)

44   On March 17 — two days after the assassination of Julius Caesar — the Roman senate passed a resolution, proposed by Cicero, granting amnesty to Caesar's assassins. In 43, however, the amnesty was revoked at the urging of Quintus Pedius, Caesar's nephew and one of the consuls in that year. (Velleius Paterculus 2.58; Cary 423)

44   (March 18.) A few days after Caesar's assassination, Mark Antony delivered his famed *laudatio* (eulogy). Although it was brief— the biographer Suetonius described it as containing *perpauca verba*, "very few words" — it turned the fury of the assembled listeners against the assassins, who were present.

44   (September 1.) Mark Antony excoriated Cicero for his failure to attend the September 1 meeting of the senate, even threatening to tear down Cicero's house as a penalty for his absence. (Ker LCL Cicero *Philippics* 18)

44   The *Lex Cassia* passed in this year, conferring upon Julius Caesar the power to create new patricians. (OCD *s.v.* lex)

44–   Cicero attacked Mark Antony in a series of 14 highly inflamma-
43   tory speeches known as the *Philippics* (delineated infra), so called
        because they were patterned after the Athenian orator Demos-
        thenes' attacks on King Philip of Macedon. (Ker LCL Cicero
        Philippics 3)

44   (September 2.) Cicero delivered his *First Philippic*, a relatively non-
        inflammatory criticism of Mark Antony.

44   (September 19.) *Vomere suo more, non dicere*: "to vomit, as usual,
        not to speak." With these words, Cicero characterized a speech
        of Antony delivered on this day, an oration in which Antony had
        bitterly criticized Cicero. (Cicero *Letters to His Friends* 12.2)

44   (November.) Cicero's *Second Philippic* was published; this speech
        was never spoken, although it was widely read by Cicero's friends,
        and presumably by others. (Ker LCL Cicero *Philippics* 62)

44   (November.) Octavian made a speech, quoted in part by Cicero in
        a letter to Atticus (16.15) in which he pledged to follow in his
        father's (*i.e.,* Julius Caesar's) footsteps, and to avenge his murder.

44   (December 20.) Cicero delivered his *Third Philippic* in a senate
        meeting. Later that day, he appeared before the people to pre-
        sent the *Fourth Philippic*. (Ker LCL Cicero *Philippics* 187, 233)

44   Shortly after Caesar's assassination, several measures were passed:
        that the hall where he was killed should be closed off; that the
        Ides of March be referred to as the Day of Parricide; and that
        the senate never be convened on any March 15 in the future.
        (Suetonius *Julius Caesar* 88)

43   (January 1.) Cicero presented his *Fifth Philippic*, in which he
        recounted, among other things, various measures in connection
        with Antony's blockade of Mutina. (Ker LCL Cicero *Philippics*
        253–254)

43   (January 4.) Cicero delivered his *Sixth Philippic* in the forum,
        before the people. (Ker LCL Cicero *Philippics* 313)

43   (January.) Cicero's *Seventh Philippic* was spoken to the senate.

43   (Late January.) The *Eighth Philippic*, in which Cicero criticized
        Antony's blockade of Mutina. (Ker LCL Cicero *Philippics* 362)

43   (Late January.) In the *Ninth Philippic*, Cicero eulogized his recently

deceased friend, the statesman Servius Sulpicius Rufus (consul in 51). (Ker LCL Cicero *Philippics* 398)

43   (March.) Cicero delivered his *Tenth Philippic*. (Ker LCL Cicero *Philippics* 419)

43   (Mid-March.) Cicero's *Eleventh Philippic* was an attack on his erstwhile son-in-law, Publius Cornelius Dolabella. (Ker LCL Cicero *Philippics* 455)

43   (Late March.) Cicero delivered his *Twelfth Philippic*, and a few days later, the *Thirteenth Philippic*. He spoke the final oration of his long career on April 21: the *Fourteenth Philippic*. (Ker LCL Cicero *Philippics* 504, 541, 605–606)

43   Lucius Cornificius prosecuted Marcus Junius Brutus for Caesar's murder. (OCD *s.v.* Cornificius)

43   Although Cicero's speeches against Mark Antony have achieved a more lasting fame, the tribune Titus Cannutius also denounced Antony vigorously. Cannutius was subsequently one of the first to die in the proscriptions of 43. (Velleius Paterculus 2.64)

43   The passage of the *Lex Titia*, which declared the Second Triumvirate a legally constituted entity. (OCD *s.v.* triumviri)

43   "Cicerculus, Ciceracius, Ciceriscus, Graeculus." All these demeaning diminutives were attached to Cicero by Quintus Fufius Calenus, during the course of a vituperative speech in this year. (Dio 46.18)

42   Hortensia, the daughter of one of Rome's leading orators, Quintus Hortensius, gave a speech in opposition to proposed tax reforms affecting women. (Cary 431)

42   The triumvirs enacted a measure which made Julius Caesar's birthday a kind of national holiday, and that any senators or their sons who failed to observe it properly would be liable to a fine of 1,000,000 sesterces. (Dio 47.18)

42   The triumvirs decreed that anyone who sought refuge in the shrine dedicated to Julius Caesar could not be forcibly removed. However, when every manner of criminal began to take advantage of this decree to avoid prosecution, the shrine was fenced in, and thus rendered inaccessible. (Dio 47.19)

41   Prior to his departure from Rome for Gaul (although he ultimately halted at Perusia), Lucius Antonius made a speech to the people wearing military garb, an apparently unprecedented act. (Dio 48.13)

33   At the age of nine, the future emperor Tiberius eulogized his recently deceased father. (Suetonius *Tiberius* 6)

33   A decree was passed which granted immunity to any citizen of the senatorial class from prosecution for piracy. The decree was also made retroactive. (Dio 49.43)

32   The consul Gaius Sosius, a backer of Mark Antony, had planned to introduce several measures hostile to the interests of Octavian, but a tribunician veto (by Nonius Balbus) prevented him from so doing. (Dio 50.3)

32   Octavian delivered a speech defending himself and criticizing the consuls Gaius Sosius and Gnaeus Domitius Ahenobarbus, who had proposed censuring him. The result: the consuls and 300 senators fled Rome. (Cary 444)

31   Prior to the Battle of Actium, Mark Antony gave a lengthy speech to his troops, emphasizing the following points:
          1. the fighting ability of his soldiers
          2. the superiority of their equipment, weapons and ships
          3. his own military abilities and leadership experience, and
      Octavian's deficiencies in these matters
          4. Octavian's cruelty and dishonesty
          Octavian also addressed his troops, in which he emphasized the fact that they would be fighting against "an accursed woman" (Cleopatra), whose role in governing Rome, should Mark Antony prevail, would spell disaster. He scornfully referred to Antony as an Egyptian, not a Roman, whose association with Cleopatra had destroyed his credibility as a Roman leader. Finally, he reminded his men of their many previous military successes. (Dio 50.16–22; 24–30)

30   The passage of the *Lex Saenia* empowered Octavian to grant patrician status on any family of his choosing; the *Lex Cassia* (45 or 44) gave similar powers to Julius Caesar. (OCD *s.v.* patricius)

3. Military Events

264 In 265, the Roman army besieged the Etruscan town of Volsinii, enslaving a number of its inhabitants in the following year. Some accounts indicate that the Romans removed some 2,000 statues from the town. (OCD *s.v.* Volsinii; Scullard RW 125)

264 At the outset of the First Punic War, the consul Appius Claudius Caudex wished to transport his army from Italy to Sicily. Seeing that the Carthaginians had heavily fortified the straits, he first attempted negotiations. When this failed, he succeeded in defeating the Carthaginians militarily, thus offering Appius Claudius easy passage into Sicily. (Polybius 1.11–12)

264– The First Punic War (against Carthage).
241

263 The consul Manius Valerius Messalla subdued the Syracusan King Hiero II, who then allied himself with Rome, during the First Punic War. His colleague, Manius, had led Otacilius Crassus in a successful assault on Syracuse, forcing the king (Hiero) to accept a treaty with Rome. (Harper's *s.v.* Otacilius; Polybius 1.16)

261 Appius Claudius Caudex led Roman military incursions into Sicily. (Velleius Paterculus 2.38)

260 The Romans defeated Carthage at the Battle of Mylae, which gave them temporary control of Sicilian waters. (OCD *s.v.* Punic Wars)

c.260 In the First Punic War, the Romans developed the *corvus*, "crow," a sort of gangplank/grappling device which enabled Roman soldiers to board Carthaginian ships. (OCD *s.v.* Punic Wars; Polybius 1.22)

259   The Romans invaded and occupied the islands of Corsica and Sardinia. (OCD *s.v.* Corsica)

256   The Battle of Ecnomus occurred, a Roman naval victory during the First Punic War, under the leadership of the consuls Marcus Atilius Regulus and Lucius Manlius Vulso. (OCD *s.v.* Punic Wars)

255   The Carthaginians, under a Spartan mercenary named Xanthippus, defeated Marcus Atilius Regulus near the Bagradas River in north Africa. Only 2,000 of Regulus' 15,000 men survived; he himself was captured by the Carthaginians. In a famous incident around 249, he was sent to Rome to negotiate prisoner releases, before voluntarily returning to Carthage, where he died. (OCD *s.v.* Regulus [1])

254   The Romans captured Panormus, an important military center in northern Sicily. (OCD *s.v.* Panormus)

250   Lucius Caecilius Metellus captured some 140 war elephants from the Carthaginians in Sicily. Using specially constructed pontoon rafts, he transported the beasts to Rome, where they were displayed in the Circus Maximus. (Dionysius of Halicarnassus 2.66)

249   Aulus Atilius Calatinus became the first Roman dictator to lead an army outside Italy, to Sicily (although consular armies had, of course, left Italian soil prior to 249). Before assuming the dictatorship, Atilius had twice held the office of consul (258, and again in 254). (Dio 36.34; MRR II 215)

249   The Roman siege of Lilybaeum (western Sicily), the first successful Roman attempt at siege maneuvers. (OCD Claudius [6])

249   The Battle of Drepana, in the First Punic War, a naval disaster for the Romans. The battle was reputedly lost because the Roman commander, Publius Claudius Pulcher, failed to heed the divine forewarnings which had been revealed to him. (OCD *s.v.* Claudius [6])

241   The Battle of the Aegates Islands (near Sicily), in which the Romans, under the command of Gaius Lutatius Catulus, defeated Carthage in the final and decisive engagement of the First Punic War. (OCD *s.v.* Catulus [1])

238   Tiberius Sempronius Gracchus (great-grandfather of the land

reformer) led a successful assault on Sardinia. (OCD *s.v.* Sardinia)

237   The Romans completed their expropriation of Sardinia from Carthage and fined the Carthaginians an additional 1200 talents (over and above the indemnity specified by the treaty ending the First Punic War). (CAH VIII 27)

235   The first closing of the gates of the Temple of Janus, traditionally emblematic of peace. One of the consuls for the year, Titus Manlius Torquatus, presided over the ceremony. Torquatus later held the posts of censor (231), consul again (224) and dictator (208). (OCD *s.v.* Torquatus [2])

230   A Roman delegation to Teuta, queen of the Illyrians, ended in disaster when the two leaders of the delegation, Gaius and Lucius Coruncanius, were assaulted, and Lucius was killed. This incident led to the outbreak of the First Illyrian War. (OCD *s.v.* Coruncanius [2])

225   The final Gallic invasion of Italy culminated in the Battle of Telamon (in Etruria), a total Roman victory. (OCD *s.v.* Telamon [2])

222   The Battle of Clastidium (northern Italy); the Romans defeated the Insubres. The outcome was decided when the Roman commander, Marcus Claudius Marcellus, overcame the chieftain of the Insubres, a certain Viridomarus, in single combat. (OCD *s.v.* Clastidium)

221   Hannibal took command of the Carthaginian armies in Spain, upon the death of his brother-in-law, Hasdrubal. (OCD *s.v.* Hannibal)

218–   The Second Punic War.
202

217   After Hannibal's victory at Lake Trasimene, he released some 6,000 native Italians, asserting that his purpose in fighting was to free Italy. By this ploy, he gained the surrender — and presumably the good will — of a number of indigenous Italians. (Frontinus *Stratagems* 4.7)

217   At the age of 17, Cato the Elder embarked upon the first of many military campaigns, this one against Hannibal during the Second Punic War. (Plutarch *Cato the Elder* 1)

216–   The First Macedonian War.
205

216   The Battle of Cannae, in the summer of 216, in which Hannibal inflicted a terrible defeat on the Romans, one of their worst military setbacks ever. (OCD *s.v.* Cannae)

216   In this year, Hannibal blockaded the town of Casilinum, on the Volturnus River. The Romans aided the town's residents by filling large jars with wheat, and placing them in the river, upstream from the town. When Hannibal discovered the ploy, and set a large chain in the river to intercept the jugs, the Romans threw edible nuts into the water, which eluded the chain. (Frontinus *Stratagems* 3.14; Livy 23.19)

216   The consul-elect Lucius Postumius Albinus suffered a crushing defeat at the hands of the Gauls, in a heavily wooded area in northern Italy. Very few of his 25,000 man army escaped with their lives. (Livy 23.24)

215   The senate's first order of business in this year was to impose a doubled tax, to raise money to pay the soldiery. (Livy 23.31)

215   With funds running low (in this and the following year) to continue to finance the Second Punic War, the Roman government devised a plan to borrow money from private contractors and to be allowed extended time for repayment. Some 19 contractors agreed to the scheme, which facilitated the conduct of government business by private funding. (Livy 23.48)

214   As the Second Punic War dragged on, funding for it became increasingly difficult to provide. The consuls for 214 decreed this extraordinary naval levy:

If a citizen's net worth were:	Then he had to provide funding for:
50,000–100,000 *asses*	six month's pay for one sailor
100,000–300,000 *asses*	one year's pay for three sailors
300,000–1,000,000 *asses*	one year's pay for five sailors
1,000,000+ *asses*	one year's pay for seven sailors

Additionally, all Roman senators were required to provide one year's pay for eight sailors. (Livy 24.11)

214   The consul Quintus Fabius Maximus Cunctator sent 370 army

deserters to Rome, where they were scourged and then thrown from the Tarpeian Rock. (Livy 24.20)

213– Marcellus' invasion of Syracuse, a city defended by Archimedes'
211   ingenious devices. (OCD *s.v.* Archimedes)

209   Quintus Fabius Maximus Cunctator recaptured Tarentum, which had fallen to Hannibal in 213. (MRR I 285)

209   New Carthage, the Carthaginian base of operations in Spain, was captured by the Romans under Publius Cornelius Scipio. (MRR I 287)

208   The Battle of Baecula in Spain. The Romans, under the command of Publius Cornelius Scipio, defeated Hannibal's brother Hasdrubal, thus enabling them to wrest Spain from Carthaginian control. (OCD *s.v.* Hasdrubal [2])

208   The death near Venusia of Marcus Claudius Marcellus, the "Sword of Rome," a title bestowed upon him for his vigorous policies against Hannibal. He had held the consulship in 222, 215, 214, 210 and 208. (He was consul suffectus in 215; he subsequently resigned the post because both he and his colleague were plebeians. One consul was supposed to be a patrician.) (OCD *s.v.* Marcellus [1])

207   The Romans again triumphed over Hasdrubal, this time at the Battle of the Metaurus River (east central Italy). (MRR I 294)

205   The Peace of Phoenice, the treaty ending the First Macedonian War. Chief negotiator for the Romans was Publius Sempronius Tuditanus, a survivor of the Battle of Cannae (216), and later censor (209). He also held the consulship (204). (OCD *s.v.* Tuditanus [1])

205   Quintus Pleminius captured and plundered Locri (in Sicily). His activities there were later investigated by the senate, but he died (*c.*195) before formal charges were filed. According to another version of the story, Pleminius was executed after an abortive attempt to bribe certain confederates to set fire to Rome, thus affording Pleminius an opportunity to escape. (Diodorus Siculus 27.4; Livy 29.21–22)

204   Publius Cornelius Scipio landed near Utica in north Africa with the Roman army, thus prompting the recall of Hannibal from Italy, in 203. (MRR I 308; OCD *s.v.* Hannibal)

203   The Battle of the Campi Magni ("Great Plains") in Africa, which pitted the forces of the Numidian general Syphax against the Romans under Scipio Africanus. The latter prevailed; Syphax fled, but was soon captured and removed to Italy, where he later died. (OCD *s.v.* Scipio {5})

202   The Battle of Zama, in North Africa, at which the Romans, under Scipio Africanus, defeated Hannibal in the final and decisive battle of the Second Punic War. (OCD *s.v.* Zama)

202   The indemnity imposed upon Carthage after the Second Punic War included a fine of 800,000 pounds of silver, to be paid over a span of 50 years, in annual installments of 16,000 pounds. (Pliny 33.51)

201   According to Livy (31.4), land distributions to Punic War veterans were proposed; this marked the first time in Roman history in which such distributions were carried out. In later years, the practice became commonplace.

200   Livy (42.34) records the military career of a soldier named Spurius Ligustinus:
   200   Joined the army; sent to Macedonia.
   198   Promoted to junior centurion.
   195   Went to Spain, under the command of Cato the Elder.
   191   Fought against King Antiochus III and the Aetolians.
   190–   In Italy.
   182
   181   Returned to Spain, under the commands of Quintus Fulvius Flaccus and Tiberius Sempronius Gracchus.
   171   Volunteered to fight in Macedonia.

200   Only a few months after the treaty ending the Second Punic War had been concluded and after some initial wavering, the Romans began preparations for another major military undertaking, this one against King Philip V and the Macedonians. (Livy 31.6, 8)

200   The Roman army, under the command of Gaius Aurelius, won a major victory over the Gauls, near Ariminum. According to Livy (31.21), 35,000 enemy soldiers died; 200 wagons filled with booty were seized by the Romans.

200   Lucius Furius Purpurio, a praetor involved in the victory over the Gauls in this year, conveyed to Rome booty in the amount of

320,000 *asses* worth of bronze, and 105,000 silver coins. (Livy 31.49; MRR I 323)

200 The proconsular governor of Spain, Gaius Cornelius Cethegus, defeated the Sedetani; 15,000 of the enemy were reported by Livy (31.49) to have died in this battle.

200– The Second Macedonian War.
196

199 Although voted the celebration of an *ovatio* by the senate, Lucius Manlius Acidinus, a commander in Spain, had to forego the honor because of the intervention of the tribune Publius Porcius Laeca. Acidinus therefore returned to Rome as a private citizen, whereupon he presented to the treasury spoils in the amount of 1200 pounds of silver and about 30 pounds of gold. (Livy 32.7)

199 Gnaeus Baebius Tamphilus, governor of Gaul in this year, imprudently attacked a Gallic tribe — the Insubres — and lost over 6700 soldiers. (Livy 32.7)

198 The Roman army serving in Greece received a large gift from King Masinissa: 200 cavalry; ten elephants; 200,000 measures of grain. (Livy 32.27)

197 The Romans triumphed over the Macedonian king Philip V at the Battle of Cynoscephalae in Thessaly, thus securing Roman control of Greece. (OCD *s.v.* Philip [3] V)

196 At the staging of the Isthmian Games, Titus Quinctius Flamininus, conqueror of King Philip V, proclaimed the Greeks to be a free people. (OCD *s.v.* Flamininus [1])

196 Hannibal fled Carthage for Syria, under the (perhaps mistaken) belief that some Roman envoys who had come to Carthage intended to take him into custody. (Nepos *Hannibal* 7)

196 A slave revolt erupted in Etruria; it was quickly put down by the praetor peregrinus, Manius Acilius Glabrio. (Livy 33.36)

196 A fierce battle between Romans and Gauls broke out near Comum. 40,000 men were said by Livy (33.26) to have been killed in the battle, a Roman victory.

195 While conducting military operations in Spain, Cato the Elder was nearly defeated; only a payment of 200 talents to a nearby

tribe, the Celtiberians, reversed the Roman fortunes. Although criticized for, in effect, bribing foreign troops, Cato's approach succeeded, and the Romans went on to claim numerous victories in this year in Spain. (Plutarch *Cato the Elder* 10)

194   Cato the Elder celebrated a triumph for his military victories in Spain in the preceding year. (Plutarch *Cato the Elder* 11)

191   Manius Acilius Glabrio, with a 20,000 man force, attacked Antiochus III at Thermopylae. The Romans emerged victorious. (MRR I 352; Plutarch *Cato the Elder* 13–14)

191   The Carthaginians offered to pay the balance of the indemnity they owed to Rome, as a result of the terms ending the Second Punic War. (The money was to have been paid over 50 years.) (Livy 36.4)

190   The Battle of Magnesia, in which the Roman army, commanded by Lucius Cornelius Scipio, defeated a much larger Syrian force under King Antiochus III. (MRR I 356)

190   Cato the Elder used his considerable influence to deny a triumph to Minucius Thermus, for the latter's Ligurian victories, on the grounds that Thermus had been guilty of unnecessarily cruel behavior in the campaigns. (CAH VIII 370)

189   The consul Marcus Fulvius Nobilior captured Ambracia (in Greece) and transferred its objets d'art to Rome. (OCD *s.v.* Nobilior). The Romans besieging Ambracia found it impossible to breach the walls, so they decided to attempt to tunnel their way into the city. When the Ambracians discerned the Roman strategy, they countered by digging a ditch to intercept the tunnelers. When the two armies met, an unusual underground battle ensued. The Romans finally prevailed by filling a perforated barrel with feathers and setting it on fire. They used bellows to fan the flames and engulf the tunnel and trenchworks in smoke, which compelled the Ambracians to withdraw. (Livy 38.7)

188   The Romans' conflicts with King Antiochus III of Syria were laid to rest by the terms of the Peace of Apamea. (OCD *s.v.* Apamea)

188   The proconsul Gnaeus Manlius Vulso pacified Galatea. The triumph which he celebrated in the subsequent year was opposed

by Cato and others, because of his suspected philhellenism and hedonistic impulses. (OCD *s.v.* Vulso [2])

186   The consul Quintus Marcius Philippus was instrumental in crushing the Bacchanalian "conspirators." (Livy 39.8 ff)

186   Marcus Fulvius Nobilior provided an elaborate 10-day period of spectacles in honor of his exploits in the Aetolian War. Actors, athletes and wild beasts were displayed. (Livy 39.22)

186   In a precedent setting move, the Roman government subsidized celebratory games organized under the supervision of Lucius Cornelius Scipio for his victory over King Antiochus III in 190. (Pliny 33.138)

185   A slave revolt broke out in Apulia. The praetor Lucius Postumius Tempsanus dealt with the situation by condemning 7,000 of the participants. Some escaped; others were executed. (Livy 39.29)

179   The propraetor Tiberius Sempronius Gracchus continued the subjugation of the Celtiberians (Spain) in a battle near the town of Alce. According to Livy, 9000 enemy soldiers fell, while the Romans lost only 109. Gracchus later won a major battle against the Celtiberians in the Chaunus Mountains; 22,000 of the enemy died on the final day of the engagement. (Livy 40.48, 50)

179   Thurrus, a powerful and influential Spanish chieftain, switched his allegiance to the Romans, and provided his new allies with crucial assistance in a number of their military ventures in Spain. (Livy 40.49)

179   The consul Quintus Fulvius Flaccus celebrated a triumph for his military success against the Ligurians. Livy (40.59) suggests that the honor was undeserved, since Fulvius had expropriated almost no money from the vanquished enemy.

178   Two triumphs were held on two consecutive days, by two different commanders: Tiberius Sempronius Gracchus, for his subjugation of the Celtiberians, and Lucius Postumius Albinus, for his victory over the Lusitanians. The Roman treasury was enriched by a combined 60,000 pounds of silver, courtesy of the two triumphators. (Livy 41.7)

177   Military campaigns against Sardinia and Istria were proposed and initiated. (Livy 41.9)

177   At the beginning of the Istrian campaign, a Roman assault on the town of Nesattium succeeded in part because the Romans were able to divert the course of a river which supplied the town with water. Two other settlements, Mutila and Faveria, fell quickly, thus bringing the entire war to a close. (Livy 41.11)

177   The consul Gaius Claudius Pulcher subdued two provinces in this year: Istria and Liguria — a rare achievement, according to Livy (41.12, 13). He celebrated a triumph in the same year.

176   The Romans under Tiberius Sempronius Gracchus subjugated the island of Sardinia. He took 230 hostages; the senate doubled the province's tax obligation. (Livy 41.17)

173   The Romans demanded an unusual war indemnity of 200,000 pounds of wax from the Corsicans, after a military operation in this year. (Livy 42.7)

172   Gaius Cicereius requested a triumph for his Corsican victories. When the senate refused to accede to this request, he nonetheless went ahead with his plans, and celebrated his triumph on the Alban Mount (13 miles southeast of Rome). Here it was permissible for rejected commanders to hold their triumphal processions without senatorial approval. (Livy 42.21)

172   Some of the preparations for war against King Perseus, carried out in 172: 50 quinqueremes to be refurbished and readied for battle; the drafting of enough sailors to man 25 ships; the drafting of 180,000 infantrymen and 400 horsemen. (Livy 42.27)

171–   The Third Macedonian War.
168

171   The consul Gaius Cassius Longinus attempted to implement his ill-conceived scheme of invading Macedonia via northern Italy. When the plan failed, Cassius managed to gain (in the following year) an appointment to a military tribunate, perhaps in this way hoping to evade the necessity of explaining his actions to the senate. (Livy 43.1 ff)

171   According to Livy (42.32), many men volunteered for military duty against the Macedonians, because of the great wealth of the Macedonian kings, and the concomitant opportunities for booty.

169   Much time was devoted in this year to the recruitment of enough soldiers to confront Perseus in the coming war. Older men (in their fifties) were considered liable for duty. (Livy 43.14)

168   The Romans, under the leadership of Lucius Aemilius Paullus, defeated Perseus at the Battle of Pydna, thus ending the Third Macedonian War. At the order of the Roman senate, Aemilius Paullus permitted his soldiers to sack 72 Macedonian towns, because they had allied themselves with Perseus. (MRR I 427; Livy 44.40 ff)

167   Aemilius Paullus paid 300,000,000 sesterces to the state treasury, after the defeat of Perseus at Pydna. He also celebrated a triumph in this year, in which much of this money was displayed. (Livy 45.40)

154   Quintus Opimius defended the town of Nicaea (in Gaul) from the onslaughts of the Ligurians. (OCD s.v. Nicaea)

151   The consul Lucius Licinius Lucullus (grandfather of the consul/epicure) was briefly incarcerated for overzealousness in enrolling soldiers for the upcoming campaigns in Spain. (OCD s.v. Lucullus)

151   Military setbacks in Spain doused the ardor for a continuing Roman presence there. Publius Cornelius Scipio Aemilianus publicly volunteered for any military post in Spain which the senate might deem appropriate. By his example, a spirit of militarism was rekindled; Aemilianus was soon joined by other eager volunteers. (Livy *Epitome* 48)

150   The propraetor Servius Sulpicius Galba treacherously persuaded the Lusitanians into surrendering to Roman might by promising them grants of land. When the unarmed Lusitanians appeared before him to work out the details of the settlement, he ordered them to be massacred. (OCD s.v. Galba [3])

150–148   The Fourth Macedonian War.

149–146   The Third Punic War, ending with the destruction of Carthage, in 146. The Romans sacked Corinth in the same year.

148   Quintus Caecilius Metellus Macedonicus defeated Andriscus in Thrace; Andriscus was a mercenary who had tried to rally the Macedonians against Roman rule. (OCD s.v. Andriscus)

148   Scipio Aemilianus persuaded the Carthaginian cavalry comman-
       der Phameas Himilco to desert to the Romans. The senate
       showed its gratitude to Phameas by giving him a purple robe, a
       horse, a suit of armor, 10,000 drachmas in coined silver, 100
       minas worth of silver plate, a furnished tent, and pledges of more
       if he continued to assist the Romans. (Appian *Punic Wars* 109;
       Livy *Epitome* 50)

147   The Lusitanian Viriathus became the leader of Spanish resistance
       to Roman hegemony, and led his troops to a number of victo-
       ries between 147 and 141. (OCD *s.v.* Viriathus)

146   Scipio Aemilianus' reduction of Carthage provoked the suicide of
       Hasdrubal's wife and two children, who leapt from a turret. Has-
       drubal was captured, and later displayed in Scipio's triumphal
       procession. (Livy *Epitome* 50; OCD *s.v.* Hasdrubal [4])

146   Scipio Aemilianus ingratiated himself to the Sicilians by pro-
       claiming that they could travel to Carthage — recently destroyed
       by Rome — and reclaim any of their temple gifts which the
       Carthaginians had stolen in previous wars. (Appian *Punic Wars*
       133)

c.146 Lucius Mummius' destruction of Corinth earned him the cog-
       nomen Achaicus; according to Velleius Paterculus (1.13), no *novus
       homo* had ever before been honored with a cognomen based on
       a military exploit.

143   The consul Appius Claudius Pulcher, victor over the Salassi (in
       Cisalpine Gaul) in this year, was nonetheless denied the honor
       of a triumph by the senate. The triumph which he celebrated in
       defiance of the senate was sanctioned and protected by the par-
       ticipation in it of his sister Claudia, a Vestal Virgin. Her pres-
       ence precluded the tribunes, or any other politicians, from inter-
       fering; for them to have done so would have been a sacrilege.
       (Suetonius *Tiberius* 2)

141   Quintus Pompeius became the first member of his famous family
       to hold the consulship. He conducted an ill-fated war against
       the Numantines, and in the following year he was forced to con-
       clude a treaty on unfavorable terms. (OCD *s.v.* Pompeius [1])

138   The death of Viriathus, the Lusitanian chieftain. Quintus Servil-
       ius Caepio bribed three of his friends to assassinate him. (CAH
       VIII 316)

138   The consul Decimus Junius Brutus conducted wide-ranging and successful military operations in Spain, earning for himself the cognomen Gallaecus. (OCD *s.v.* Brutus [2])

138   An army deserter named Gaius Matienius was punished with a sustained beating; he was then sold as a slave for the paltry sum of one sestertius. (Livy *Epitome* 55)

138   The three assassins of Viriathus — Audax, Minurus and Ditalco — were expelled from Rome and denied a reward for their deed. (Livy *Epitome* 55)

137   The Roman army based in Spain under the consul Gaius Hostilius Mancinus was surrounded by hostile Numantines. Skillful diplomacy by Tiberius Sempronius Gracchus extricated the Romans from a potentially disastrous outcome. (Plutarch *Tiberius Gracchus* 5)

136   Marcus Aemilius Lepidus Porcina (consul 137) initiated a campaign against the Vaccaei in Spain, despite senatorial opposition. When he suffered a major setback, he was recalled to Rome, where he was stripped of his consulship and fined. (Appian *Spanish Wars* 82–83)

135–   Slave revolt in Sicily.
132

134   Publius Cornelius Scipio Aemilianus was sent to Spain, to deal with the military situation in Numantia. (MRR I 490)

133   The capitulation of the Spanish town of Numantia to the Romans, under Publius Cornelius Scipio Aemilianus, thus marking the end of the Spanish Wars (154–133). Numantia was the last outpost of Spanish resistance. (OCD *s.v.* Numantia)

132   The consul Publius Rupilius quelled the slave revolt in Sicily. In consort with a ten-man senatorial commission, he then reorganized the province, with a new charter. Rupilius was also active in this year in prosecuting the surviving supporters of Tiberius Gracchus. (OCD *s.v.* Rupilius)

131   Aristonicus of Pergamum led an uprising against Rome after the death of King Attalus III (who had bequeathed Pergamum to the Romans). One of the consuls for 131, Publius Licinius Crassus

Mucianus, was killed while giving battle to Aristonicus' forces. In the following year, however, the rebellion was quelled by a Roman army under the command of Marcus Perperna. (OCD *s.v.* Crassus [1])

130   The consul Marcus Perperna (a plebeian novus homo) defeated and captured Aristonicus in Asia. Perperna died soon after; the Asian campaign was completed in the following year by his successor, Manius Aquillius. (MRR I 502, 504)

129   One of the consuls for 129, Gaius Sempronius Tuditanus, defeated the Iapydes in Illyria. Tuditanus was also the author of treatises on Roman politics and military history. (OCD *s.v.* Tuditanus [2])

129   The Romans took control of Halicarnassus (southwestern Turkey), birthplace of the historians Herodotus and Dionysius. (OCD *s.v.* Halicarnassus)

125   A previously loyal Italian town, Fregellae (about 60 miles southeast of Rome) revolted. The uprising sprang from Roman refusal to consider granting citizenship rights to the town's residents. The Romans destroyed Fregellae and resettled its survivors in a new colony, Fabrateria Nova. (OCD *s.v.* Fregellae)

122   The subjugation of the Balearic Islands (east of Spain) was completed by the proconsul Quintus Caecilius Metellus, in consequence of which he received the cognomen Baliaricus. (OCD *s.v.* Metellus [4])

*c.*121   The Romans, under Quintus Fabius Maximus, defeated the Arvernian Gauls in a battle in which Gallic losses reputedly numbered 120,000, while only 15 Romans were killed. According to Pliny the Elder (7.166), Fabius Maximus shook off a lingering fever by participating vigorously in this battle.

121   The consul Gnaeus Domitius Ahenobarbus defeated the Allobrogian Gauls at Vindalium (in southern France). (OCD *s.v.* Domitius [2])

*c.*119   The Romans captured and occupied one of Pannonia's major towns, Siscia. (OCD *s.v.* Siscia)

118   The consul Quintus Marcius Rex defeated an Alpine tribe, the Styni, and later celebrated a triumph for this victory. (Livy *Epitome* 62; Sage/Schlesinger LCL Livy [Vol. XIV] xx)

113   This year heralded several major Roman defeats in Gaul, includ-
       ing: Noreia (113); Rhone Valley (109); Garonne Valley (107), and
       the worst disaster of all, the Battle of Arausio in 105. (Gardner
       LCL Cicero *Pro Caelio*, etc. 578)

110   A Roman army under the command of Aulus Postumius Albinus
       was defeated in Africa by King Jugurtha. The king forced the
       surviving Roman legionnaires to submit to the humiliation of
       marching under a yoke of spears (*sub jugum*), a gesture of sub-
       servience. (OCD *s.v.* Postumius [4])

109   Quintus Caecilius Metellus Numidicus, consul in this year, gained
       several military victories over Jugurtha. Nonetheless, the
       Jugurthine command was taken from him two years later, and
       granted to Gaius Marius. (OCD *s.v.* Metellus [6])

108   Marcus Minucius Rufus defeated the Scordisci (a tribe living in
       the Danube region). He was noted for beautifying Rome with
       porticos, including the Porticus Minucia. (OCD *s.v.* Minucius
       [4])

107   Gaius Marius began implementing his reform of the recruitment
       of soldiers, emphasizing volunteerism rather than conscription.
       (OCD *s.v.* Marius [1])

105   The Battle of Arausio (in Gaul), the worst Roman defeat since
       Cannae, over a century earlier. Some reports indicated that the
       Romans lost 80,000 soldiers in the disaster. (OCD *s.v.* Arausio)

105   The wars against King Jugurtha came to a conclusion when
       Jugurtha was kidnapped and brought to Rome. He was executed
       in the following year. (OCD *s.v.* Jugurtha)

105   The general Marcus Aurelius Scaurus was captured by the Cim-
       bri and summoned to appear before their tribal council. When
       he expressed the view that the Romans were invincible, a hot-
       headed Cimbrian youth named Boiorix assaulted and killed him.
       (Livy *Epitome* 67)

104   (January 1.) On the day on which he took office as consul for the
       second time, Gaius Marius celebrated a triumphal procession.
       One of his prized "displays": the captured Jugurtha. (Velleius
       Paterculus 2.12)

c.104 Several revolts erupted in Italy at about this time: 30 slaves at
       Nuceria formed an abortive conspiracy, and 200 in Capua. A

third, also apparently in Capua, occurred when a wealthy man named Titus Vettius organized 400 of his slaves to resist with violence creditors whom he owed seven talents for the purchase of a slave girl. This incident eventually evolved into a minor uprising, ultimately put down by Lucius Licinius Lucullus. (Diodorus Siculus 36.2, 2a)

102   The Battle of Aquae Sextiae, in Gaul, in which Roman forces under Gaius Marius virtually annihilated the Teutones and the Ambrones. (OCD s.v. Marius [1])

102   Marcus Antonius (grandfather of the triumvir) was granted a special command to deal with bands of pirates who roamed the eastern Mediterranean. (MRR I 568)

102–   A servile uprising in Sicily was ultimately quashed by Manius
99   Aquillius. During one of the battles in this conflict — in 101— Aquillius dispatched Athenion, the leader of the insurrection. (OCD s.v. Aquillius [2])

101   The Battle of Vercellae, in which the combined forces of Gaius Marius and Quintus Lutatius Catulus decimated the Cimbrian Gauls. After defeating the Cimbrians, Marius reputedly drank from Bacchic cups, à la Bacchus himself— an act of which Pliny the Elder (33.150) disapproved.

c.100   Titus Didius was instrumental in enlarging the Roman province of Macedonia; for this service, he was awarded a triumph, in 99. (OCD s.v. Didius [1])

92   Gaius Sentius, governor of Macedonia, lost a battle against the Thracians, but later atoned for the defeat by triumphing in a subsequent engagement. (Cicero In Pisonem 84; Livy Epitome 70)

91   A massacre of Roman citizens living in the northern Italian town of Asculum resulted from an inflammatory diatribe against them delivered by a Roman entrepreneur and agent named Gaius Servilius. This unfortunate incident is cited by some historians as the spark that ignited the Social Wars. (Cary 319)

91   At the outbreak of the Social Wars, the following Italian tribes revolted against the Romans: the Picentes, Vestini, Marsi, Paeligni, Marrucini, Samnites and Lucanians. (Livy Epitome 72)

91–   The Social Wars in Italy, caused by the Roman refusal to grant cit-
89   izenship to its Italian allies.

90   The Samnites defeated the consul Lucius Julius Caesar. They also occupied the town of Nola, and killed the Roman praetor there, Lucius Postumius. (Livy *Epitome* 73)

90   Rebels in the Social Wars captured the south central town of Venafrum, and killed the soldiers stationed there. (OCD *s.v.* Venafrum)

89   The Samnite leader Marius Egnatius, according to Livy "the most outstanding enemy general" of the Social Wars, was killed in battle. (Livy *Epitome* 75)

89   Lucius Cornelius Sulla attacked the city of Pompeii, which had remained loyal to the Italians during the Social War. (OCD *s.v.* Pompeii)

89   The consul Gnaeus Pompeius Strabo (father of Pompey the Great) blockaded and captured Asculum, thus ending the Social War in the north of Italy. (OCD *s.v.* Pompeius [3])

88   Manius Aquillius (consul in 101) was captured by King Mithridates VI. (Livy *Epitome* 78)

88   Gaius Marius, attempting to sail for Africa from Rome, was forced to land and hide in the marshes at the headwaters of the Liris River, near Minturnae (central Italy). The Minturnians sheltered him and gave him a new ship and funding for the continuation of his voyage. (Livy *Epitome* 77)

88   This year marked the first time that a Roman consul was killed at the hands of Roman soldiers, when Quintus Pompeius Rufus lost his life during a mutiny. (OCD *s.v.* Pompeius [2])

87   An attempted assassination of Pompey by his tentmate Lucius Terentius failed when Pompey, who had been informed of the plot, slipped away during the night on which the attempt was to have been made. (Plutarch *Pompey* 3)

87   A tragic incident of the civil war which erupted in this year: two (unnamed) brothers, on opposing sides, met in combat. Neither recognized the other until one of them killed his brother and was stripping the corpse of its armor. When the survivor realized that he had slain his own brother, he committed suicide. (Livy *Epitome* 79)

87   One of Gaius Marius' last military forays, and one of his cruelest,

occurred in this year: he besieged and plundered Rome's port city, Ostia, and put most of its residents to death. (Livy *Epitome* 80; Plutarch *Marius* 42)

86   Sulla's battles against King Mithridates VI, at Chaeronea and Orchomenus (both in Greece), wherein the Romans prevailed on each occasion. (Cary 334)

86   Sulla besieged and captured Athens. (Cary 333)

85   Gaius Flavius Fimbria occupied Pergamum (then under Mithridates' control) and nearly captured him. In the following year, Fimbria committed suicide after his army deserted him for Sulla. (Livy *Epitome* 83; Plutarch *Sulla* 25)

84   Lucius Cornelius Cinna (consul 87–84) was killed in a military mutiny. According to Plutarch (*Pompey* 5), he pled for his life by offering his killer his valuable signet ring. But the assassin refused, saying that his purpose was not to seal documents, but to eliminate a tyrant.

83   Pompey organized three legions from the area around Picenum, to aid Sulla in his march upon Rome. (Plutarch *Pompey* 6)

83   Sulla defeated in battle near Capua the consuls Gaius Norbanus and Lucius Cornelius Scipio Asiagenus. (Velleius Paterculus 2.25)

82   At the age of 26, Gaius Marius (son of the seven-time consul) entered upon the consulship. He unsuccessfully opposed Sulla's troops at the Battle of Sacriportus. (OCD *s.v.* Marius [2])

82   Sulla attacked and demolished Praeneste, a town destined to become a fashionable imperial resort/retirement community.
      To commemorate this victory, he instituted annual circus games, still celebrated in Velleius Paterculus' time, over 100 years later. (Velleius Paterculus 2.27)

82   The ancient city of Norba (southeast of Rome) was destroyed by Sullan forces. (OCD *s.v.* Norba)

82   The praetor Lucius Junius Brutus Damasippus murdered several notable Romans in this turbulent year, including Gaius Papirius Carbo, whose brother Gnaeus was consul in this year; and Quintus Mucius Scaevola, the renowned jurist, orator and legal scholar. (Velleius Paterculus 2.26)

82   Pompey was on the point of subduing the Sicilian town of Himera
      (for its fealty to Sulla's enemies) when its leader, Sthenius, offered
      to serve as the scapegoat. Pompey was so impressed with his
      bravery and character that he pardoned the entire town, includ-
      ing Sthenius. (Plutarch *Pompey* 10)

82   The Battle of Colline Gate, which Sulla won, a victory which paved
      the way for his subsequent military dictatorship. (Cary 337)

81   Pompey routed the army of Gnaeus Domitius Ahenobarbus in
      Africa, eradicating nearly all of his 20,000-man contingent. He
      secured and pacified Numidia and Libya for Sulla, all within 40
      days. (Plutarch *Pompey* 12; MRR II 77)

c.81   Despite Sulla's misgivings, he allowed Pompey to celebrate a tri-
      umph for his Sicilian and African victories. According to Plutarch
      (*Pompey* 14), Pompey wanted to enter the city in a chariot pulled
      by four elephants; however, the gates were not wide enough to
      accommodate the elephants, so he had to settle for a horse-drawn
      chariot.

80–   Quintus Sertorius ruled Spain as a virtual military dictator, turn-
72   ing back several Roman attempts to oust him. Ultimately, he was
      murdered by a jealous subordinate, Marcus Perperna. (OCD *s.v.*
      Sertorius)

78   Publius Servilius Vatia (consul in 79) attacked Cilicia in an effort
      to subdue the Mediterranean pirates whose stronghold was
      located there; he prevailed. (Velleius Paterculus 2.39; OCD *s.v.*
      Servilius [2])

78   A farmer's rebellion erupted in Faesulae, a reaction against Sullan
      colonists living in the area. To deal with the situation, the sen-
      ate sent both consuls — Marcus Aemilius Lepidus and Quintus
      Lutatius Catulus. (Gruen 14)

77   Marcus Aemilius Lepidus (father of the triumvir) launched a mil-
      itary attack on Rome. He was repulsed at the Mulvian Bridge
      by a force under the command of Quintus Lutatius Catulus,
      who, ironically, had been his consular colleague the year before.
      Lepidus fled to Sardinia, where he died. (OCD *s.v.* Lepidus [2])

77   A watershed year in Pompey's career: although he did not hold the
      consulship, he was assigned a proconsular command to deal with
      Quintus Sertorius' uprising in Spain. (OCD *s.v.* Pompeius [4])

76   Pompey was nearly killed in battle (at the Sucro River) against Sertorius' troops. He escaped only by abandoning his war-horse, with its golden trappings and ornaments; the horse, thus decked out, served as a distraction to its rider's pursuers. (Plutarch *Pompey* 19)

76–71 Pompey spent these years in Spain, dealing with the seditious activities of Sertorius. (OCD *s.v.* Pompeius [4])

75   Publius Servilius Vatia (consul in 79) defeated the marauding Isaurians; in commemoration of this victory, he was awarded the cognomen Isauricus. (Livy *Epitome* 93)

75   Pompey and Quintus Caecilius Metellus Pius blockaded Quintus Sertorius in Saguntum and eventually forced him to flee the city. (OCD *s.v.* Saguntum)

74   King Mithridates VI destroyed a Roman fleet of 100 ships near Chalcedon. The Roman commander, Marcus Aurelius Cotta, thus gave way to Lucius Licinius Lucullus, who warred against Mithridates for the next eight years. However, he was unable to deliver the coup de grace, and was removed from his post in 67. (OCD *s.v.* Lucullus [2]; Mithridates VI)

74   Marcus Fonteius began a gallic governorship. Later (*c*.70) accused of extortion, he was defended by Cicero. (MRR 104; OCD *s.v.* Fonteius)

74   Mark Antony's father — also named Mark Antony — was granted a military command against the pirates, whom he failed to suppress. Shortly thereafter, he was defeated in Crete, whence his derisive cognomen Creticus. (OCD *s.v.* Antonius [2])

73–71 Spartacus' slave rebellion, ultimately crushed in 71 by a large Roman army led by Marcus Licinius Crassus. The initial Roman response was a weak one: in 72, armies under the command of the consuls Lucius Gellius Publicola and Gnaeus Cornelius Lentulus Clodianus suffered humiliating defeats at the hands of Spartacus' adherents. (CAH IX 330)

73   Gaius Scribonius Curio (consul in 76) celebrated a triumph for his military accomplishments in Macedonia. (OCD *s.v.* Curio [1])

72   The Battle of Cabira, in which Lucullus defeated the forces of

King Mithridates. Although the king escaped, the Roman victory enabled them to seize and occupy Pontus. (Cary 352)

72   When Pompey captured Sertorius' assassin, Marcus Perperna, the latter attempted to save his life by offering to present to Pompey certain documents which would implicate a number of leading Romans in a plot to overthrow Sulla's constitutional reforms. The indignant Pompey destroyed both the papers and Perperna. (Shipley LCL Velleius Paterculus 112)

71   Six thousand slaves, who had served with Spartacus in the rebellion of 73–71, were crucified. The crosses were erected along the Appian Way, grim warnings to other slaves or rebels who might have been contemplating a similar uprising. (Cary 365)

71   (December 29.) Pompey celebrated a triumph for his role in crushing the Sertorian and Spartacan uprisings. (Plutarch *Pompey* 22)

c.71   When Crassus returned to Rome after defeating Spartacus, the senate decreed that he should be granted an ovation, not a triumph, since his victory over slaves and gladiators was not considered particularly arduous or dangerous. Crassus had the decree nullified, thereby receiving no official recognition whatever for his victory. (Aulus Gellius 5.6; Plutarch *Life of Crassus* 11)

69   Lucullus' invasion of Armenia led to the first contact between the Romans and the Parthians, a near eastern nomadic tribe, and one of the more implacable enemies whom the Romans ever encountered. (OCD *s.v.* Lucullus [2])

69   The Battle of Tigranocerta, in Armenia, a major victory for Lucullus over King Mithridates. According to Frontinus (*Stratagems* 2.14), Lucullus' army numbered only 15,000 — much smaller than Mithridates' forces — but he used that apparent disadvantage effectively, by attacking before the enemy's unwieldy line was ordered for battle.

c.68   This was the high-water mark for the Mediterranean pirates who preyed upon Italian shipping: they kidnapped two praetors defeated a Roman navy off Ostia, and interfered with shipments of corn to Rome. (Cary 349)

68–   Quintus Caecilius Metellus Creticus (consul in 69) fought against

67   pirates headquartered in Crete; he succeeded in his task with grim efficiency. (OCD *s.v.* Metellus [8])

67   The first, and more obscure, Battle of Zela was fought. King Mithridates VI routed a Roman force under the command of Gaius Valerius Triarius. (The Battle of Zela won by Julius Caesar occurred some 20 years later.) (OCD *s.v.* Zela)

66   Pompey's decisive victory over King Mithridates occurred at Nicopolis, in Pontus. According to Frontinus (*Stratagems* 2.1), Pompey lured Mithridates into a night battle, aligning his forces in such a way that the light of the moon shone into the eyes of the enemy.

64   Lucius Licinius Lucullus returned to Rome from his command in the east, having been superseded by Pompey. (OCD *s.v.* Lucullus)

63   After a three-month siege, Pompey captured Jerusalem. (Scullard GN 106)

63   A brief respite from war permitted the Romans to observe the *augurium salutis*, a ceremony in which the people inquired of the gods whether it would be appropriate for them to pray for prosperity. The *augurium salutis* was celebrated so infrequently because the rites could be conducted only when the Romans were neither fighting wars, nor preparing to do so. (Dio 37.24)

62   Proposals to grant Pompey the command against Catiline failed. In the forefront of the opposition: Cato the Younger, whose vetos (as tribune) proved decisive. (MRR II 174–175)

62   The Battle of Pistoria, in which Catiline and his conspiratorial army were defeated; Catiline fell during the fighting. (OCD *s.v.* Catiline)

61   The Allobrogian chieftain Catugnatus inflicted several losses on Roman forces in this year, including those under the command of the provincial governor Gaius Pomptinus. Pomptinus, however, eventually brought the situation under control, although he did not capture Catugnatus. (Dio 37.48; MRR II 176)

60   While en route to his provincial governorship in Macedonia, Gaius Octavius, the father of Octavian, decimated a band of fugitives, the remnants of the armies of Spartacus and Catiline, near Thurii. (Suetonius *Augustus* 3)

58   Julius Caesar attacked Ariovistus' German forces during a time of
      the waning of the moon, knowing that the enemy had a super-
      stitious belief against fighting with the moon in that stage. (Fron-
      tinus *Stratagems* 2.16)

57   Cicero proposed granting Julius Caesar an unprecedented 15-day
      supplicatio (thanksgiving), in honor of his Gallic victories of 58
      and 57. (Gardner LCL Cicero *Pro Sestio* and *In Vatinium* 26)

56   Decimus Junius Brutus defeated the Veneti in a naval battle. The
      Romans disabled the enemy ships by cutting their sails and rig-
      gings, using long poles tipped with knives for the purpose. (Dio
      39.40, 43)

55   The consuls Pompey and Crassus stirred up popular resentment
      when they both began planning expensive, post-consular mili-
      tary campaigns: Pompey in Spain and Crassus in the east. Pom-
      pey eventually decided to remain in Rome, but Crassus pro-
      ceeded to Syria. (Dio 39.39)

55   (November.) Crassus' proposed Parthian war was opposed by the
      tribune Gaius Ateius Capito. To prevent Crassus from leaving
      Rome to embark upon this campaign, Ateius announced unfa-
      vorable omens, which Crassus disregarded. Ateius was later accused
      of fabricating the omens, but his action was defended by Cicero,
      who argued that the disaster at Carrhae (in 53) could have been
      avoided if Crassus had respected the pronouncement, fraudulent
      or not. (OCD *s.v.* Capito [1]; Cicero *De Divinatione* 1.29)

54   Ambiorix, a chieftain of the Eburones (in eastern Gaul), won a
      decisive battle against Roman legions under the command of
      Quintus Titurius Sabinus and Lucius Aurunculeius Cotta. (OCD
      s.v. Ambiorix)

54   Crassus' forces captured an insignificant Mesopotamian town
      called Zenodotia. But Crassus did not refuse the honorary title
      of Imperator for this action, a decision which brought him a
      good deal of disgrace and derision, since many felt that he had
      done nothing to deserve the honor. (Plutarch *Crassus* 17)

54   Many of Crassus' officers harbored doubts about the efficacy of a
      war against the Parthians, including Gaius Cassius Longinus,
      one of the ringleaders in the assassination of Julius Caesar some
      ten years after this. (Plutarch *Crassus* 18)

53   The Battle of Carrhae, in which the Romans lost badly to the Parthians. (MRR II 230)

53   Gaius Cassius Longinus (the tyrannicide) rallied the surviving remnants of the army after Carrhae, thus enabling the Romans to retain control of Syria. (Velleius Paterculus 2.46)

52   Julius Caesar's siege of Alesia in Gaul, and his defeat of Vercingetorix. (OCD *s.v.* Alesia)

49   (January.) Julius Caesar crossed the Rubicon River without first dismissing his army, thus initiating a civil war (49–45).

49   Caesar's forces captured Corfinium, in one of the early engagements of the civil war. Corfinium's republican defender was Lucius Domitius Ahenobarbus (consul in 54). (Dio 41.10; OCD *s.v.* Domitius [4])

49   Siege operations were conducted against Massilia, a Gallic town which had remained loyal to Pompey at the outset of the civil war. The (ultimately successful) blockade was carried out by two of Caesar's lieutenants, Gaius Trebonius and Decimus Junius Brutus. (Dio 41.19)

49   Julius Caesar defeated the Pompeian sympathizers Lucius Afranius and Marcus Petreius, near Ilerda (Spain). He not only pardoned all his captives, but pledged that he would not attempt to compel them to oppose Pompey. It was as a result of this action that the noted antiquarian Marcus Terentius Varro became a partisan of Caesar. (Dio 41.23)

49   Caesar faced a military mutiny at Placentia. The soldiers gave weariness as their official reason for rebelling, but in reality, they were disappointed in the lack of booty. Caesar responded with a long speech in which he defended his leadership. Afterwards, he executed the ringleaders and won back the loyalty of the rest. (Dio 41.35)

49   The Caesarian staff officer Gaius Scribonius Curio was soundly defeated in battle in north Africa. The loss of this battle, along with two of his legions, represented a major setback for Caesar, especially occurring as it did, at the outbreak of the civil war of 49–45. (Cary 400–401)

49   Quintus Valerius Orca, legate of Julius Caesar, was sent to Sardinia

to take possession of that island in Caesar's name. Valerius succeeded in so doing. Gaius Asinius Pollio, dispatched to Sicily with similar orders, was also successful. (Appian *Civil Wars* 2.40)

48   The Battle of Dyrrhachium, in Greece. Pompey's forces were able to fend off Caesar's advancing army, partially because the scarcity of food had emaciated Caesar's troops. (OCD *s.v.* Dyrrhachium)

48   Shortly after turning back Caesar at the Battle of Dyrrhachium, Pompey styled himself *Imperator* ("commander"), an honorary title originally accorded to victorious generals by their troops. (Dio 41.52)

48   The Battle of Pharsalus, in Greece in the summer of 48; it was the decisive showdown of the Civil Wars between Pompey and Julius Caesar. Caesar claimed the victory; Pompey was assassinated soon after, in Egypt. (OCD *s.v.* Pharsalus; Pompeius [4])

48   Of the many Pompeian partisans whom Caesar captured and pardoned after the Battle of Pharsalus, perhaps the most notable was Marcus Junius Brutus, who later spearheaded the Ides of March conspiracy that cost Caesar his life. (Dio 41.63)

48   A certain Granius Petro, a Caesarian soldier captured in Africa by the Pompeians, was told by his captors that he would be spared. His response: Caesar's soldiers gave mercy, but did not receive it. Thereupon, he committed suicide by falling on his sword. (Plutarch *Caesar* 16)

47   The Pontic king Pharnaces defeated a Caesarian force under Gnaeus Domitius Calvinus, at Nicopolis. This success emboldened Pharnaces to challenge Caesar himself, at the Battle of Zela, an overwhelming victory for the Romans. (OCD *s.v.* Calvinus [2])

47   The Battle of Zela, in Asia Minor, won by Julius Caesar. The speed with which Caesar triumphed occasioned his famous *veni, vidi, vici* boast: "I came, I saw, I conquered." Frontinus (*Stratagems* 2.2) states that Caesar's troops won in part because they occupied high ground, thus rendering their spear throwing more effective.

47   Caesar quelled a military mutiny by promising the rebels land and money, and also by releasing them from service, telling them that he had no more need of them. His conciliatory approach

shamed many of them into dropping their complaints, and even volunteering to re-enlist. (Dio 42.54–55)

47   The Pompeian sympathizers in Africa gained confidence and optimism partially because their commander was Quintus Caecilius Metellus Pius Scipio; they believed that no one named Scipio could be defeated in Africa. To counter this, Caesar enlisted to his cause a man commonly known as Salvito, but also sometimes called Scipio. (Dio 42.58; Suetonius *Julius Caesar* 59)

47   Caesar's assault on the African town of Hadrumentum came to naught when his army was repelled by the town's defenders. (Dio 42.58

46–   Julius Caesar celebrated five triumphs in these years, for his Gal-
45   lic, Pontic, Alexandrian, African and Spanish victories. With the spoils from these successes, he enriched the Roman treasury by some 600,000,000 sesterces. (Velleius Paterculus 2.56)

46   The Battle of Thapsus, in north Africa, one of the bloodiest battles of the civil wars of 49–45. Julius Caesar's forces prevailed. One of the consequences: the demise of Cato the Younger, who committed suicide in Utica rather than submit to a Caesarian amnesty. (Cary 406)

46   Shortly after the Battle of Thapsus, Marcus Petreius (victor over Catiline at the Battle of Pistoria in 62) died with the Numidian king Juba in a suicide pact. (OCD *s.v.* Juba [1])

46   As governor of Transalpine Gaul, Decimus Junius Brutus quelled a revolt of one of the local tribes, the Bellovaci. (OCD *s.v.* Brutus [6])

46   Julius Caesar granted a triumph to Marcus Aemilius Lepidus (the future triumvir) for his military activities in Farther Spain, even though Lepidus had not accomplished anything noteworthy there. (Dio 43.1)

46   Caesar rewarded his soldiers for their loyalty by giving them a largesse of 20,000 sesterces apiece. (Dio 43.21)

45   The Battle of Munda (in Spain), which brought to a close the civil wars of 49–45. It was the final battle of Julius Caesar's long military career. (Cary 407)

44–   During Mark Antony's siege of Mutina, the blockaded com-
43   mander, Decimus Brutus, used carrier pigeons to send messages
       to the consuls camped in the region. Pliny the Elder (10.110)
       remarks that Antony's siege tactics were useless for intercepting
       documents transmitted in this manner.

44   (March 15.) Caesar's assassination on this date occurred a mere
       four days before he had planned to leave Rome to initiate a mil-
       itary campaign against the Parthians. (Appian *Civil Wars* 2.110)

44   (Late spring.) Mark Antony appealed to the senate to allow him
       to retain a bodyguard. This contingent ultimately swelled to
       6,000 men; despite the senate's objections, Antony refused to
       reduce the size of the guard. (Appian *Civil Wars* 3.5)

44   (October.) Mark Antony traveled to Brundisium to attempt to
       assume command of four legions stationed there. However, they
       derided his offer of 400 sesterces per man, especially since
       Antony's rival, Octavian, was paying four times that sum. (Dio
       45.13; Ker LCL Cicero *Philippics* 185)

44–   Lucius Staius Murcus and Quintus Marcius Crispus led the siege
43   of Apamea, a town in Syria held by the Pompeian sympathizer
       Quintus Caecilius Bassus. (OCD *s.v.* Bassus [1])

43   Octavian seized the consulship. As he marched toward Rome with
       his army, he sent a centurion ahead to demand ratification of his
       usurpation of the office. The biographer Suetonius states that this
       centurion, while relaying Octavian's demands to the Senate, laid
       his hand on the hilt of his sword and said: *Hic faciet, si vos non
       feceritis* ("This will do it [*i.e.* make him consul] if you don't").

43   Marcus Junius Brutus captured Mark Antony's brother Gaius at
       Apollonia; Gaius was executed in the next year, probably at Bru-
       tus' order. (Dio 47.24)

44–   Mark Antony besieged Decimus Junius Brutus at Mutina (in Cisal-
43   pine Gaul) in these years. He was driven off by an army under
       the command of Aulus Hirtius and Gaius Vibius Pansa, the con-
       suls in 43. (MRR II 334–335)

43   Pontius Aquila, one of the Caesarian assassins, died in the Battle
       of Mutina. He was subsequently honored with a commemora-
       tive statue, and it was further decreed that his heirs should be

reimbursed for the personal funds which he had spent to equip the troops. (Dio 46.40)

43   Decimus Brutus was voted a triumph for his resistance to Mark Antony at Mutina, although as Velleius Paterculus (2.62) wryly notes, his success was due in large part to *alieno beneficio* "someone else's help" (*i.e.* Aulus Hirtius).

43   Lucius Munatius Plancus celebrated a triumph for his Gallic campaigns in this and the preceding year. (OCD *s.v.* Plancus [1])

42   After defeating Bessi (in Thrace), Brutus assumed the title Imperator, thinking that it might give him added credibility in the inevitable showdown with Octavian and Mark Antony. (Dio 47.25)

42   The Battle of Philippi (actually two separate engagements), in Greece, in which Octavian defeated Caesar's assassins Brutus and Cassius. (OCD *s.v.* Philippi)

42   *Sequar eum quem mea occidit tarditis*—"I will follow him whom my tardiness has killed." These were the last words of Gaius Cassius' aide, spoken immediately before he committed suicide. He was motivated to do this by the sight of Cassius' severed head, and his own failure to report Brutus' military successes in a timely manner. (Velleius Paterculus 2.70)

41   Lucius Antonius (Mark Antony's younger brother) celebrated a triumph on the first day of this year, although his victories over various Alpine tribes were deemed relatively insignificant. Antonius also assumed the consulship on this day. (Dio 48.4)

41–40 (Winter.) Octavian besieged and captured the central Italian town of Perusia, then held by Lucius Antonius. After capturing Perusia, Octavian carried out a brutal repression of its citizens. According to some reports, 300 men were executed on the Ides of March of this year, as partial revenge for the murder of Caesar. (Suetonius *Augustus* 15). Velleius Paterculus (2.73) reports that much of Perusia's devastation was self-inflicted, notably by a citizen named Macedonicus, who set fire to the city and then committed suicide.

40   Quintus Labienus and the Parthian chieftain Pacorus joined to defeat Mark Antony's legate Decidius Saxa in Syria. The Parthians

later dubbed Labienus *Parthicus Imperator* ("Parthian general"). Labienus was the son of Titus Labienus, Caesar's trusted Gallic legate. (CAH X 47; OCD *s.v.* Labienus [2])

40   During the campaign against Sextus Pompeius, Quintus Salvidienus Rufus aroused the derision of his troops for attempting to ferry them from Rhegium to Sicily on leather boats. (The craft apparently resembled large floating shields.) So he decided to transport the men in more conventionally constructed ships, a plan that also backfired when Pompey's naval skills proved superior. (Dio 48.18)

Originally a partisan of Octavian, he made overtures to Mark Antony in this year. When these matters were later revealed to Octavian, he vilified Salvidienus before the senate, who thereupon declared Salvidienus a public enemy. (Velleius Paterculus 2.76; OCD *s.v.* Salvidienus)

40   Titus Sextius, governor of Numidia, dreamt that a bull buried in the district encouraged Sextius to exhume the bull and display its head on a pole. When he later discovered the bull at the place revealed in the dream, he interpreted it as a sign that he should invade Africa Vetus. He eventually succeeded, and briefly ruled both provinces, until surrendering them to Gaius Fuficius Fango, Octavian's representative. (Dio 48.21–22; OCD *s.v.* Sextius [1])

40   The murder of Arabio, by Titus Sextius. Arabio, an African prince, ultimately allied himself with Sextius when the latter was a provincial governor in Africa. Sextius, however, grew suspicious of Arabio's intentions, and so dispatched him, an action which caused most of Sextius' cavalry to desert. (Dio 48.23)

40   Menodorus (or Menas), a freedman of Sextus Pompeius, captured Sardinia, forcing its governor, Marcus Lurius, to flee. (Dio 48.30)

40   Tiberius Claudius Nero (father of the future emperor Tiberius) attempted to instigate a rebellion in Campania. His efforts came to naught, however, when Octavian arrived on the scene and quickly quelled the uprising. (Velleius Paterculus 2.75; OCD *s.v.* Nero [3])

*c.*40   Sextus Pompeius executed Lucius Staius Murcus (one of Caesar's Gallic legates), despite the fact that the latter had considerably augmented the size of Pompeius' fleet by joining his own navy with Pompeius'. Velleius Paterculus (2.77) states that false accusations against Murcus led to his demise.

39   The battles of the Cilician Gates and Mount Amanus, both Roman victories over the Parthians, under the command of Publius Ventidius. In 38, Ventidius defeated the Parthians again, at the Battle of Gindarus. According to Frontinus (*Stratagems* 2.2), he held back his troops until the advancing Parthians were within 500 paces, thus nullifying their considerable archery skills. The Parthian leader Pacorus died in this battle, 15 years to the day (according to Dio 44.21) after Crassus fell at Carrhae. Ventidius was later honored with a memorable and magnificent triumph in Rome.

38   Gnaeus Domitius Calvinus, governor of Spain, punished a cowardly centurion named Vibillius by the use of the *fustuarium*, a method of execution in which the condemned man was beaten to death by his fellow soldiers. (Velleius Paterculus 2.78; Shipley LCL Velleius Paterculus 216)

37   Marcus Agrippa oversaw a major fleet and harbor construction effort, in preparation for the upcoming naval struggle with Sextus Pompeius. (Dio 48.49)

36   (November 13.) Octavian celebrated an ovation (minor triumph) for his victory over Sextus Pompeius. (Suetonius *Augustus* 22)

36   Mark Antony made several abortive attempts to defeat the Parthians, and so avenge the Roman setback at their hands in the Battle of Carrhae (53). (Cary 441–442)

36   A major storm off Cape Palinurus destroyed many of Octavian's ships. (Dio 49.1)

36   The Battle of Naulochus (off Sicily), in which Octavian's admiral Marcus Agrippa defeated Sextus Pompeius, Octavian's last viable republican opponent. This engagement ranked as one of the largest naval encounters in Roman history, with a total of 600 ships taking part. (MRR II 403; Scullard GN 169)

36   Lucius Cornificius led three legions on a dangerous march from Tauromenium to Tyndaris (in Sicily). The journey was complicated by the numerous nagging injuries suffered by Cornificius' men when they were struck by stones and spears launched at

them from great distances by Sextus Pompeius' soldiers. Eventually, however, Cornificius successfully rendezvoused with Agrippa. (Dio 49.6–7)

36   A major military mutiny erupted among Octavian's troops. Octavian handled the situation by discharging the mutinous soldiers, while promising even greater rewards in money and land for those who remained loyal. (Dio 49.14)

36   Publius Canidius Crassus successfully campaigned against the Iberians and the Albanians (in Asia), overcoming kings Pharnabazus and Zober, respectively. (Dio 49.24)

36   The Romans made effective use of the *testudo*, in a battle against the Parthians (the *testudo* being a military formation in which the soldiers packed themselves closely together, crouched down, and raised their shields over their heads, thus forming a shelter against enemy arrows and spears.) The Parthians, having never seen this maneuver before, assumed that the Romans were either dead or exhausted. When the enemy drew near, however, the Romans jumped to their feet and handily defeated the unwary Parthians. (Dio 49.29)

35   Shortly after the Battle of Naulochus, Sextus Pompeius fled to the east, where he was executed by Marcus Titius, one of Mark Antony's henchmen. Octavian ordained circus games to commemorate the deed. (Dio 49.18; MRR II 409)

35   Cleopatra provided Mark Antony with money and supplies, to compensate for his losses in the disastrous Parthian campaigns. (Antony's wife Octavia had also organized relief supplies, but these he rejected.) (OCD *s.v.* Cleopatra; Scullard GN 173)

35–   Octavian's military campaigns in Illyria.
34

34   Mark Antony's troops invaded Armenia and captured the king, Artavasdes. (MRR II 411)

32   Provinces and regions which supported Octavian in the imminent civil war with Antony: Italy, Gaul, Spain, Illyricum, Africa (except for Cyrene), Sardinia, Sicily. Antony drew support from: Asia, Thrace, Greece, Macedonia, Egypt, Cyrene. (Dio 50.6)

31   Mark Antony was beset by desertions prior to the Battle of Actium,

and as a result, he became suspicious of those men who remained. He executed or harassed several of these, including Iamblichus, an Arabian king; Quintus Postumius, a senator; and Quintus Dellius. The latter, who had served under Dolabella, Cassius and Antony before joining Octavian, was termed by the historian Valerius Messalla a *desultor bellorum civilium*, "a turncoat of the civil wars." (Dio 50.13; OCD *s.v.* Dellius)

31   The Battle of Actium, a naval confrontation in which the forces of Octavian and Marcus Agrippa overcome Mark Antony and Cleopatra. (OCD *s.v.* Actium)

28   Marcus Licinius Crassus (grandson of the triumvir) killed a king of the Bastarnae, whereupon he demanded the *spolia opima* (the right to consecrate the captured spoils to a deity, usually Jupiter or Mars). (Dio 51.24)

27   Octavian received a crown of oak leaves, awarded to him for showing clemency to enemy soldiers after the Battle of Actium. (Shipley LCL Velleius Paterculus 349)

27   Octavian's intended journey to Britain was cancelled, when he tarried in Gaul en route, to stamp out the beginnings of an insurgence there. (Dio 50.22)

4. Literary Milestones

240   Livius Andronicus, a Romanized Greek brought as a slave from Tarentum to Rome, was the first to produce Latin comedy and tragedy in Rome, at the celebration of the Ludi Romani in 240. (OCD *s.v.* Livius Andronicus)

*c.*235   Gnaeus Naevius' first play was produced. (OCD *s.v.* Naevius)

*c.*222   Caecilus Statius was brought as a slave from Gaul to Rome, where he became a noted comic playwright. (OCD *s.v.* Caecilius [1])

216   The historian Quintus Fabius Pictor was sent to Greece to consult the Delphic oracle, after Rome's disastrous defeat at the Battle of Cannae. (OCD *s.v.* Fabius Pictor)

207   Livius Andronicus was requested to compose a hymn of expiation, to counteract omens unfavorable to the government. (Livy 22.1; OCD *s.v.* Livius Andronicus)

206   The poet/playwright Gnaeus Naevius was incarcerated for attacking the powerful and influential family of the Metelli in his plays. Quintus Caecilius Metellus, one of the consuls in 206, thus implemented his famous threat: *Dabunt malum Metelli Naevio poetae*: "The Metelli will make trouble for the poet Naevius." (OCD *s.v.* Naevius)

205   Hannibal ordered the construction of a lengthy bilingual (Punic and Greek) inscription in which he recounted his accomplishments. The inscription was placed in the temple of Juno Lacinia, near Croton (southern Italy). (Livy 28.46)

*c.*204   The probable date of the production of one of Plautus' best known comedies, *Miles Gloriosus* (*Bragging Soldier*). (OCD *s.v.* Plautus)

204   The poet Quintus Ennius, a Calabrian, arrived in Rome, with the assistance of Cato the Elder, to author tragic plays and teach Greek. (CAH VIII 403)

204   The poet Naevius was imprisoned in this year, as a result of his battles with the powerful Caecilii Metelli. He wrote two plays during his incarceration. (OCD *s.v.* Naevius)

200   Publius Licinius Tegula composed an expiatory hymn to be sung this year (three times by nine young women), in response to various prodigies and omens. (Livy 31.12)

c.200   The senator Quintus Fabius Pictor, a veteran of the Second Punic War, authored the first prose history of Rome, a work spanning from the origins of the city to Fabius' own times. It survives in fragmentary form. (CAH VIII 419; OCD *s.v.* Fabius Pictor)

c.184   The poet Quintus Ennius received Roman citizenship, with the help of the son of Marcus Fulvius Nobilior. (Grant *s.v.* Ennius)

167   One thousand Achaeans were deported from Greece to Italy; included in their number was the noted historian Polybius. It is generally assumed that Polybius composed his 40-volume history of Rome during his stay in the city. The (300 surviving) exiles were returned to Greece in 151. (Cary 141, 210)

167   Lucius Aemilius Paullus, triumphant general in the Third Macedonian War, transferred to Rome the massive personal library of the defeated Macedonian king Perseus. (Livy 45.28 ff)

166–
160   Productions of the plays of the comic playwright Terence were undertaken. The first of these, *Andria* (produced in 166), benefited from the invaluable patronage of the established comic poet Caecilius Statius, whom Terence impressed with a personal recitation of the script. (OCD *s.v.* Terence)

160   Productions of Terence's *Adelphi* and *Hecyra* were given in consort with funeral games commemorating the death of Lucius Aemilius Paullus. (Balsdon 250)

c.160   The probable date of Cato's book on agriculture, *De Agri Cultura*. (OCD *s.v.* Cato [1])

c.160   The playwright Terence left Rome, never to return. Terence's reasons may have been twofold: 1. to escape charges of plagiarism (there had been rumors that large portions of his plays were ghostwritten); 2. to learn more about Greek culture, thus to incorporate it more effectively into future plays. (Suetonius *Terence* 4–5)

c.150   Books 1–6 of Polybius' *Histories* were published. The publication date of the remaining books (7–40) is unknown. (OCD *s.v.* Polybius)

134   The satirist Lucilius accompanied Scipio Aemilianus to Numantia, and the onset of Aemilianus' military activities there. He had arrived in Spain in 139. (Velleius Paterculus 2.9)

133   The consulship of Lucius Calpurnius Piso Frugi, who authored a history of Rome to 146; he dated the moral decline of Rome to 154, at which time *pudicitiam subversam*, "chastity was subverted." This same Calpurnius, as tribune in 149, proposed the establishment of a special court to try cases of extortion. (OCD *s.v.* Piso [1])

c.132   The satirist Lucilius began writing poems. (OCD *s.v.* Lucilius [1])

c.130   The poet Volcacius Sedigitus composed a canon of the ten best Latin writers of comedy. (OCD *s.v.* Volcacius [1])

c.123   The Pontifex Maximus Publius Mucius Scaevola reputedly systematized and published the *Annales Maximi*, annual chronicles of political and religious events dating to the earliest days of the Roman Republic. (OCD *s.v.* Annals, Annalists)

c.123   The probable date of publication of the last five of Lucilius' 30 books of satires. (The rest were collected and published after his death.) (OCD *s.v.* Lucilius [1])

c.121   Lucius Coelius Antipater introduced the genre of the historical monograph in Rome, with his account of the Second Punic War, in seven books. Fragments remain. (OCD *s.v.* Coelius [1])

c.120   The trial of Quintus Mucius Scaevola (for provincial mismanagement) was satirized by Lucilius. (OCD *s.v.* Lucilius)

103   The death of Sextus Turpilius, an author of comic plays. Thirteen titles are known, but no texts survive. (OCD *s.v.* Turpilius)

94   The death of Lucius Attius, a poet. He coined the famous phrase *Oderint dum metuant* ("Let them hate [me] as long as they fear [me]"), often associated in later times with dictators and tyrants. (Harper's *s.v.* Attius)

c.92   The death of the freedman Aurelius Opilius, an author and teacher of philosophy and rhetoric. He was a Plautine specialist. (OCD *s.v.* Opilius)

c.91   Cicero composed two books on rhetoric, the *De Inventione*; both books have survived. The treatise was unsophisticated and in later years, Cicero himself denigrated it. (CAH IX 756)

c.90   The Greek author and sculptor Pasiteles came to Rome, whereupon he was granted citizenship. (OCD *s.v.* Pasiteles)

c.89   Gaius Novius and Lucius Pomponius gave literary form to Atellan farces, heretofore slapstick improvisational stage plays. (OCD *s.v.* Novius)

88   The Greek philosopher/author Philo of Larissa immigrated to Rome, where he became one of Cicero's most influential teachers. (OCD *s.v.* Philon of Larissa)

87   The philosopher/scientist/historian Posidonius of Rhodes was sent to Rome to represent Rhodian interests before Gaius Marius. He became a mentor of sorts to Cicero and Pompey. (OCD *s.v.* Posidonius)

86   Lucius Ateius Praetextatus Philologus, an Athenian, was brought to Rome, where he became a leading scholar, and author of some 800 books. (OCD *s.v.* Ateius Praetextatus Philologus)

86–   Sometime within this period, the first Latin textbook on rhetoric
82   appeared: *Rhetorica ad Herennium*. Although once ascribed to Cicero, scholarly consensus now concludes that it is the work of an unknown author. (OCD *s.v.* Rhetorica ad Herennium)

84   Sulla transferred to Rome the manuscripts of Aristotle. They had been in the possession of a certain Apellicon, ruler of Delos. (OCD *s.v.* Aristotle)

83   A fire on the Capitoline Hill destroyed the prophetic Sibylline books. A new collection was produced, based on references and quotations from various sources. (OCD *s.v.* Sibylla)

79   Cicero departed Rome for Athens and Rhodes, where he spent several years studying oratory and philosophy. (OCD *s.v.* Cicero [1])

78   The most accomplished historian of the Sullan era, Lucius Cornelius Sisenna, held the praetorship. (OCD *s.v.* Sisenna)

c.77   The death of Titus Quinctius Atta, writer of comedies and poems. Only fragments of his work survive. (OCD *s.v.* Atta)

73   The Greek poet Parthenius of Nicaea was brought to Rome; he had been captured during the Third Mithridatic War. He became a mentor to several noted Latin poets, including Gaius Cornelius Gallus, Gaius Helvius Cinna, and possibly Vergil. (OCD *s.v.* Parthenius; Grant *s.v.* Parthenius)

71   When Pompey was about to assume the consulship for the first time, he asked Marcus Terentius Varro to compose a manual for him on the proper method of addressing the senate and proposing measures to that body. Since Pompey was primarily a military man, he felt that he needed this information in order to discharge his duties successfully. (Aulus Gellius 14.7)

c.70   Gaius Licinius Macer, Claudius Quadrigarius and Valerius Antias all published accounts of Roman history. (Cary 465)

c.68   The death of the philosopher Antiochus of Ascalon, a friend of Lucullus. He greatly influenced Cicero, who often quoted him in his writings. (OCD *s.v.* Antiochus [1])

68–   Cicero wrote hundreds of (still extant) letters to his friend Atti-
44   cus over the span of these years.

63   Lucius Orbilius Pupillus emigrated from Beneventum to Rome, where he flourished as a teacher and author. Many of his writings display an attack mode; politicians, students, teachers and others fell under his critical eye. (OCD *s.v.* Orbilius Pupillus)

c.63   The Greek poet Aulus Licinius Archias completed a lengthy epic on the accomplishments of Lucius Licinius Lucullus in Asia. (Pompey, as a rival of Lucullus, salved his wounded pride by engineering the prosecution of Archias and, by extension, his circle of Roman friends.) (Cicero *Pro Archia* 21; Gruen 267)

62   The poet Archias began a laudatory poem on Cicero's consulship. Cicero saw the preliminary draft, which he termed *magna res et iucunda*, "a great and pleasing piece of work." (Cicero *Pro Archia Poeta* 28)

c.62   The death of Quintus Roscius Gallus, considered the best actor of his day. In his prime, he reputedly earned an annual salary of 500,000 sesterces. (OCD *s.v.* Roscius [3]; Pliny 7.128) *c.*62   The poet Catullus arrived in Rome, where he soon fell passionately in love with Clodia, the "Lesbia" of many of his most well known poems.(OCD *s.v.* Catullus)

*c.*62   Pompey prevailed upon his educated freedman, Pompeius Lenaeus, to translate into Latin King Mithridates' writings on medicine. (OCD *s.v.* Lenaeus)

60   Cicero sent a Greek version of his account of his consulship to Atticus, for Atticus' comments. Interestingly, Cicero completed the Greek version before the Latin. (Cicero *Letters to Atticus* 1.19)

59   Cicero received a shipment of books written by Alexander of Ephesus, whom the orator described as a *poeta ineptus*, "worthless poet." (Cicero *Letters to Atticus* 2.20)

59–   Catullus authored his series of poems detailing his relationship
54   with Lesbia.

57   Cicero secretly composed a short treatise in which he denounced his political enemies, notably Julius Caesar and Crassus. Fearing the consequences if the book should be published, he sealed it and gave it to his son, with instructions that it not be opened until after his death. (Dio 39.10; Cicero *Letters to Atticus* 2.6)

57   A revival of Afranius' (b. *c.*150 B.C.) comic play *Simulans* (*The Pretender*) took place in this year. According to Cicero, one of its lines — about the end of a disreputable character's life — was patently and loudly directed at Publius Clodius, who was in the audience. (Cicero *Pro Sestio* 118)

57–   Catullus served on the staff of Gaius Memmius, governor of Bithy-
56   nia in these years. Catullus' fellow neoteric poet Gaius Helvius Cinna reputedly also accompanied Memmius. (CAH IX 750; OCD *s.v.* Cinna [3])

56   (January 17.) Cicero dictated a letter to his brother Quintus on this day, a departure from his customary procedure of writing letters to his brother in his own hand. Eye problems caused him to rely on a scribe. (Cicero *Letters to His Brother Quintus* 2.2)

*c.*56   The poet Helvius Cinna wrote a poem in honor of the departure of Gaius Asinius Pollio for Greece. The poem — entitled *Proempticon*— has not survived. (Grant *s.v.* Cinna)

55   The final performance of the noted tragic actor Clodius Aesopus occurred in this year, at the dedication of Pompey's theater. He was a friend and tutor of Cicero. (OCD *s.v.* Aesopus)

55   Cicero composed *De Oratore* (*On the Orator*), a treatise on the nature and function of the art of oratory. (OCD *s.v.* Cicero [1])

55   (October 15). Vergil assumed the toga of manhood; the poet Lucretius reputedly died on the very same day. (OCD *s.v.* Virgil)

54   Cicero referred to the poet Lucretius only once, in a letter written in 54 to his brother Quintus. In it, he described Lucretius' *De Rerum Natura* as a work *multis luminibus ingenii multae tamen artis*: "[containing] many ingenious insights, very skillfully written." (CAH IX 747)

54   (September.) In another letter to his brother Quintus, Cicero remarks that he had bought an estate for him at Arpinum (their birthplace). The purchase price: 100,000 sesterces. (Cicero *Letters to His Friends* 3.1)

54   Cicero's brother Quintus claimed to have written four tragedies in 16 days while in Gaul. Marcus doubted his brother's claim; he suspected a certain amount of "borrowing" was involved. (Cicero *Letters to His Brother Quintus* 3.5)

c.54   The probable date of the composition of Julius Caesar's book on grammar (*De Analogia*). Although no longer extant, it is known that Caesar dedicated the work to Cicero. Its famous advice to writers: *ut tamquam scopulum sic fugias inauditum atque insolens verbum*. "Just as you would avoid a sharp rock, so avoid an unusual or nonstandard word." (Aulus Gellius 1.10; Hendrickson LCL Cicero *Brutus* 216)

53   The date of the grant of freedom to Marcus Tullius Tiro, Cicero's secretary and editorial assistant. (OCD *s.v.* Tiro)

52–51   (Winter.) Julius Caesar wrote his *Commentaries*, on the wars in Gaul.

50   The censors Appius Claudius Pulcher and Lucius Calpurnius Piso Caesoninus expelled the historian Sallust from the Roman senate, for immoral behavior, possibly his illicit affair with the wife of Titus Annius Milo in 52. The next year, however, Julius Caesar appointed Sallust as a quaestor, thus restoring him to the ranks of the senate. (Dio 40.63; MRR II 248)

50   Pompey wrote a letter to the senate in which he reviewed and defended his official acts; he took pains to point out that the army and powers which he was then retaining devolved upon him from the senate, as unsolicited perquisites. (Appian *Civil Wars* 2.28)

49   (January 1.) Gaius Scribonius Curio delivered a letter written by Julius Caesar to the consuls (Lucius Cornelius Lentulus Crus and Gaius Claudius Marcellus). In this letter, Caesar outlined the many services he had performed for Rome and his willingness to compromise with his political adversaries, to avoid a civil war. (Dio 41.1)

       Curio carried the letter to Rome from Ravenna, where Caesar wrote it; he covered the approximately 150 miles in three days. (Appian *Civil Wars* 2.32)

49   Lucius Cornelius Balbus (nephew of the Balbus defended by Cicero in 56) served as an ambassador and diplomatic representative of Julius Caesar. He later wrote an account of his experiences. (OCD *s.v.* Balbus [4])

49   Aulus Caecina (son of the Caecina defended by Cicero in 69) wrote an anti–Caesarian treatise in this year, subsequently resulting in his banishment by Caesar in 48. (OCD *s.v.* Caecina [1])

c.49 Vergil moved from Rome to Naples to study philosophy, a relocation possibly motivated by the outbreak of the civil war. (Grant *s.v.* Vergil)

48   Cicero inadvertently came across a bundle of unsent letters written by his brother Quintus to various friends. The letters were filled with harsh criticisms of Marcus; the reason for Quintus' (temporarily) hostile attitude toward his brother has never been explained. (Williams LCL Cicero *Letters to His Brother Quintus* 386)

48   After the Battle of Pharsalus, Caesar's troops discovered numerous letters written by Pompey; many of these letters provided detailed information about Caesar's enemies. Caesar did not read them; instead, he ordered them to be burned, so as to avoid the necessity of punishing the individuals named in the letters.

47   The date of publication of Atticus' history of Rome, replete with chronological listings of the chief magistrates. (Nepos *Atticus* 18)

47   Julius Caesar selected Marcus Terentius Varro to organize and
      administer his proposed public library. (OCD *s.v.* Varro [2])

46   Sallust, newly appointed to the office of praetor, was almost killed
      by some of Caesar's soldiers, disgruntled because of their disap-
      pointment in not receiving as much booty as they expected after
      their exertions on Caesar's behalf in the east. (Dio 42.52; MRR
      II 291)

46   Cicero wrote three books on the art of oratory: *De Optimo Genere
      Oratorum*; *Brutus*; *Orator*. (CAH IX 758–759)

46   An unknown author — possibly Sallust — sent a pamphlet to Julius
      Caesar urging him to follow a path of moderation, reconcilia-
      tion and reform in domestic affairs. (CAH IX 693)

46   Marcus Junius Brutus authored a laudatory essay on Cato the
      Younger. Cicero felt that it gave Cato too much credit for bring-
      ing down the Catilinarian conspirators, at the expense of Cicero's
      role in the matter. (Cicero *Letters to Atticus* 12.21; Rolfe LCL
      Suetonius *Augustus* 250)

*c.*46 Julius Caesar published several (now lost) pamphlets called the
      Anticatones, responses to Cicero's laudatory essays on Cato the
      Younger. In one of them, according to Plutarch, Caesar accused
      Cato of sifting through the ashes of cremated corpses, in search
      of gold that had melted with them in their funeral pyres.

*c.*46 Publilius Syrus began writing and producing mimes in Rome.
      (Grant *s.v.* Publilius Syrus)

45   In one of his letters to Julius Caesar, Cicero commended the lit-
      erary talents of a freedman named Apollonius, who was at the
      time writing a book about Caesar's accomplishments. Apollo-
      nius, a freedman of Crassus, composed the book in Greek.
      (Cicero *Letters to His Friends* 13.16; CAH IX 789)

45   Caerellia, an educated woman mentioned occasionally in Cicero's
      letters, spent some of this year and the next making copies of a
      number of his treatises. (CAH IX 784) In a scathing speech
      directed at Cicero by Quintus Fufius Calenus in 43, he accused
      Cicero of divorcing his second wife so that he could freely pur-
      sue an adulterous affair with Caerellia. (Dio 46.18)

45   The historian Sallust retired from public life to devote himself to
      his literary endeavors. (CAH IX 767

45   Decimus Laberius, author of mimes, appeared as an actor in several
        stage productions of his compositions. For this service, Julius Cae-
        sar awarded him 500,000 sesterces. (Suetonius *Julius Caesar* 39)

45–   The death of Cicero's daughter Tullia in 45 resulted in his author-
44   ship of numerous philosophical treatises in these years: *Conso-
        latio*; *Hortensius*; *De Finibus Bonorum et Malorum*; *Academics*;
        Tusculan Disputations; *De Natura Deorum*; *De Senectute*; *De
        Amicitia*. (OCD *s.v.* Cicero [1])

44   (August 19.) In a letter to Atticus (16.7), Cicero introduced the
        term *scholium*, to refer to an explanatory note. The word is cur-
        rently used (usually in its plural form, scholia) to describe anno-
        tations and commentaries made by medieval scholars in the mar-
        gins of manuscripts. (OCD *s.v.* scholia)

44   On September 1, Mark Antony criticized Cicero for his failure to
        attend a meeting of the senate. Cicero appeared on the follow-
        ing day and delivered the first of his 14 *Philippics*, diatribes against
        Antony. (KER LCL Cicero *Philippics* 18)

44   (November.) Cicero completed his final philosophical treatise, *De
        Officiis*. (OCD *s.v.* Cicero [1])

44   In his *Second Philippic*, Cicero referred to Julius Caesar as *divus*
        ("divine"), apparently the first example in Roman literature of
        such a titled applied to an individual ruler. *Divus* later became
        a standard epithet of many Roman emperors.

44   In one of the more striking contradictions in Roman literature,
        Cicero drafted his vitriolic *Second Philippic* against Mark Antony,
        while at the same time completing his treatise *De Amicitia* (*On
        Friendship*).

c.43   The probable date of publication of Varro's treatise on the Latin
        language, *De Lingua Latina*. (OCD *s.v.* Varro [2])

43   Varro's name was included on the proscription lists, courtesy of
        Mark Antony. He escaped death with the help of Quintus Fufius
        Calenus (consul in 47), but his massive personal libraries were
        pillaged. (OCD *s.v.* Varro [2]; Aulus Gellius 3.10)

43   During the siege of Mutina, Octavian was said to have been so
        devoted to oratory and literature that he read, wrote and practiced

public speaking every day, even though serious military matters constantly demanded his attention. (Suetonius *Augustus* 84)

43   Sallust's *War with Catiline* was published (although some scholars suggest a publication date as late as 40); two years later, his *War with Jugurtha* appeared. (OCD *s.v.* Sallust [1])

43   The consulship of Aulus Hirtius, one of Julius Caesar's staff officers; the eighth book of Caesar's *Gallic War* is widely attributed to him. (OCD *s.v.* Hirtius)

43   Quintus Fufius Calenus ridiculed Cicero's literary efforts, claiming that Cicero started his history of Rome not with the earliest known events — the standard procedure — but with his own consulship. (Dio 46.21)

43   Lucius Cornelius Balbus (nephew of the Balbus defended by Cicero) staged a *fabula praetexta* (Roman historical drama) about his own exploits in the civil wars of 49–48. Cicero sarcastically remarks that Balbus was so moved by the portrayal of his heroics that he wept openly during the performance. (Cicero *Letters to His Friends* 10.32)

42   While studying in Athens, the poet Horace was induced to join Brutus' army as a military tribune. He survived the Battle of Philippi, but a twofold tragedy awaited him upon his return to Italy: his father had died, and the family estate had been confiscated by the triumvirs. (Grant *s.v.* Horace)

41   Vergil's ancestral farm was confiscated from his father by the triumvirs, and allocated to military veterans who had fought in the civil war of 49–45. (OCD *s.v.* Virgil)

41   Horace returned from Greece to Rome, where he obtained a post as a quaestor's clerk. He devoted his nonworking hours to writing poetry. (Bennett vi)

c.40   Horace began work on his *Epodes*, which were published about ten years later. (OCD *s.v.* Horatius Flaccus)

39   Gaius Asinius Pollio established the first public library in Rome. (OCD *s.v.* Pollio)

c.38   Vergil's *Eclogues* were published. (OCD *s.v.* Virgil)

38   Vergil introduced Horace to the literary patron Gaius Maecenas, the conduit of imperial financial support for writers of Rome's literary Golden Age. (OCD *s.v.* Horatius Flaccus)

c.37–   Horace completed work on his *Satires*.
30

37   Varro's book on agriculture, *De Re Rustica*, was published. (OCD *s.v.* Varro [2])

37   A famous diplomatic journey — from Rome to Brundisium — was chronicled by Horace in one of his *Satires* (1.5). Chief travelers included Maecenas and Lucius Cocceius Nerva, who assisted in negotiating the Pact of Tarentum in this year.

c.34   The apparent date of publication of the first edition of Cornelius Nepos' *Lives of Illustrious Men*. A revised and expanded edition appeared sometime before 27. (OCD *s.v.* Nepos)

c.33   Some scholars believe that Cicero's letters to Atticus were published at about this time. His correspondence with friends and acquaintances had been published earlier. (OCD *s.v.* Cicero [1])

33   Horace took possession of the Sabine farm where he wrote much of his poetry. (Scullard GN 246)

c.32   Gaius Oppius, a political operative of Julius Caesar and Octavian, wrote an essay around 32 B.C. in which he argued that Cleopatra's son Caesarion had not been fathered by Caesar. (OCD *s.v.* Oppius)

31   At the age of 12, Ovid left his hometown of Sulmo to journey to Rome to complete his education. (Thornton v.)

31   Mark Antony authored his only literary work, *De Sua Ebrietate* (*On His Propensity for Drinking*). Although not extant, it appears to have been a defense of his behavior or lifestyle. (OCD *s.v.* Antony)

c.30   Tibullus began writing and publishing poetry.

c.30   Dionysius of Halicarnassus arrived in Rome at about this time. He spent the next 22 years gaining proficiency in Latin and Roman literature, and collecting information for the massive Roman history which he wrote. (Cary LCL Dionysius of Halicarnassus [Vol. I] vii)

29   Vergil finished his *Georgics*, poems on farming. (OCD *s.v.* Virgil)

29   Octavian, en route from the east to Rome, was forced by illness to slow his journey through Campania. At the town of Atella, Vergil visited him and recited for him the recently completed *Georgics*. (CAH X 119)

29   Varius Rufus' tragic play *Thyestes* was performed at a festival celebrating Octavian's victory at Actium. The play received a warm reception. (OCD *s.v.* Varius Rufus [2])

29–19 Vergil spent this decennium writing the *Aeneid*. (OCD *s.v.* Virgil)

28   Gaius Julius Hyginus was appointed chief librarian of the newly established Palatine Library. (OCD *s.v.* scholarship, Latin)

*c.*27 Livy embarked upon his life's work, a monumental 142-volume treatise on the history of Rome, *Ab Urbe Condita*. The project occupied him for the next 40 years. (OCD *s.v.* Livius [2])

5. Art and Architecture

263 Manius Valerius Maximus Messalla, consul in 263, adorned a portion of the senate house with a painting depicting his role in the liberation of Messana (Sicily), during the First Punic War. (Pliny 35.22)

260 A column commemorating Gaius Duilius' naval victory at the Battle of Mylae was set up in the Roman forum.

254 The Columna Rostrata was fashioned and erected on the Capitoline Hill; it was a column decorated with beaks of ships captured during the early years of the First Punic War. (Pliny 34.20)

c.250 Mile markers on Roman roads came into use. (OCD s.v. milestones)

c.244 The Via Appia (Appian Way) was extended as far as Brundisium. (OCD s.v. Via Appia)

238 In this year, paving was first employed in street surfacing in the city of Rome. (Ward-Perkins 328)

c.238 A temple in honor of the goddess Libertas was constructed on the Aventine Hill. (OCD s.v. Libertas)

221 Gaius Flaminius (consul in 223) constructed Rome's second chariot racetrack: the Circus Flaminius. It was sited near the Campus Martius. (OCD s.v. Circus)

c.221 Watchtowers and turrets built in Spain by Hannibal could still be viewed in Pliny's time, nearly 300 years later. Likewise, Hannibalic mineshafts still existed. (Pliny 33.96; 35.169)

220 Work began on the Via Flaminia, an important road leading north from Rome. (OCD s.v. Via Flaminia)

121

215   Two Capitoline Hill temples were dedicated: one in honor of Venus of Eryx, the other for Mens. Presiding over the dedication of the former was Quintus Fabius Maximus, who had vowed it when he was dictator. (Livy 23.30)

214   Tiberus Sempronius Gracchus arranged to have scenes painted on the Temple of Liberty depicting the celebrations that took place in Beneventum, after he successfully defeated the Carthaginian Hanno in battle near the town. (Livy 24.16)

212   When Marcus Claudius Marcellus captured Syracuse in this year, he removed a number of its art objects to Rome. The same sort of transfer occurred in 211, when Capua fell, and again in 209, with the capture of Tarentum. (CAH VIII 397–398)

212   The military tribune Lucius Marcius discovered a Carthaginian portrait shield in Spain; the shield (which once belonged to Hasdrubal) was transported to Rome, where it was displayed on the Capitoline Hill until its destruction in the fire of 83. (Pliny 35.14; MRR I 275)

204   A temple dedicated to the eastern cult goddess Cybele was constructed on the Palatine Hill. (Ward-Perkins 329)

200   Plautus' play Stichus was performed at the Plebeian Games, on a temporary wooden stage which stood in the Circus Flaminius. The stage had to be easily disassembled, since chariot races were also featured in the Circus during this festival. (Bieber 167)

196   Triumphal arches were erected in Rome, by Lucius Stertinius, to commemorate his victories in Spain. (Livy 33.27)

193   The construction of the Porticus Aemilia, a warehouse; it was the first known Roman building to employ concrete vaulting. (Ward-Perkins 60)

191   A Palatine temple in honor of Magna Mater was dedicated. It was constructed primarily of stuccoed tufa. (CAH VIII 385)

190   Publius Cornelius Scipio Africanus built a triumphal arch which was adorned with seven gilded statues and two horses. (Harper's s.v. arcus triumphalis)

189   The censors made provisions for the paving with flint of a short stretch of the Appian Way, near Rome. (Livy 38.28)

189   Publius Cornelius Scipio Nasica erected on the Capitol an image
       of a golden chariot drawn by six horses. (Livy 38.35)

189   Marcus Fulvius Nobilior transferred most of the art treasures of
       Ambracia to Rome. However, he left certain clay works attrib-
       uted to the noted 4th century B.C. painter Zeuxis of Heraclea.
       (Pliny 35.66)

187   Construction started on the Via Aemilia, a northbound road.
       (OCD s.v. Via Aemilia)

187   A mast in the Circus Maximus toppled onto a statue of Pollentia,
       destroying it. This unsettling omen was expiated by the addi-
       tion of an extra day to the circus games, and by the construc-
       tion of two new statues, both gilded. (Livy 39.7)

187   Gnaeus Manlius Vulso, celebrator of a triumph in this year, report-
       edly introduced decorated dinner couches and bronze tables into
       Rome at the same time. (Pliny 34.14)

184   Cato the Elder initiated the building of the Basilica Porcia, thought
       to be the first structure of its kind in Rome. In 179, a second
       basilica (the Aemilia) arose. (OCD s.v. Basilica; MRR I 392)

184   Cato spent 20,000,000 sesterces in refurbishing Rome's sewer and
       drainage systems. (CAH VIII 386)

181   The temple of Pietas was dedicated by Gaius Acilius Glabrio on
       the site of a house once belonging to his grandmother. There was
       a story that the grandmother had been imprisoned for some
       offense, and that when Glabrio's mother visited her, she offered
       her nourishment from her own breasts. The guards would not
       allow her to carry food into the cell. (Livy 40.34; Pliny 7.121)

179   The censorship of Marcus Aemilius Lepidus and Marcus Fulvius
       Nobilior was noted for its numerous construction projects,
       including:
           1. A breakwater at Tarracina.
           2. An auditorium at the Temple of Apollo.
           3. The cleaning and refurbishing of the Temple of Jupiter
       on the Capitoline Hill.
           4. A harbor and bridge pilings on the Tiber. (The pilings
       were placed for the Pons Aemilia, built in 142.)
           5. the Basilica Aemilia.

6. a fishmarket.

7. two porticos.

The two censors also wanted to initiate the construction of an aqueduct, but the project was scuttled due to the opposition of Marcus Licinius Crassus; part of the proposed aqueduct would have been built on his property. These censors also initiated economic, religious and political reforms. (Livy 40.51; Sage/Schlesinger LCL Livy [Vol. XII] 158–159)

179 An inscription commemorating the final defeat of King Antiochus III in 190 was placed above the doors of the Temple of Jupiter. (Livy 50.52)

174 The censors for 174, Quintus Fulvius Flaccus and Aulus Postumius Albinus, initiated a number of construction projects in and around Rome, including:

  1. Paving the city streets with flint.

  2. Building sidewalks next to roads outside the city.

  3. Renovating portions of the Circus Maximus, including the placement of starting gates and lap counters.

  4. Constructing and renovating various porticos.

  (Livy 46.27)

174 An inscription commemorating the subjugation of Sardinia was placed in the Temple of Mater Matuta. In the text, it was noted that 80,000 enemy soldiers had been killed or captured. (Livy 46.28)

173 The censor Quintus Fulvius Flaccus undertook the construction of the Temple to Fortuna Equestris. In order to achieve his objective of making it the nonpareil of Roman temples, he decided to provide it with marble roof tiles. These he obtained by plundering the marble tiles from the Temple of Juno Lacinia in Bruttium. Upon learning of the pillage, the senate was outraged, and ordered the tiles to be returned to Bruttium.

  Flaccus was devastated. In the following year, when one of his sons was killed and another contracted a terminal illness, he hanged himself. (Livy 47.3; 28)

169 The Basilica Sempronia was constructed, at the direction of the censor Tiberius Sempronius Gracchus. (Livy 44.16)

168 The praetor Gnaeus Octavius initiated the construction of a double stoa in the Campus Martius; it was used as a repository for

art objects seized by the Romans during the Third Macedonian War. (CAH VIII 385)

168   After defeating King Perseus, the Roman commander Lucius Aemilius Paullus requested the Athenians to send him their best painter, to prepare a visual record of his triumphal procession. They selected Metrodorus, a choice of which Paullus heartily approved. (Pliny 35.135)

163   The porticus Octavia was constructed. (CAH IX 836)

160   The consul Marcus Cornelius Cethegus made the first of many attempts to drain the Pomptine Marshes, a wetlands area south of Rome. It was a project not successfully accomplished until modern times. (OCD *s.v.* Pomptine Marshes)

159   The censors Publius Cornelius Scipio Nasica and Marcus Popillius Laenas removed all statues of ex-magistrates from the forum, except those whose placement had been authorized by senatorial or popular decree. (Pliny 34.30; OCD *s.v.* Scipio [10])

154   The Roman senate ordered the destruction of a partially completed stone theater; had it been built, it would have been the city's first permanent theater. (Duff 115)

*c.*150 The Roman colony of Cosa was the site of the oldest known triple arch (dated *c.*150) in Italy. (MacKendrick 107)

149   The Temple of Jupiter on the Capitoline Hill was the first building in Rome to be furnished with a diamond-pattern floor, in this year. (Pliny 36.185)

148   The northern portion of the Via Egnatia was extended to Dyrrhachium (Greece). (OCD *s.v.* Dyrrhachium)

*c.*148 The consul Spurius Postumius initiated construction of the Via Postumia, a northern Italian road. (OCD *s.v.* Via Postumia)

*c.*147 The construction of the Temples of Jupiter Stator and Juno Regina, under the supervision of the Greek architect Hermodorus. Both were fashioned of Greek marble and adorned with equestrian statues. (CAH VIII 385)

146   The Romans sacked the city of Corinth, in the process removing many of its artistic treasures and transporting them to Rome.

During the general violence, some Roman soldiers reportedly had so little regard for the city's art works that they used paintings for gaming boards. (Strabo 8.6.23)

146   So unappreciative of the unique character of Greek art was the Roman commander Lucius Mummius that, after the sack of Corinth, he instructed those in charge of shipping captured paintings and statues to Rome that if they lost them, they would be responsible for providing replicas. (Velleius Paterculus 1.13)

146   Ceilings in private homes were gilded for the first time. (Pliny 33.57)

145   Lucius Mummius Achaicus (sacker of Corinth) constructed the rudiments of a theater for the staging of plays celebrating his triumphal return to Rome. (Bieber 168)

145   The Comitia Tributa began meeting in the Roman forum, thus illustrating the importance of the forum as the center of government and politics. (OCD *s.v.* Forum)

144   The first high-level aqueduct was begun, the Aqua Marcia, under the supervision of the praetor Quintus Marcius Rex. (OCD *s.v.* Rex [1])

142   Lucius Mummius Achaicus dedicated a temple in Rome in honor of Hercules Victor. (OCD *s.v.* Hercules)

140   The Marcian aqueduct was extended to the Capitol, despite Sibylline prophecies prohibiting the delivery of water to this part of Rome. (Livy *Epitome* 54)

*c.*130   Construction began on the Via Egnatia, a trans–Hellenic Roman road stretching from the Adriatic coast to Byzantium. (OCD *s.v.* Via Egnatia)

122   Gaius Gracchus reportedly constructed temporary seats for a gladiatorial show he sponsored, the first time such an amenity for spectators had been provided in Rome. In the same year, he ordered the demolition of amphitheater seats that had been built for the aristocrats, because they blocked the view of ordinary citizens wishing to view the games. (Plutarch *Gaius Gracchus* 12; Wiedemann 20)

121   The consul Lucius Opimius rededicated the Temple of Concord,

after having overseen the execution of 3,000 of Gaius Gracchus' partisans. (Plutarch *Gaius Gracchus* 17)

121   The arch of Fabius was erected, at the southeastern end of the forum. (Watts LCL Cicero *Pro Archia*, etc. 426)

c.120   The construction of the first triumphal arch in Rome (Fornix Fabianus), at the direction of Quintus Fabius Maximus Allobrogicus. (OCD *s.v.* Fabius [8])

115   Rome's Temple of Juno was struck by lightning. (Pliny 2.144)

114   A certain Sulpicia was selected by a vote of Roman matrons to be the most chaste woman in the city. She thereby received the right to dedicate a statue of Venus Verticordia. (Pliny 7.120)

109   The Mulvian Bridge in Rome was rebuilt in stone. (MRR I 545)

c.106   Marcus Minucius Rufus (consul in 110) supervised the construction of the porticus Minucia, a building used in imperial times for the storage and distribution of grain. (OCD *s.v.* Minucius [4])

c.100   Concrete became the material of choice for the interiors of buildings. (Scullard GN 187)

c.100   Lucius Licinius Crassus, the leading orator of his day, ordered six 12-foot Hymettus marble columns to adorn the atrium of his Palatine mansion. Crassus was subsequently nicknamed the *Venus Palatina*, "Palatine Venus," an apparent reference to his home's luxurious furnishings. (Pliny 36.7)

99   A stage built for shows sponsored by Claudius Pulcher in this year was decorated with painted roof tiles so realistic that crows tried to land on them. (Pliny 35.23)

97   The censor Marcus Antonius decorated the speaker's platform in the Forum with military trophies obtained in Cilicia. (MRR II 6)

c.88   Lucius Licinius Lucullus purchased a copy of a famous painting by Pausias of Sicyon, for two talents. The painting was a portrait of Pausias' paramour Glycera. (Pliny 35.125)

83   The monumental Temple of Jupiter Optimus Maximus was

destroyed by fire; Sulla subsequently undertook its restoration. Large areas of the Capitoline Hill were also destroyed by fire. (Rolfe LCL Aulus Gellius [Vol. I] 150)

83   In gratitude for his Campanian victory over the consuls Norbanus and Scipio Asiagenus in this year, Sulla gave public thanks at a temple of Diana in the region. According to Velleius Paterculus (2.25), an inscription and a bronze tablet commemorating the event remained affixed to the temple in his own time, over 100 years later.

83–   The sanctuary of Fortuna Primigenia at Praeneste was refurbished,
82   a project noteworthy in view of the fact that most of the money for such endeavors was spent in Rome. (Cary 461)

80   To create space for the enlargement of the senate house, Sulla razed a portion of the assembly's meeting place, in the process removing statues of Pythagoras and Alcibiades; the two statues had been standing there for nearly 250 years. (Pliny 34.26)

c.80   According to Pliny the Elder (36.189), it was during Sulla's dictatorship that mosaics were first employed in Roman construction.

78   The tabularium was built, a repository for records and documents. (OCD *s.v.* tabularium)

78   Pliny the Elder states that this was the first year in which Numidian marble was imported to Rome; one of the consuls for 78, Marcus Aemilius Lepidus, employed this kind of marble in the door-sills of his home. According to Pliny, Lepidus' home was considered the finest in Rome. Yet 35 years later, his dwelling would not have even ranked among the 100 most luxurious houses in the city. (Pliny 36.49, 109)

78   Marcus Aemilius Lepidus (consul in this year) adorned his home with shields portraying battle scenes of various sorts (à la the shields of Achilles and Aeneas as described in the *Iliad* and *Odyssey*, respectively). (Pliny 35.12)

75   Ciceronian humor: While quaestor in Sicily in this year, Cicero dedicated some silver plate to the gods; he requested the silversmith to engrave them with his first two names (Marcus and Tullius) and then the image of a chickpea, the Latin word for which is *cicero*. (Plutarch *Cicero* 1)

75   Decimus Junius Silanus brought to Rome a painting of the personified Nemea, by the noted Athenian artist Nicias. The painting was later displayed in the curia. (Pliny 35.131)

c.75   The duumvirs Quinctius Vulgus and Marcus Porcius constructed Pompeii's second (smaller) theater; it had a seating capacity of about 1,500. (Bieber 174)

73   A colossal statue of Apollo, 45 feet high, was brought to Rome from Pontus in this year. It reportedly cost 500 talents to fabricate. (Pliny 34.39)

71   Lucius Licinius Lucullus brought to Rome from the island of Apollonia a 50-foot-tall statue of Apollo. He displayed it in a triumphal procession commemorating his military victories in Macedonia in 72. The statue was later set up on the Capitoline Hill. (Pliny 4.92)

c.70   Construction of the amphitheater in Pompeii, the oldest known surviving structure of its kind. (Bieber 177–178)

c.70   Quintus Lutatius Catulus first employed strips of linen cloths to serve as awnings in theaters. (Pliny 19.23)

69   Quintus Lutatius Catulus (consul in 78) dedicated the rebuilt Capitoline temple, a project which he oversaw. When he dedicated the restored temple of Jupiter in the same year, he provided awnings to shield the spectators from the sun. (Pliny 19.23; Balsdon 257)

65   During his aedileship, Julius Caesar restored the images of Marius and statues of Victory. They were gilded and inscribed with descriptions of Marius' victories over the Cimbri, in 101. (Plutarch *Caesar* 6)

62   Cicero purchased a home on the Palatine Hill, at a cost of 3,500,000 sesterces.

62   Construction was completed on the Pons Fabricius, a bridge over the Tiber River. An inscription carved into an arch of this bridge states: "Lucius Fabricius, the son of Lucius, the roads commissioner, took charge of the construction." (MRR II 174)

62   Realistic portraiture on Roman coins began, when a mint official named Coelius Caldus distributed coins bearing the likeness of his grandfather, a tribune in 107.

62   Pompey visited the theater at Mytilene, which (according to Plutarch) he used as the model for the theater which he constructed in Rome some seven years later. (Plutarch *Pompey* 42)

61   Cicero's brother Quintus purchased a home on the Argiletum, for nearly 1,000,000 sesterces. (Cicero *Letters to Atticus* 1.14)

58   The aedile Marcus Aemilius Scaurus reputedly built a three-story colonnaded wooden theater, with a seating capacity of 80,000. (Bieber 168)

58   All the paintings at Sicyon, including many by the noted artist Pausias, were sold to liquidate municipal debt; the art was subsequently transferred to Rome by the aedile Marcus Aemilius Scaurus. (Pliny 35.127) Scaurus' aedileship was marked by many excesses, including a provision for 3000 statues for use — apparently as props — in a temporary theater. (Pliny 34.36)

58–   During his time in Cyprus as the governor there, Cato the Younger
56   sold off all the statues he found, except for one, an image of the philosopher Zeno. (Pliny 34.92)

57   (October.) Cicero decided to sell his Tusculan home, claiming that he had no need for a residence outside Rome. Ironically, he had stated to Atticus in a letter in 68 that no place was as restful as his Tusculan villa. (Cicero *Letters to Atticus* 4.2)

56   (March.) In a letter to his brother Quintus (2.4), Cicero remarked that he had houses under construction at three (unnamed) locations, and that he was renovating his other properties.

55   Construction of the Theater of Pompey, Rome's first permanent theater. The structure's dedication in 52 was marred by the slaying of several elephants, an act which the spectators thought unnecessarily cruel.
      According to Dio, a rumor circulating at the time indicated that the theater was actually financed and constructed by a certain Demetrius, a wealthy freedman of Pompey. (Dio 39.38)

55   Julius Caesar's legions built a temporary wooden bridge across the Rhine River. Caesar's description of the construction of this bridge appears in Book IV of his *Gallic War*.

54   Julius Caesar purchased land in central Rome for his proposed

expansion of the forum — the cost: 100,000,000 sesterces. (Pliny 36.103)

54   Cicero wrote to his brother Quintus that he had erected a statue of him near the temple of Tellus in Rome. (Cicero *Letters to His Friends* 3.1)

52   The Curia, Rome's senate house, was burned in the rioting that followed the assassination of Publius Clodius. The rostra (speaker's platform) was also destroyed. (CAH IX 840)

52   Gaius Scribonius Curio oversaw the construction of two wooden theaters, facing in opposite directions and built on pivots.
     When the theaters were not in use for plays, they could be rotated toward one another, to form an amphitheater for gladiatorial shows. (Pliny 36.117)

50   Julius Caesar provided the consul Lucius Aemilius Paullus with 1500 talents (from Caesar's Gallic spoils) with which to build a lavish new basilica in the forum. (Plutarch *Caesar* 29) According to Appian (*Civil Wars* 2.26), the 1500 talents was in reality a bribe, to ensure Paullus' neutrality in the controversy over Caesar's continuing Gallic command.

50   The tribune Gaius Scribonius Curio proposed an ambitious road construction and maintenance program; he did so not because he thought the proposal practical, but because he wished to pick a quarrel with Pompey who, he believed, would oppose him. This was precisely the outcome. (Appian *Civil Wars* 2.27)

49   Julius Caesar erected a large altar of burnished stones at the summit of the Pyrenees, as a commemoration of his various Spanish victories. (Dio 49.24)

c.48 The Romans began developing the marble quarries near Luna, in Liguria (northern Italy). (Harper's *s.v.* Luna)

46   Work was begun on the first major expansion of the Roman forum, at the behest of Julius Caesar. (Harper's *s.v.* Forum)

46   Julius Caesar constructed a wooden amphitheater in Rome, the city's second such building. (Harper's *s.v.* amphitheater)

46   By senatorial decree, a chariot belonging to Caesar was placed on the Capitol, as was a statue depicting him standing upon a

representation of the known world, with the inscription that he was a demigod. (Dio 43.14)

46   Outside the temple of Venus Genetrix, Caesar dedicated paintings of Ajax and Medea. He purchased these works — by Timomachus of Byzantium — for 80 talents.

The cult statue was dedicated at the same time, even though its sculptor, Arcesilaus, had not completely finished it. (Pliny 35. 26; 136; 156)

c.46   The probable completion date of the Basilica Julia, in the forum, constructed under the supervision of Julius Caesar. (Mackendrick 138)

c.45   A statue of Caesar inscribed with the words *Deo Invicto* ("to the unconquered god") was set up in the temple of Quirinus. (Winstedt LCL Cicero *Letters to Atticus* [Vol. III] 96)

44   Shortly after the assassination of Caesar, a commemorative column was sited in the Forum. (Suetonius *Julius Caesar* 85)

44   (April.) A low-born rabble rouser named Herophilus (or Amatius) created a brief stir by constructing an altar in the forum, in front of a commemorative pillar dedicated to Caesar. Mark Antony quickly intervened, and summarily executed Herophilus. (Ker LCL Cicero *Philippics* 11)

44   Mark Antony instigated the placement of a statue of Julius Caesar in the forum; it was inscribed with the words *Parenti Optime Merito* ("to the best deserving father [*i.e.*, of his country]"). The episode is generally viewed as a ploy by Antony to attract Caesar's partisans to his side. (CAH X 11)

44   Several rostra were constructed and placed at the western end of the Roman forum. This was done at the direction of Julius Caesar. (OCD *s.v.* rostra)

44   Brutus began minting coins depicting his own image, along with daggers and a cap, the latter traditionally given to slaves upon manumission. (Dio 47.25)

44   When Brutus and Cassius arrived in Athens, they were given a hero's welcome; bronze statues of the two were fashioned and placed next to those of Harmodius and Aristogiton, the assassins of the Athenian tyrant Hipparchus in 514 B.C. (Dio 47.20)

42   Octavian vowed to build a temple in honor of the avenging Mars (Mars Ultor), if granted victory at the Battle of Philippi against Caesar's assassins; he prevailed, but he did not fulfill his vow until 40 years later. (Harper's *s.v.* Mars)

42   A certain Lucullus offered 1,000,000 sesterces to the artist Arcesilaus to fashion a statue of Felicitas. (Pliny 35.156)

40–   The construction of a temple dedicated to the deified Julius Cae-
27   sar.

39   Gnaeus Domitius Calvinus rebuilt and decorated the Regia, a project funded by the spoils from his recently concluded Spanish campaigns. He also borrowed some statues from Octavian to display in the Regia; their promised return did not materialize, since Octavian feared that demanding them back would appear sacrilegious. (Dio 48.42)

37   Horace traversed the full extent of the Via Appia (Appian Way, some 360 miles). (*Satire* 1.5)

37   Marcus Agrippa created a harbor in Campania by cutting canals from the sea to two nearby inland lakes, Avernus and Lucrinus. (Dio 48.50)

36   The Regia (home of the pontifex maximus in the Roman forum) was rebuilt under the auspices of Gnaeus Domitius Calvinus, in connection with his Spanish triumph. Carrara marble was employed, the first known usage of this particular material in Roman construction. (OCD *s.v.* Calvinus [2]; Ward-Perkins 333)

36   Octavian vowed to construct a temple of Apollo, replete with a surrounding portico. (Velleius Paterculus 2.81)

c.36   A solid gold statue — the first of its kind — was removed from a temple of Anaitis (near Cappadocia) by Mark Antony, during his war against the Parthians. (Pliny 33.83)

33   The aedileship of Marcus Vipsanius Agrippa, in which he undertook the supervision of several building projects; included in these: the construction of a new aqueduct, the Aqua Julia. In the previous year, he had overseen the refurbishing of another aqueduct, the Aqua Marcia. (Dio 49.42)

33   This year saw the completion of the Roman sewer system — called by Pliny the city's *opus omnium maximum*, "greatest work of all," because of its durability and efficiency. (Pliny 36.105 ff.)

31   Fire swept through Rome and destroyed or damaged a number of structures, including the Circus Maximus, a temple of Spes and the temple of Ceres. Arson was suspected. The likely perpetrators: freedmen whose net worth exceeded 200,000 sesterces, and who had recently been ordered to surrender one-eighth to the government. (Dio 50.10; Strabo 8.6.23)

c.30   The Temple of Saturn in the Roman forum was rebuilt, under the supervision of Lucius Munatius Plancus. (Ward-Perkins 66)

29   (August 18.) The temple in honor of the deified Julius Caesar (*Divus Julius*) was dedicated. It was located in the eastern end of the Roman forum. (Augustus *Res Gestae* 3.19; Shipley LCL *Res Gestae* 375)

29   The Temple of Deified Julius [Caesar] was dedicated. (CAH X [chronological table])

29   A dedicatory arch inscribed with the words *Re Publica Conservata* (*The Republic Saved*) was erected in Rome, in honor of Octavian's presumed rescue of the Roman republic from the clutches of Mark Antony and others. (CAH X 122)

29   Work began on Octavian's mausoleum, some 43 years before its owner would permanently occupy it. (CAH X [chronological table])

29   Octavian remodeled a wall in the curia so that it could accommodate a painting of the (personified) Nemean forest sitting on a lion — a reference to Hercules' first labor. (Pliny 35.27)

29   The porticos of Philippus were constructed, under the supervision of Lucius Marcius Philippus (suffect consul in 38). (Rackham LCL Pliny [Vol X] 310; OCD *s.v.* Philippus [6])

28   (October 9). The dedication of the Temple of Apollo on the Palatine; this temple served as a major repository for Greek and Latin books. (Harper's *s.v.* Bibliotheca; Suetonius *Augustus* 29)

28   Gaius Calvisius Sabinus celebrated a triumph in this year, for his Spanish victories. He used a portion of the war booty for repairs

to the Via Latina, an important road leading south and east from Rome. (CAH X 133)

28 In connection with Octavian's post–Actium festivities, a wooden stadium was built in the Campus Martius, for the staging of gladiatorial shows. (Dio 53.1)

27 The construction of the Pantheon began, under the supervision of Marcus Agrippa. Pliny the Elder (34.13) reports that the capitals of the Pantheon's columns were fabricated of Syracusan metal.

27 Augustus ordered repairs on various roads, including the celebrated Via Flaminia. (Dio 53.22)

6. Miscellaneous

264 The first gladiatorial show was presented in Rome; it featured three pairs of gladiators, in conjunction with the funeral of a certain Junius Brutus Pera. (Wiedemann 5)

256 The consul Marcus Atilius Regulus killed a 120-foot-long snake on the Bagradas River, in north Africa, during the First Punic War. (Pliny 8.37)

252 Lucius Caecilius Metellus captured about 140 Carthaginian elephants and sent them to Rome on specially constructed rafts. Once there, however, the Romans did not know what to do with them; some, apparently, were killed, while others were put on display. (Pliny 8.17)

246 The Romans founded a Latin colony at the important harbor town of Brundisium. (Scullard *Roman World* 124)

246 A daughter of the noted censor Appius Claudius Caecus was fined 25,000 pounds of bronze coinage for wishing destruction on a group of people who jostled her as they were all leaving a theatrical performance. (Aulus Gellius 10.6)

241 The pontifex maximus Lucius Caecilius Metellus (consul 251, 247) rescued the Palladium (a sacred statue of Athena) from a fire in the Temple of Vesta, where the image was stored. He was blinded by the conflagration. (OCD *s.v.* Metellus [1])

234 According to the *Cambridge Ancient History* (VIII 343), Rome recorded male citizen populations in the following years as:

234:	270,713	204:	214,000
225:	291,200	194:	143,704
209:	137,108	189:	258,318

179:	258,794	147:	322,000
174:	269,015	142:	327,442
169:	312,805	136:	317,933
164:	337,452	131:	318,823
159:	328,316	125:	394,736
154:	324,000		

231 A certain Spurius Carvilius Ruga divorced his barren wife — although he loved her dearly — because he had taken an oath that he would marry primarily for the purpose of fathering children. (Aulus Gellius 4.3)

220 The Plebeian games, held in November, were instituted. They evolved into one of the city's more important annual festivals. (Cary 241)

219 The first Greek physician, Archagathus, arrived in Rome. According to Pliny the Elder (29.12), he was so ruthless in his surgical techniques that he earned the disreputable moniker *Carnifex* ("Executioner").

217 The Romans minted gold coins for the first time; each coin was worth 20 sesterces. (Pliny 33.47)

217 Pliny the Elder (2.200) records that as many as 57 earthquakes shook Italy in this year, including one of great magnitude during the Battle of Lake Trasimene. Neither side in this battle — Carthaginians or Romans — noticed, however; they were too intent upon the military exigencies of the moment.

216 Aulus Gellius (3.15) preserves an anecdote about an aged Roman matron whose son had reportedly been killed at the Battle of Cannae. However, when her son — who survived the battle — returned home, her shock at seeing him caused her sudden death.

216 The three sons of Marcus Aemilius Lepidus — Lucius, Marcus and Quintus — sponsored funeral games in their father's memory. The games lasted three days and featured 22 pairs of gladiators. (Livy 23.30)

214 The Tiber River flooded twice in this year, causing tremendous losses of lives and property. (Livy 24.9)

213 Marcus Postumius, an unscrupulous entrepreneur, bought a fleet of unseaworthy ships, filled their holds with worthless cargo, and

then intentionally sunk them. He hoped in this way to collect an indemnity from the Roman government, which had promised to pay shipowners for such losses. (Livy 25.3.9–11; Boren 75–76)

213   Quintus Fabius Maximus (son of the dictator) was elected one of the consuls for this year. A famous anecdote relates a visit paid by the father to his son, then encamped at Suessula (in Campania). The father did not dismount from his horse until his son so ordered; as he jumped to the ground, he exclaimed: "I wanted to discover, my son, whether you really knew that you were a consul." (Aulus Gellius 2.2; Livy 24.44)

213   Livy (25.1) remarks that Roman devotion to their gods began to wane, as the Punic War continued with no end in sight. An interest in foreign cults and deities correspondingly increased.

c.213   Roman coinage was standardized: 2½ bronze asses, at two ounces apiece, to one sestertius; four sesterces to one denarius. These three denominations became the staples of Roman currency. (Boren 68)

212   In response to an oracular command, the Romans established the Ludi Apollinares, games in honor of Apollo. (Harper's *s.v.* Apollo)

210   A devastating fire swept through many sections of Rome; it damaged shops, private homes and the shrine of Vesta. Since the blaze started in several quarters of the city simultaneously, arson was suspected. A group of Capuan noblemen ultimately confessed to the crime. (Livy 26.27)

210f.   The career of an early novus homo and protégé of Scipio Africanus, Gaius Laelius:

210–206	Served in Spain, in various command positions.
204–202	Fought in Africa, including at Cirta and Zama.
197	Aedile.
196	Praetor.
190	Consul.
189	Proconsul in Gaul.
174	Negotiated with King Perseus.
170	Ambassador to Celtic tribes.

(OCD *s.v.* Laelius [1])

209   The interval between *lustra*—ritual purifications of the Roman state—was set at five years. (OCD *s.v.* censor)

209   Cato the Elder's notions on the preferability of a frugal and disciplined lifestyle were reinforced by his meeting with a Pythagorean philosopher named Nearchus, who taught that pleasures, especially bodily, were inherently evil. (Plutarch *Cato the Elder* 2)

205   The cult of the eastern goddess Cybele was brought to Rome. (OCD *s.v.* Cybele)

205   Marcus Pomponius Matho and Quintus Catius traveled to Delphi to represent the Roman government in the presentation of war spoils (from the Battle of the Metaurus River) to Apollo's temple: a 200-pound golden crown, decorated with battle scenes and silver trophies. (Livy 28.45)

204   The so-called "Black Stone of Pessinus," symbolizing the eastern cult goddess Magna Mater, was transported to Rome and placed in the Temple of Victory. (CAH VIII 453) The ship bearing the paraphernalia associated with this goddess became stranded on a sandbar as it sailed up the Tiber River. A noblewoman named Claudia miraculously extricated it, having been granted the strength by the gods, as a reward for her chastity. (Suetonius *Tiberius* 2)

203   When Quintus Fabius Maximus Cunctator died in this year, he had been an augur for 62 years. (OCD *s.v.* Fabius [5])

201   The senator Quintus Terentius Culleo, a captive of the Carthaginians, was freed by Scipio Africanus in this year. When Scipio celebrated his triumph in Rome, Culleo marched in the procession wearing a freedman's cap, a token of his gratitude to Scipio. Culleo later held the offices of tribune (189) and praetor (187). (OCD *s.v.* Culleo)

200   Marcus Valerius Laevinus (consul in 210) died in this year. His sons Publius and Marcus gave him an elaborate four-day funeral, replete with a gladiatorial show in which 25 pairs of combatants fought. (Livy 31.50)

199   The Carthaginians were required — by the terms of the treaty ending the Second Punic War — to pay to Rome annual installments

of a large indemnity. Impoverishment and corruption in Carthage sometimes affected the payments, however; in 199, the quality of the silver coinage offered to the Romans was so substandard that the quaestors returned it to Carthage. (CAH VIII 467)

198   Representatives of King Attalus I of Pergamum brought to Rome a golden crown weighing 246 pounds, as a token of gratitude for Roman assistance in dissuading King Antiochus III from invading Attalus' territory. (Livy 32.27)

198   As consul, Sextus Aelius Paetus Catus maintained such a modest lifestyle that he ate his meals off earthenware plates, even though offered silver table settings by Aetolian ambassadors. He never owned any silver vessels until near the end of his life, when he accepted two bowls as a gift from his father-in-law. (Pliny 33.142)

196   For the first time, three priests charged with supervising the feasts of the gods were elected — their title: *tresviri epulones*. The first three office holders: Gaius Licinius Lucullus; Publius Manlius; Publius Porcius Laeca. (Livy 33.42; MRR I 338)

196   A number of farmers who had illegally permitted their herds to graze on public lands were tried in Rome. Three were convicted and fined; the money thus collected was used to construct a temple in honor of Faunus, on the Tiber island. (Livy 33.42)

194   Features of Cato the Elder's Spanish triumph, celebrated in this year: 25,000 pounds of silver; 123,000 silver denarii; 540,000 silver Oscan coins; 1400 pounds of gold. (Livy 34.46)

189   Livy states that the relative value of gold to silver at this time was one to ten, a ratio that held true until the early empire, when one to twelve became the norm. (Harper's *s.v.* argentum)

189   An unusual year for Tiber inundations: according to Livy (38.28), twelve floods occurred, affecting particularly the Campus Martius and other low-lying portions of Rome.

187   Tiberius Sempronius Gracchus married Cornelia, daughter of Publius Cornelius Scipio Africanus; they parented the reformer tribunes Tiberius and Gaius Gracchus. (Livy *Epitome* 38)

187   A serious epidemic ravaged both the city of Rome and the outlying districts in this year; three days of prayer and supplication were decreed, as a potential remedy. (Livy 38.44)

187   *Athletarum certamen*—a "contest of athletes" (probably boxers, wrestlers and foot racers) was held for the first time in Rome. (Livy 39.22)

c.187 Luxuries from the east began filtering into Rome at about this time: bronze couches with costly cloth draperies; ornate furniture; elaborate banquets. (Livy 39.6)

183   The pontifex maximus Publius Licinius Crassus died; his funeral was celebrated with a gladiatorial show featuring 120 combatants, a public dinner and a distribution of meat to the citizenry. (Livy 39.46)

182   (April 20.) A violent spring storm struck Rome on this date; heavy winds toppled statues and dislodged roofs from buildings. (Livy 40.2)

181   A clerk of the praetor Quintus Petilius unearthed two stone chests, one which once contained the remains of Rome's second king, Numa Pompilius; the other held two bundles of books, seven in Latin and seven in Greek. The subject of the Latin books was pontifical law; the Greek books were concerned with Pythagorean philosophy. Ultimately the books were deemed subversive, and consigned to the flames. (Livy 40.29) In the anti-Hellenic spirit of the times, the senate ordered the philosophical writings to be burned. (Boren 84)

181   A six-month long drought struck central Italy; during this time, no crops could be grown. (Livy 40.28)

181   One of the consuls for the year, Marcus Baebius Tamphilus, oversaw the transfer of some 40,000 Ligurians to Samnium. (OCD *s.v.* Baebius)

180   The death of Lucius Valerius Flaccus, the friend and mentor of Cato the Elder. They were colleagues in the consulship (195) and the censorship (184). (OCD *s.v.* Flaccus [4])

180   The consul Gaius Calpurnius Piso died in office, ostensibly of a plague then ravishing the city. However, his wife Quarta Hostilia

was later convicted of killing him and arranging for her son (and Piso's stepson) Quintus Fulvius Flaccus to take his place as consul. (Livy 40.37)

179   One of the censors, Marcus Aemilius Lepidus, received a grant from the senate of 20,000 *asses* to produce games and festivities, in connection with the dedication of temples to Juno and Diana. (Livy 40.52)

179–   The winter of 179-178 was unusually cold and snowy. Many trees
178   better suited for fairer weather perished. (Livy 40.45)

176   One of the newly elected consuls for the year, Gnaeus Cornelius Scipio Hispallus, contracted a paralytic disease of some sort and soon died. Many Romans viewed this as a troublesome portent. (Livy 41.16)

175–   According to Pliny the Elder (7.156), this was the only quinen-
171   nium in Roman history in which no senator died.

174   Titus Quinctius Flamininus sponsored a gladitorial show in conjunction with his father's funeral; the show featured 74 gladiators, who fought over a span of three days. (Livy 28.10 ff)

174   A plague struck central Italy, equally debilitating to people and animals. It affected slaves with particular virulence, but a number of noted Roman citizens succumbed to it as well, including several augurs and pontiffs. (Livy 41.21)

174   After describing numerous internal dissensions among eastern potentates and their subjects (occurring in 174), Livy concludes the discussion by noting that it would be pointless to continue relating these events, since his focus is upon Roman history. (Livy 41.25)

174   A severe earthquake in the Sabine region destroyed numerous buildings; a day of prayer was decreed in consequence. (Livy 41.28)

173   A swarm of locusts ravaged Apulia. To deal with the situation, a praetor-elect named Gnaeus Sicinius recruited a large band of men, who systematically captured and disposed of the insects. (Livy 42.10)

171   Pliny the Elder (7.36) reports a bizarre story of a girl's transformation into a boy, an event observed by the child's parents.

169   The censor Tiberius Sempronius Gracchus purchased for the state the house of his famous father-in-law, Publius Cornelius Scipio Africanus. (Livy 44.16)

169   The aediles Publius Cornelius Scipio Nasica Corculum and Publius Cornelius Lentulus continued the trend of increasingly lavish public entertainments by displaying 63 leopards and 40 bears and elephants. (Livy 44.18)

168   On the evening before the Battle of Pydna, Gaius Sulpicius Gallus (consul 166) created a considerable stir among the troops by accurately forecasting a lunar eclipse. Sulpicius Gallus also published a book on eclipses. (OCD *s.v.* Gallus [2])

168   After subduing King Perseus, Lucius Aemilius Paullus transferred from Macedonia to Rome some 300,000,000 sesterces in booty. According to Pliny the Elder (33.56), direct taxation of Roman citizens was ended in the following year, because of this large influx of foreign capital.

167   (Autumn.) Because of a lull in the campaign against Perseus, the Roman commander Lucius Aemilius Paullus decided to tour some of the famous places in Greece. Included on his itinerary: Athens, Corinth, Sicyon, Argos, Epidaurus, Sparta and Olympia. (Livy 45.28)

167   Lucius Aemilius Paullus arranged for the sale of 150,000 Epirotes captured during the Third Macedonian War. A life of slavery awaited most of them. (Livy 45.34)

167   Aemilius Paullus sponsored in Amphipolis a lavish festival, replete with actors, athletes and noted race horses, as well as sumptuous sacrifices to the gods. A well known axiom of the time: Paullus, who knew how to win wars, was no sluggard either when it came to organizing banquets and games. (Livy 45.32)

167   Aemilius Paullus' triumphant return to Rome after defeating Perseus was marred by the sudden deaths of two of his sons, aged 12 and 14. (Livy 45.50)

167   According to Polybius (30.13), a Greek orchestra performing traditional music was greeted with indifference by its Roman audience, during a holiday in this year.

164   King Perseus, defeated by Lucius Aemilius Paullus in 168, died at Alba Fucens, where he had been imprisoned. (Velleius Paterculus 1.11)

160   The death of Lucius Aemilius Paullus (consul in 182 and in 168); he left an estate valued at 1,500,000 sesterces. (Stockton 7) His lavish funeral was attended by people from all walks of life, not only dwellers in Rome, but inhabitants of nearby towns also came to pay their respects. (Diodorus Siculus 31.25)

160   According to Livy (*Epitome* 46), the consul Marcus Cornelius Cethegus oversaw a successful effort to drain the Pomptine Marshes (southeast of Rome), and convert the acreage thus reclaimed into productive farmland. Other sources (*e.g.*, OCD *s.v.* Pomptine Marshes) indicate that the ancient drainage efforts failed.

156   According to Pliny the Elder (33.55), the Roman government owned 17,410 pounds of gold and 22,070 pounds of silver, as well as 6,135,400 coined sesterces. By the year 91, the weight of silver had increased to 1,620,831 pounds.

155   The Cilician grammarian Crates introduced the Romans to grammatical studies in this year. (Rolfe LCL Aulus Gellius [Vol. 1] 453)

154   With the death of the elder Tiberius Sempronius Gracchus, his widow Cornelia assumed the role of raising and educating her three surviving children. She gained lasting fame as an independent and capable Roman matron. So devoted was she to her family and to the management of her household that she refused an offer of marriage from the wealthy King Ptolemy VII. (OCD *s.v.* Cornelia [1])

c.152   At age 86, Masinissa, the vigorous king of the Numidians, fathered a child. (Livy *Epitome* 50)

c.152   Cato the Elder's son, Marcus, died. Despite the father's long and successful career in politics and business, he possessed limited financial resources, and hence could provide only a modest funeral for his son. (Livy *Epitome* 48)

c.150   By this time, most educated Romans were bilingual (in Latin and Greek).

*c.*149   In this year, three Roman ambassadors were sent to Bithynia, to mediate in a local dispute there. One of the envoys had numerous battle scars on his head; the second walked with a limp; the third was regarded as unintelligent. Cato the Elder, upon learning of the composition of the delegation, remarked that it possessed "neither head, nor feet, nor brains." (Livy *Epitome* 50)

148   *Incendium maximum*— a huge fire — engulfed central Rome in this year, destroying much of the Regia. (Livy *Epitome* 50; Julius Obsequens 19)

146   According to Polybius (18.35), Carthage was the richest city in the world at the time of its destruction by the Romans in this year.

146   The complete destruction of Carthage by Rome occurred in the African city's 700th year of existence. The Roman author of the devastation, Scipio Aemilianus, is said to have wept over the demise of one of the ancient world's great cities. (Appian *Punic Wars* 132)

146   Appian (*Punic Wars* 135) calls Scipio Aemilianus' triumphal procession (for crushing Carthage) the "most spectacular in Roman history." According to Pliny the Elder (33.141), Scipio displayed, among other items, 4370 pounds of silver, the sum total owned by the Carthaginian government and people.

143   The Romans took control of gold mines formerly belonging to the Salassi, a Gallic tribe. (Strabo 4.206)

140   The longtime Roman nemesis Viriathus was assassinated in this year. His funeral was celebrated with a gladiatorial show featuring 200 pairs of combatants, as well as military honors and numerous sacrifices. (Diodorus Siculus 33.21a; Appian *Spanish Wars* 75)

139   All astrologers were expelled from Rome; it was thought that they preyed upon the gullible and the unwary for their own private gain. This was the first of nine known expulsions of astrologers between 139 B.C. and A.D. 93. (OCD *s.v.* astrology)

137   One of the consuls for this year, Marcus Aemilius Lepidus Porcina, found it difficult to perform his military duties because of extreme obesity and a concomitant inability to engage in physical

activities. (His agnomen Porcina may be translated as "Porky.")
(Diodorus Siculus 33.27)

133   One of the consequences of the assassination of Tiberius Gracchus
      was a directive from the Sibylline Books to the senate that a del-
      egation be sent to Sicily, to visit religious shrines and offer
      sacrifices. (Diodorus Siculus 34.10)

132   The execution of the Greek philosopher/orator Diophanes, who
      had served as a tutor to Tiberius and Gaius Gracchus. (Plutarch
      Tiberius Gracchus 20)

131   Publius Licinius Crassus Mucianus, consul in this year, was said
      to have possessed five important attributes: wealth, nobility, elo-
      quence, legal knowledge and the office of pontifex maximus.
      (Aulus Gellius 1.13)

129   The powerful and influential Scipio Aemilianus died unexpect-
      edly, on the very day when he had been scheduled to deliver a
      major speech before the senate. Rumors of foul play abounded,
      but a consensus developed that he died a natural death. (Scullard
      GN 32) He left an (unnamed) heir 32 pounds of silver. (Pliny
      33.141)

129   The death by suicide of Blossius of Cumae, a noted Stoic philoso-
      pher and close friend of Tiberius Gracchus. (OCD *s.v.* Blossius)

c.123 A woodpecker landed on the head of the praetor Aelius Tubero
      while he was presiding at court. He easily caught the bird, and
      then consulted the augurs for any prophetic messages. They
      replied that disaster was imminent for Rome if the bird escaped,
      but for Tubero if it were killed. The patriotic praetor immedi-
      ately dispatched it, and soon thereafter *implevit prodigium*, "he
      fulfilled the portent," evidently meaning that he met his end.
      (Pliny 10.41; Rackham LCL Pliny [Vol. III] 319)

121   A certain Septumuleius brought the severed head of Gaius Grac-
      chus to the consul Lucius Opimius, to collect the prescribed
      bounty: a measure of gold equal to the head's weight. In a par-
      ticularly macabre touch, Septumuleius had surreptitiously stuffed
      lead into the mouth, to increase the bounty due him. (Pliny
      7.48)

121   According to Pliny (33.141), Quintus Fabius Maximus Allobrogi-

cus, consul in this year, was the first Roman to own 1000 pounds of silver.

121   A certain Pomponius, a friend of Gaius Sempronius Gracchus, stood on a bridge (à la the legendary Horatius Cocles) and single-handedly held off the violent pursuers of Gracchus; Pomponius then committed suicide. (Velleius Paterculus 2.6)

115   During his consulship, Marcus Aemilius Scaurus used his considerable influence to prohibit the consumption of dormice, shellfish and imported birds at banquets. (Pliny 8.223)

115   At the funeral of Quintus Caecilius Metellus Macedonicus, his four sons bore his body to the rostra. Of these four, one had held the consulship and the censorship; the second had been consul; the third was consul in this year; and the fourth was a candidate for the consulship, an office which he subsequently attained. Velleius Paterculus' comment (1.11): *Hoc est nimirum magis feliciter de vita migrare quam mori*: "This is assuredly not to die, but to pass happily out of life." (Trans. Shipley)

111   A highly destructive fire engulfed Rome.

109   Jugurtha's parting comment upon leaving Rome —*urbem venalem ... si emptorem invenerit* ("[Rome] is a city for sale if a buyer could be found") was prompted by his observation of the rampant bribery which had corrupted the political process. (Livy *Epitome* 64)

c.109   Gaius Marius married Julia, the aunt of Julius Caesar. (OCD *s.v.* Marius [1])

106   The consul Quintus Servilius Caepio plundered the town of Tolosa in southern Gaul, in the process securing a huge amount of gold and silver — hundreds of thousands of pounds, according to some accounts. The horde mysteriously disappeared en route to Rome; Caepio was widely believed to have stolen it, but this rumor was never confirmed. (OCD *s.v.* Caepio [1])

105   Publius Rutilius Rufus, consul in this year, turned to gladiatorial trainers to instruct inexperienced replacement troops recruited to fill the ranks of the army, recently depleted by the disastrous Battle of Arausio. (Wiedemann 7)

103   The residents of Ameria and Tuder reputedly saw celestial armies fighting in the sky, with the one from the eastern horizon triumphing. (Pliny 2.148)

103   The wearing of gold rings by Roman officials was generally discouraged; according to Pliny the Elder (33.12), Gaius Marius did not adorn his hand with one until his third consulship, in 103.

102   Aulus Gellius (1.6) quotes portions of a speech entitled *De Ducendis Uxoribus* (*On Marriage*), delivered by one of the censors for 102, Quintus Caecilius Metellus Numidicus. In the speech, Metellus advised his mostly male audience that, while wives were annoyances, nonetheless *sine illis ullo modo vivi possit*: "Life cannot in any way be lived without them."

c.101   According to Livy (*Epitome* 68), a certain Publicius Malleolus, upon his conviction for matricide, was sewn into a sack and throw into the sea. Livy states that this was the first time in which this kind of punishment was meted out, but Dionysius of Halicarnassus and Valerius Maximus both report that similar fates befell parricides during the monarchy.

93   A school devoted to the study of Latin rhetoric opened, but it remained in business for only one year, before being closed by the censors Gnaeus Domitius Ahenobarbus and Lucius Licinius Crassus (MRR II 17)

93   The praetor (later dictator) Sulla displayed 100 fighting lions, the first time such a large number of these animals was seen in Rome. (Pliny 8.53)

91   Lucius Marcius Philippus, consul in this year, was said to have suggested that only 2,000 Roman citizens owned any property. (Cary 454)

91   According to Pliny (2.199), a devastating earthquake occurred near Mutina, in Cisalpine Gaul. Many farm buildings were destroyed, along with much livestock.

91   Marcus Livius Drusus owned 10,000 pounds of silver when he held the tribuneship in this year. (Pliny 33.141)

89   Sulla married Caecilia Metella, thus gaining an alliance with the powerful family of the Caecilii Metelli. She and her husband

became the parents of twin children, a boy and a girl. Their praenomina (Faustus and Fausta, "lucky") supposedly symbolized the good fortune with which Sulla believed he had been blessed throughout his life. (OCD *s.v.* Metella)

88   Efforts to enlist the support of Quintus Mucius Scaevola against Marius failed, when the aged but still highly regarded jurist refused to participate in an attack on the man who saved Rome from the Gauls. (OCD *s.v.* Scaevola [3])

87   Marcus Licinius Crassus (the future triumvir) fled to Spain with three friends and ten servants, to escape persecution by Marius and Cinna, who had executed Crassus' father and brother. (Plutarch *Crassus* 4)

87   The death of Pompey's father, Gnaeus Pompeius Strabo. Plutarch (*Pompey* 1) says that he was killed by a lightning bolt, and that his corpse was abused by the populace, who hated him.

86   Pliny the Elder (2.99) records that a *clipeus ardens*—"burning shield"—sped across the sky from west to east, showering sparks as it went.

86   Titus Pomponius (at the age of about 24) departed from Rome to Athens, due to the turmoil in Italy at the time. Some 20 years later, he returned to Rome, having lived so noble a life in Athens that he acquired his famed cognomen, Atticus. (Nepos *Atticus* 2)

86   Pompey married Antistia, the daughter of Publius Antistius, who presided over Pompey's trial for mismanagement of public funds in this year. Most observers saw a connection between the marriage and Pompey's acquittal in the trial. (Plutarch *Pompey* 4)

*c.*85   The probable date of birth of Marcus Junius Brutus. Some Romans thought that Julius Caesar was his father, since Caesar's affair at the time with Brutus' mother Servilia was common knowledge. (Appian *Civil Wars* 2.112; OCD *s.v.* Servilia)

83   Julius Caesar married Cornelia, the first of his four wives. She was the daughter of Lucius Cornelius Cinna, Sulla's bitter enemy. Hence, the union did not please Sulla, who tried to compel Caesar to divorce his new wife. Caesar refused, and soon thereafter he left Italy, for an overseas stint with the army, apparently a

safer environment for him than Rome. (Harper's *s.v.* Julius Caesar)

*c.*83   Marcus Pupius Piso Frugi Calpurnianus (quaestor in 83, and later consul in 61) divorced his wife Annia, Cinna's widow, in order to favorably impress Sulla. (Velleius Paterculus 2.42; OCD *s.v.* Piso [4])

82   (May 28.) Pliny the Elder records that two noted orators were born on this day: Marcus Caelius Rufus and Gaius Licinius Calvus.

82   After defeating Gaius Marius (son of the seven-time consul) at the Battle of Sacriportus, Sulla adopted his famous cognomen Felix ("Lucky"). (Velleius Paterculus 2.37)

82   When Lucius Cornelius Sulla swept into Rome as a military dictator, one of his first acts was the promulgation of a proscription list, whereby he exterminated his enemies and seized their property. This was the first instance in Roman history of a proscription. (OCD *s.v.* Proscriptio; Sulla [1])

82   The stage debut of an actress named Galeria Copiola. She lived a long life, performing at games dedicating Pompey's theater (55), and also — at the age of 104 — at theatrical productions staged in A.D. 8. (Pliny 7.158)

82   Pompey divorced Antistia, in order to marry Aemilia, who was already married and pregnant by her husband Manius Acilius Glabrio. These machinations were orchestrated by Sulla, Aemilia's stepfather, who wanted Pompey bound to him by a marriage tie. Aemilia died soon after, in childbirth. (Plutarch *Pompey* 9)

82   Marcus Marius Gratidianus (nephew and supporter of Gaius Marius) met his end at the hands of Catiline, who reportedly tortured him cruelly before decapitating him. (Q. Cicero[?] *Handbook of Electioneering* 10)

82   Gaius Marius (son of the seven-time consul) transferred to Palestrina 14,000 pounds of gold from a temple on the Capitoline, a move reportedly necessitated by a fire. In the following year, Sulla returned the gold to Rome. (Pliny 33.16)

82   One of the chief objectives of the Sullan proscriptions: the 150+ silver plates in the possession of private citizens, plates that weighed over 100 pounds each. (Pliny 33.145)

81   Conveyed in Sulla's triumphal processions were 29,000 pounds of gold and 121,000 pounds of silver, the bounty from his various military victories. (Pliny 33.16)

81   The Ludi Victoriae Sullae — Games for Sulla's Victory — were established, to commemorate Sulla's victory at the Battle of the Colline Gate in the previous year. (Balsdon 247)

c.81 When Sulla auctioned off the property of proscription victims, the total amount of money raised thereby came to 350,000,000 sesterces — much of which Sulla kept for himself. (Livy *Epitome* 89)

81   Caecilia Metella, wife of Sulla, died in this year, from some unspecified lingering disease. Sulla divorced her shortly before her death, and forcibly removed her from his house, fearing contagion and contamination. (OCD *s.v.* Metella [1])

81   Pompey arrived in Utica (north Africa) with nearly 1000 ships and six legions. Shortly after landing, some of his soldiers stumbled upon a valuable buried treasure. As word of the find spread, many other soldiers began digging randomly, hoping for similar luck. Pompey merely laughed at the sight of so many men aimlessly clawing at the ground. No more valuables were discovered, however, and the men soon returned to military discipline, having become bored with their fruitless searching. (Plutarch *Pompey* 11)

c.81 Gaius Scribonius Curio, a Sullan partisan, acquired Gaius Marius' home at Baiae during the proscriptions. Curio later became consul (76) and a defender of Publius Clodius in the Bona Dea affair (61). (OCD *s.v.* Curio [1])

c.81 Lucius Cornelius Chrysogonus, a freedman of Sulla, ingeniously contrived to have the name of a dead man entered on the proscription lists, so that the deceased's relatives could purchase his property for a pittance. (OCD *s.v.* Chrysogonus)

c.81 Sulla reputedly bestowed the title Magnus ("Great") on Pompey, for the latter's victories in Sicily and Africa during the Sullan civil wars. (Plutarch *Pompey* 13)

c.80 Mucia Tertia wed Pompey, to whom she remained married until c.61. In 39, she attempted to assist her son Sextus in his negotiations with Octavian. (OCD *s.v.* Mucia Tertia)

80   The Olympic games for this year featured only foot races, since Sulla had removed all the other athletes (*e.g.*, boxers, wrestlers, equestrians) to Rome, to participate in the celebrations commemorating his victories against Mithridates VI and in the Social War. (Appian *Civil Wars* 1.99)

77   Marcus Aemilius Lepidus (consul in 78) fled to Sardinia after his attack on Rome failed. There he died, it is said, because of his depression over learning of his wife's adulterous behavior. (Plutarch *Pompey* 16)

76   As an example of the wildly fluctuating price for corn in the late republic, one might refer to statements made by Cicero in his second speech against Verres (3.92.214–215): he noted that in 76, Sicilian corn was cheap, whereas in the following year, the price had skyrocketed.

76   Publius Gabinius led a delegation of Roman officials to Erythrae, to gather oracular pronouncements from the Sibylline texts stored there. (MacDonald LCL Cicero *In Catilinam*, etc. 414)

75   During his aedileship, Quintus Hortensius arranged for a grain distribution at reduced prices. Cicero, however, mocked the action, stating that the already high grain prices masked the fact that Hortensius' discount really amounted to nothing at all. (Cicero *In Verrem* 2.3.215)

74   The aedile Marcus Seius arranged for the sale of grain at an *as* per peck, a very low price. (Cicero *On Duties* 2.58)

74   A blow to Cicero's considerable ego: when he was returning to Rome from his distinguished service as a quaestor in Sicily, he expected a hero's welcome. A chance encounter en route with an old friend, however, destroyed his pretensions, when the friend asked: "Cicero! Where have you been for so long?" (Plutarch *Cicero* 6)

70   Crassus made a sacrifice to Hercules, during the course of which he provided public meals on 10,000 tables, and gave the people three months' worth of grain. (Plutarch *Crassus* 12)

69   Cicero's brother Quintus married Pomponia, sister of Atticus. They remained married for 25 years, although the union was rumored to have been an unhappy one. (OCD *s.v.* Cicero [3])

68   (November 27.) Cicero's father — also named Marcus Tullius Cicero — died. (Cicero *Letters to Atticus* 1.6)

c.68   Julius Caesar's wife Cornelia died about this time, as did his aunt Julia; the latter had been married to Gaius Marius for more than twenty-five years. Caesar delivered a famous eulogy in his aunt's honor. (CAH IX 342; OCD *s.v.* Marius [1])

67   Cicero's eleven-year-old daughter Tullia was engaged to Gaius Calpurnius Piso Frugi, whom she married in 63. (Cicero *Letters to Atticus* 1.3)

67   Julius Caesar married Sulla's granddaughter Pompeia. He divorced her in 61, on a suspicion of adultery with Publius Clodius. (OCD *s.v.* Julius Caesar)

67   During the debate over the proposed military command for Pompey against the pirates, a raven flying overhead suddenly plummeted into the crowd. According to Plutarch (*Pompey* 25), the force of the debaters' loud voices caused airflow disruptions to surge upward, thus becoming a danger to birds that might encounter the man-made turbulence.

c.67   According to Pliny the Elder (10.45), a certain Marcus Aufidius Lurco became the first Roman to raise and sell fattened peacocks. He earned some 60,000 sesterces in this endeavor.

66   According to Pliny the Elder (2.100), a spark fell from a star toward the earth, increasing in magnitude as it plummeted, until it became as large as the moon. It then returned to the sky, assuming the shape of a torch.

c.66   Cato the Younger, whose term as a military tribune in Asia had expired, traveled in the east for a time, before returning to Rome. As he entered Antioch in Syria, he noticed a large throng of people; Cato assumed that his entry into the city was the reason for the assemblage. His embarrassment was great when he learned that the crowd was awaiting the arrival of a certain Demetrius, a slave and confidant of Pompey. Cato's friends laughed heartily when the misunderstanding came to light, but Cato himself failed to see the humor. (Plutarch *Cato the Younger* 13)

65   During his aedileship, Julius Caesar sponsored lavish wild beast fights, gladiatorial shows and theatrical productions. (Suetonius

Julius Caesar 10). Caesar also reportedly pioneered the use of all silver trappings and equipment at funeral games and mock beast hunts. (Pliny 33.53)

65   The birth of Cicero's only son, also named Marcus Tullius Cicero. Although he played a fairly prominent role in politics and military affairs (consul in 30), he never achieved the distinction earned by his father. Seneca (*De Beneficiis* 4.30) asserted that he became consul only because of his famous family name.

65   Titus Pomponius Atticus departed Greece, after residing there for over 20 years. He was accompanied to his ship by a throng of friends expressing their sorrow over his leaving. (Nepos *Atticus* 4)

64   Publius Sittius, a businessman and friend of Cicero, traveled to Mauretania in this year, where he concluded various dealings with a local king, to restore his recently depleted finances. (OCD *s.v.* Sittius)

63   According to Varro (quoted in Pliny 33.137), the Egyptian king Ptolemy XII owned at this time 8000 horses and sponsored banquets for 1000 guests, for whom he furnished a like number of golden goblets.

*c.*63   The first of three marriages of Cicero's daughter Tullia (to Gaius Piso). She later married Furius Crassipes (*c.*56) and finally Cornelius Dolabella (50). The marriage to Dolabella took place while Cicero was away from Rome; he strongly disapproved of this union. (OCD *s.v.* Tullia [2])

63   Shorthand writers, the Roman equivalent of court reporters, were employed for the first time during the senatorial debate over the Catilinarian conspiracy. (Plutarch *Cato the Younger* 23)

63   The death of Quintus Caecilius Metellus Pius (consul in 80), who had held the office of pontifex maximus. The vacancy created by his death enabled Julius Caesar to gain election as his successor. (Plutarch *Caesar* 7)

63   Two of the principle debaters in the matter of the Catilinarian conspiracy — Julius Caesar and Cato the Younger — were interrupted when a messenger brought a note to Caesar. Cato demanded that Caesar read it aloud, whereupon Caesar merely handed it to his antagonist. It turned out to be a rather steamy

love letter to Caesar from Cato's stepsister, Servilia. Not surprisingly, Cato dropped his demand that the text of the message be revealed to the senate. (Plutarch *Cato the Younger* 24)

63   Julius Caesar's opposition to the death penalty for the Catilinarian conspirators almost cost him his own life, when a group of Cicero's bodyguards nearly assassinated him. His life was saved on this occasion by his friend Gaius Scribonius Curio, who somehow managed to extricate him from the midst of the would-be killers. (Plutarch *Caesar* 8)

63   Lucius Licinius Lucullus celebrated a triumph (for his Asiatic victories) that had been postponed for three years, due to the political opposition of Pompey and others. (MRR II 169)

62   In a letter to Atticus (1.12), Cicero described his great remorse over the death of Sositheus, a mere slave but also an accomplished *anagnostes* (one who entertained the master by readings and recitations).

61   As Julius Caesar was preparing to leave Rome to take up his Spanish governorship, he remarked that he was so far in debt that he would need 25,000,000 sesterces simply to have nothing. (Appian *Civil Wars* 2.8)

61   On the occasion of Pompey's triumphal procession in this year, he donated 200,000,000 sesterces to the state treasury, the spoils of his many conquests. (Pliny 37.16)

61   According to Cicero, one of the consuls for 61, Marcus Valerius Messalla Niger, purchased a home for the hefty sum of 3,400,000 sesterces. (Cicero *Letters to Atticus* 1.13)

61   For the first time, a midday intermission was observed at gladiatorial shows. Prior to this, the shows continued for the entire day, without interruption. (Dio 37.46)

c.60   The death of Quintus Lutatius Catulus, consul in 78, censor in 65. He was one of the (more qualified) candidates defeated by Julius Caesar in the election for pontifex maximus in 63. (OCD *s.v.* Catulus)

60   Faustus Cornelius Sulla, son of the dictator, sponsored a lavish gladiatorial show in his father's memory, and also provided baths and bathing oil to the populace. (Dio 37.51)

60   A terrible storm struck Rome, uprooting trees, destroying houses, splintering boats docked on the Tiber River and causing bridges and a theater to collapse. Some Romans took these events as a forewarning of future catastrophes that would beset the republic. (Dio 37.58)

59   Lucius Licinius Lucullus, long a force in Roman political and military affairs, retired from public life to devote himself to literary and intellectual pursuits. (OCD *s.v.* Lucullus [2])

59   Julius Caesar married Calpurnia, his fourth (and last) wife. It was a political marriage, designed to strengthen the ties between Caesar and Calpurnia's father, Lucius Calpurnius Piso Caesoninus, one of the consuls in 58. (OCD *s.v.* Calpurnia [2])

59   Diodotus, a stoic philosopher, died in this year and left Cicero a bequest of 10,000,000 sesterces. (The figure appears in one of Cicero's letters to Atticus [2.20], and is presumed erroneous by many commentators; they suggest an emendation to 100,000.)

58   Publius Clodius treacherously abducted Tigranes, an Armenian prince, and one of Pompey's hostages. There seems to have been no apparent motive for Clodius' action, other than (perhaps) to embarrass Pompey. (OCD *s.v.* Clodius [1])

58   Titus Pomponius Atticus was adopted by the dying Quintus Caecilius; Atticus thus fell heir to three-fourths of the older man's fortune, a share worth 10,000,000 sesterces. (Nepos *Atticus* 5)

58   In a move against various cult practices in Rome, the consuls ordered the altars of the Egyptian deity Isis to be destroyed. (Scullard GN 213)

58   While traveling from his praetorian province (Macedonia) to Rome, Gaius Octavius died. He was the father of Octavian (the future emperor Augustus). (OCD *s.v.* Octavius [4])

58   After Cicero had been exiled from Rome, he made his way to Macedonia, where he sank into a deep depression over his situation. While there, he met a former acquaintance, an Athenian philosopher named Philiscus. Philiscus gave him advice on coping with his misfortunes, and succeeded in helping him to view his future more optimistically. (Dio 38.18–30)

58   The aedile Marcus Aemilius Scaurus displayed 150 female leopards in a parade which he sponsored. (Pliny 8.64)

58   Among the natural curiosities Marcus Aemilius Scaurus displayed in Rome during his aedileship were the bones of some unidentified sea monster: 40 feet long, with ribs larger than an elephant's, and a spine eighteen inches in diameter. (Pliny 9.11)

57   In a letter to Atticus (4.3), Cicero described some of the devastation wrought by Publius Clodius' henchmen: the terrorizing of workmen repairing Cicero's house; the destruction of the nearly refurbished portico of Catulus; the burning of the home of Cicero's brother Quintus.

57   (November 11). *Clamor, lapides, fustes, gladii*: "shouting, rocks, clubs, swords." When Cicero was walking with friends down Rome's Via Sacra on this day, he was harassed by a gang of Publius Clodius' hooligans; they employed the tactics enumerated above. (Cicero *Letters to Atticus* 4.3)

57   In a letter to Atticus (4.2), Cicero noted that the consuls had made the following valuations on three of his properties:
his house in Rome: 2,000,000 sesterces
his Tusculan villa: 500,000 sesterces
his Formian villa: 250,000 sesterces

57   A famine struck Rome, causing a riot in which the populace thronged around the senate house and threatened mayhem and murder unless action were taken to alleviate the situation. This event led to Pompey's appointment as *curator annonae*, a post giving him wide powers to oversee the supply and distribution of corn. (OCD *s.v.* annona)

c.57   Mark Antony divorced his cousin Antonia, in order to marry his third wife, Fulvia. It was also Fulvia's third marriage. (Ker LCL Cicero *Philippics* 5)

56   (February 12.) Titus Pomponius Atticus married his wife Pilia.

56   (April 6). Cicero left Rome for a projected month-long tour of his various rural villas. (Gardner LCL Cicero *Pro Caelio*, etc. XIX)

c.56   Cicero's daughter Tullia was engaged to a certain Furius Crassipes, whom she subsequently married in this year. They were divorced in 51. (Cicero *Letters to His Friends* 1.7; OCD *s.v.* Tullia)

*c.*56   Cato the Younger lent his second wife, Marcia, to the orator Quintus Hortensius, in order that the latter could strengthen the political bonds between them by fathering a child with Marcia. This Marcia was a daughter of Lucius Marcius Philippus, consul in 56; he consented to the extramarital arrangement. (Plutarch *Cato the Younger* 25)

55   Pompey sponsored lavish public entertainments, which included displays (and in some cases, killing) of apes, a lynx, a rhinoceros, 20 elephants, 600 lions and 410 leopards. (Wiedemann 60) These entertainments hardly received a rave review from Cicero, who felt that the play actors gave poor performances, the props were overdone (600 mules in a production of *Clytemnestra*; 3000 bowls in the *Trojan Horse*), the athletic exhibitions a waste of time, and the mock beast hunts predictably revolting. (Cicero *Letters to His Friends* 7.1)

55   Prior to his departure from Rome to a Syrian governorship, Marcus Licinius Crassus' inventory of his property revealed a net worth of 7,000 talents. (Scullard GN 182)

54   Aurelia, Julius Caesar's mother, died. (OCD *s.v.* Aurelia)

54   Octavia, the older sister of Octavian, married Gaius Claudius Marcellus (consul in 50) in this year. When Marcellus died in 40, she married Mark Antony. (OCD *s.v.* Octavia)

54   Julia, daughter of Julius Caesar and wife of Pompey, died. Even in death, there was controversy. Julia was buried in the Campus Martius, an act which provoked the ire of the consul Lucius Domitius Ahenobarbus. He argued that it was sacrilegious for her to be laid to rest in hallowed ground. Domitius' complaints, however, amounted to nothing. (Dio 39.64) In the same year, Caesar's grandson (by Pompey and Julia) died. (Velleius Paterculus 2.47)

54   To demonstrate his friendship for Caesar, Crassus invited him to dinner a few days before he (Crassus) departed for Syria. (Plutarch *Cicero* 26)

52   The mysterious disappearance of 2,000 pounds of gold from the

throne of Jupiter on the Capitoline Hill occurred in this year. It was apparently decided that the slight to the god could only be expiated by replacing the lost gold with 4000 pounds. The temple official suspected of the theft committed suicide before he could be brought to trial. (Pliny 33.14–15)

52   Pompey married Cornelia, widow of Publius Licinius Crassus (son of the triumvir) and daughter of Quintus Caecilius Metellus Pius (consul for the last half of 52, with Pompey.) (OCD *s.v.* Cornelia)

*c.*52   Julius Caesar sponsored a lavish public banquet in memory of his daughter Julia. (Suetonius *Julius Caesar* 26)

51   Marcus Tullius Cicero (son of the orator) accompanied his father to Cilicia, when the elder Cicero went there as the governor. En route, they visited Athens. The son was only 14 years of age at the time. (Balsdon 235)

51   Attica, daughter of Cicero's confidant Titus Pomponius Atticus, was born in this year. At the age of 14 (in 37) she married Marcus Vipsanius Agrippa. (OCD *s.v.* Attica)

50   (November.) Cicero's secretary Tiro contracted malaria in the town of Patras, and was bedridden for several months. (Balsdon 228)

*c.*50   Cicero had hopes that his daughter Tullia might marry Tiberius Claudius Nero (future father of the emperor Tiberius), but the marriage never took place. (OCD *s.v.* Nero [3])

49   The death of the aged Marcus Perperna, at 98. He had held the consulship in 92, and had outlived all but seven men who had served in the senate during his year in office. (Pliny 7.156)

49   The anti–Caesarian Lucius Domitius Ahenobarbus, captured by Caesar at Corfinium, attempted suicide by drinking poison. He apparently had a change of heart midway through the ordeal, however, and managed to survive the poison's effects. (Pliny 7.186)

49   *Nec fuit aliis temporibus res publica locupletior.* "At no other time was the republic wealthier." (Pliny 33.56)

49   When Caesar decided to include elephants in an exhibition of wild animals, he ordered a moat to be dug around the periphery of

the arena, to prevent the beasts from charging into the crowd — as had occurred during a similar display sponsored by Pompey in 55. (Pliny 8.21)

49   When Caesar entered Rome at the outset of the civil war, he expropriated from the treasury 15,000 bars of gold, 30,000 of silver, and 30,000,000 coined sesterces. (Pliny 33.56)

49   Roman denarii began to be coined at the rate of 40 from one pound of gold. (Pliny 33.47)

49   Late in the year, two groups of Roman boys engaged in a mock battle; one side called itself the Pompeians, the other, the Caesarians. Perhaps prophetically, the latter triumphed. (Dio 41.39)

c.49   An equestrian by the name of Lucius Axius advertised and sold pigeons at a price of 400 denarii per pair. (Pliny 11.110)

48   Early in this year, Julius Caesar crossed from Italy to Greece with a portion of his army, leaving Mark Antony to transport the remainder. However, when they did not arrive in due course, and Caesar had received no explanation for the delay, he decided to return to Italy incognito, to investigate. On the day on which he sailed, such a violent storm broke that the ship's captain wanted to return to shore. Caesar then revealed his identity, saying: "Cheer up. Your passenger is Caesar." Caesar or not, the fury of the storm eventually forced them to return to port. (Dio 41.46)

48   As magister equitum, Mark Antony provided numerous entertainments for the general populace, always funded by Julius Caesar. (Dio 42.27)

48   Mark Antony experimented with harnessing lions to a chariot, and successfully did so. Pliny the Elder (8.55) states that Antony's symbolic purpose was to demonstrate that even noble creatures could submit to the authority of a yoke.

48   A major portion of the great library at Alexandria was destroyed as a result of the civil war (by accident, according to Aulus Gellius 7.17).

48   Marcus Calpurnius Bibulus (consul in 59 with Julius Caesar) died, having exhausted himself in a futile effort to prevent Caesar and

Mark Antony from pursuing Pompey into Greece. (OCD *s.v.* Bibulus)

48   Upon viewing Pompey's severed head in Egypt, Julius Caesar bewailed the fate of his rival and bitterly criticized those who had murdered him. Many Romans, however, ridiculed Caesar's crocodile tears on this occasion, knowing full well that Caesar would likely have dispatched Pompey himself, had he captured him after the Battle of Pharsalus. (Dio 42.8)

48   The death of Marcus Caelius Rufus, at the hands of Caesarian partisans. Caelius, a paramour of the notorious Clodia in the 50s, and once defended by Cicero in a court case, had become disenchanted with Caesar over the latter's failure to promote Caelius' political career. When Caelius tried to organize resistance to Caesar, he met his end. (Dio 42.25)

48–   It was widely rumored that Julius Caesar spent several months
47   during the winter of 48–47 on an excursion down the Nile River in the company of Cleopatra. (Cary 404)

*c.*47   Pearls became common accoutrements in Rome at about this time. (Pliny 9.123)

46   Cicero divorced Terentia, his wife of 30 years. A subsequent marriage to the young Publilia did not succeed. After the divorce, Terentia twice remarried, and lived to the age of 103. (Duff 267)

46   Julius Caesar enjoyed no fewer than four triumphs, which included displays of elephants, bulls, a giraffe and 400 lions. (Wiedemann 60) He also displayed a strange beast called a cameleopard, an animal that resembled a camel in most ways, except that it was spotted, in the manner of a leopard. (Dio 42.23)

46   The first exhibit of a naumachia — mock naval battles — occurred in Rome, under the direction of Julius Caesar. (OCD *s.v.* naumachia)

46   A senator (whose name is given as Fulvius Sepinus [Dio] or Furius Leptinus [Suetonius]) desired to fight in a gladiatorial show during the entertainments sponsored by Caesar. Caesar, however, forbade this, although he did permit equestrians and other notables to take part. (Dio 43.23)

46   In one of his triumphal processions in this year, Caesar displayed among the captives Arsinoe, Cleopatra's sister. The spectators disapproved, not only because of the impropriety of parading a woman in a triumph, but also because of Arsinoe's royal blood-lines. Caesar later released her. The fierce Gallic chieftain Vercingetorix (captured by Caesar six years earlier) appeared in the same procession, but he was not as fortunate as Arsinoe: he was executed after the festivities. (Dio 43.19)

46   Caesar's extravagant expenditures for his triumphs and games inspired a certain amount of discontent among the populace, and also the army. One particularly egregious example of con-spicuous consumption: he ordered expensive silk curtains — sun-screens — to be stretched above the spectators at a show. (Dio 43.24)

46   Octavian received prizes and decorations at Caesar's African tri-umph, even though he (Octavian) had not participated in any of the battles, because of his age. (Suetonius *Augustus* 8)

46   Immediately prior to committing suicide, Cato the Younger ordered his son to join with Julius Caesar. When the son inquired about the reason for this request, Cato replied that the political realities of the time required his son to acquiesce to Caesar's power, but that for Cato himself, it was too late for such a change of allegiance. (Dio 43.10)

46   Cato the Younger committed suicide in Utica (north Africa), rather than submit to a Caesarian amnesty. He posthumously obtained the cognomen Uticensis, because of his death and burial in Utica. (Dio 43.11-12)

45   (September 13.) Julius Caesar decided to designate his grand-nephew Octavian as heir to three-fourths of his estate; he also adopted Octavian as his son. He earlier had intended to name Pompey as his heir, but changed his mind when the civil war broke out in 49.
      Two other grandnephews, Lucius Pinarius and Quintus Pedius, were designated as heirs of the other one-fourth of the estate. (Suetonius *Julius Caesar* 83)

45   Porcia, daughter of Cato the Younger, married Brutus, the anti-Caesarian conspirator. She reputedly was involved in the plan-

ning of the Ides of March (44) assassination of Caesar. (OCD *s.v.* Porcia)

44   At the Lupercalian festival (held annually on February 15), an inebriated Mark Antony jokingly offered Julius Caesar a crown. Although a trivial gesture, it reinforced the popular notion that Caesar was aiming at kingship. Marcus Aemilius Lepidus demonstrated his disapproval of Antony's actions. (Suetonius *Julius Caesar* 79; MRR II 318)

44   Mark Antony's daughter Antonia, although only a child, was offered in marriage to one of the son's of Antony's future colleague in the tribunate, Marcus Aemilius Lepidus. The marriage did not take place. (OCD *s.v.* Antonia [1])

44   Gaius Helvius Cinna, a tribune in this year, was a noted victim of mistaken identity: the angry mob bent upon avenging Julius Caesar's murder mistook this Cinna for one of the assassins, Lucius Cornelius Cinna, and lynched him. (OCD *s.v.* Cinna [3])

44   The assassination of the Dacian king Burebistas, against whom Caesar had planned a military campaign at the time of Burebistas' death. (OCD *s.v.* Burebistas)

44   Octavian made a per capita donative to the citizens of Rome of 300 sesterces, in accordance with the terms of Caesar's will. He made a second donative in 29, this one in the amount of 400 sesterces. (Augustus *Res Gestae* 3.15)

43   (Spring.) The senate decreed a thanksgiving of 50 (Appian *Civil Wars* 3.74) or 60 (Dio 46.39) days to celebrate the defeat of Mark Antony at the Battle of Mutina.

43   Octavian was betrothed to Servilia, daughter of Publius Servilius Isauricus (praetor in 54, consul in 48). Although the engagement did not last, Servilia remained in Octavian's good graces, and even served as a military legate for him. (OCD *s.v.* Servilius [2])

43   The death of Atia, mother of Octavian, occurred in this year. (OCD *s.v.* Atia [1])

43   Cicero admitted that he received 20,000,000 sesterces in legacies over the course of his long public career. (*Second Philippic* 40)

43   Suetonius (*Augustus* 27) records the story of a certain Titus Vinius Philopoemen, apparently a man of low birth, who concealed his (unnamed) patron during the proscriptions, thereby saving his life. Octavian later elevated Vinius to equestrian status for this act of courage and loyalty. Dio's account (47.7) differs slightly; he indicates that the proscribed man's wife, Tanusia, arranged to have her husband hidden at Vinius' home.

43   A certain Hosidius Geta survived the proscriptions when his son planned his funeral, as if he had already been killed, and thus they deceived the would-be assassins. (Dio 47.10)

43   An act of particular brutality during the proscriptions: Mark Antony ordered the head and right hand of Cicero to be displayed in the forum. Antony's wife Fulvia stuck several of her hairpins into the dead orator's tongue. (Dio 47.8)

43–   Turia, the wife of a future consul (Quintus Lucretius Vespillo),
42   concealed and protected her husband during the proscriptions of the Second Triumvirate. A famous inscription containing a eulogy of a Turia — the *Laudatio Turiae*— may refer to her. (OCD *s.v.* Turia)

42   The members of the Second Triumvirate established a cult to propagate the worship of the recently assassinated Julius Caesar, now known as *Divus Julius*, "Deified Julius." (MRR II 358)

42   In a letter written shortly before the Battle of Philippi, Marcus Junius Brutus expressed his disgust at the wearing of gold brooches by the military tribunes. (Pliny 33.39)

42   A virtual year-long celebration was begun after the Battle of Philippi, in gratitude for the avenging of Julius Caesar's assassination. (Dio 48.3)

42   The plebeian aediles substituted gladiatorial games for the customary chariot races at the celebration of the festival of Ceres in this year. (Dio 47.40)

42   Cleopatra received the right to call her son Ptolemy the king of Egypt. She claimed that the child's father was Julius Caesar, and she referred to him as Caesarion. (Dio 47.31)

c.42   Hot springs allegedly erupted at one of Cicero's villas, shortly after his death. One of his freedmen, Marcus Tullius Laurea, wrote a poem about the event. (OCD *s.v.* Laurea)

41   So powerful was Cleopatra's sway over Mark Antony that she persuaded him to order her older sister Arsinoe to be put to death, thus removing a potential obstacle to Cleopatra's continuing sovereignty in Egypt. (Scullard GN 171; Harper's *s.v.* Arsinoe)

41   Octavian divorced his wife Claudia (daughter of Fulvia, Mark Antony's wife at the time), asserting that her virginity was still intact. He claimed that his reason for this action was his inability to get along with his mother-in-law, but it appears that he also wished to distance himself from Antony, for political reasons. (Dio 48.5)

40   Octavian married Scribonia — his second wife, her third husband — but divorced her in the following year. According to Suetonius, Octavian had wearied of her constant nagging. She was the sister of Sextus Pompeius' father-in-law, Lucius Scribonius Libo; Octavian was doubtlessly attempting to align himself with Pompeius by way of this union. (Dio 48.16)

40   Tiberius Claudius Nero, his wife Livia, and his son (also named Tiberius Claudius Nero) fled Italy as Octavian consolidated his power there. Dio Cassius (48.15) duly notes the irony: Livia later became Octavian's wife and the younger Claudius his stepson and successor. Velleius Paterculus (2.75) uses this incident as an example of the rapidity with which changes occur in human life.

40   Marcus Agrippa supervised the celebration of the Ludi Apollinares, including two days of chariot races and a production of the Troy Games. (Dio 48.20)

40   Mark Antony's infatuation with Cleopatra began to blossom. Dio calls him "the Egyptian woman's slave." A few years later, in 37 in Antioch, they formalized their political and social ties. (Dio 48.24; OCD *s.v.* Cleopatra VII)

40   The demise of Julius Caesar's assassins was officially marked by the celebration of a commemorative festival. (Dio 48.32)

40   Sphaerus, a former slave and Octavian's childhood caregiver, died in this year; Octavian gave him a public funeral. (Dio 48.33)

39   Octavian divorced Scribonia and married Livia Drusilla; the marriage lasted for over 40 years, until Octavian's death in A.D. 14. (Suetonius *Augustus* 62)

39   The three-year-old Marcus Claudius Marcellus, a nephew of Octavian, was betrothed (briefly) to Sextus Pompeius' daughter, in an apparent effort to build political ties between the two men, and to seal the Treaty of Misenum. (Dio 48.38; OCD *s.v.* Marcellus [7])

39   Mark Antony remained in Greece for some time, during which he behaved erratically. He styled himself the "young Dionysus" and demanded that others refer to him by that title; he became engaged to the goddess Athena and extracted from the Athenians a dowry of 4,000,000 sesterces. (Dio 48.39)

38   "The lucky have children in three months"—a witticism, later proverbial, applied to Octavian, whose wife Livia was already six months pregnant with her former husband's child when Octavian married her in the previous year. (The baby, Nero Claudius Drusus, was conceived in 39, born in 38.)

c.38   Pliny the Elder relates a fantastic story about a certain Gabienus — *fortissimus classium*, "bravest man in the navy"—and a partisan of Octavian in the Sicilian War against Sextus Pompeius. Pompeius captured him and ordered his throat slit. Gabienus lingered for a day between life and death, claiming to have been to the Underworld, where the gods informed him of the righteousness of Pompeius' cause.

37   Octavian's two-year-old daughter Julia was betrothed to Mark Antony's son, an obvious move to strengthen to bonds between the two triumvirs. Antony, in turn, betrothed his daughter (by Octavia) to Gnaeus Domitius Ahenobarbus, despite the fact that Ahenobarbus was one of the tyrannicides. (Dio 48.54; OCD *s.v.* Julia)

37   Mark Antony formally recognized the twin children he fathered (*c.*40) with Cleopatra, renaming them Alexander Helios (Sun) and Cleopatra Selene (Moon). (Scullard GN 172)

c.37   The probable date of the marriage of Mark Antony and Cleopatra.

36   After defeating Sextus Pompeius and returning to Rome, Octavian announced that certain houses which he owned would become public property, thus (apparently) granting to the citizens easier access to him, as he retained one of these dwellings as his principal residence. (Velleius Paterculus 2.81)

33   The death of Tiberius Claudius Nero, father of the future emperor Tiberius (reigned A.D. 14–37), and first husband of Livia Drusilla. In 39, Octavian had compelled Livia to divorce Claudius Nero, so that he could marry her. (OCD *s.v.* Livia Drusilla)

33   Marcus Agrippa donated replicas of seven eggs and a like number of dolphin images to serve as lap counters in the Circus Maximus. (Dio 49.43. Livy [42.27] states that egg replicas were first used for this purpose in 174.)

33   Agrippa evicted astrologers and their coteries from Rome. (Dio 49.43)

33   Agrippa oversaw the distribution of many benefactions to the citizens, including free olive oil and salt, and free admission to the public baths. He also arranged for tickets redeemable for money or clothing to be scattered among theater-goers. (Dio 49.43)

32   Although Mark Antony divorced Octavia in this year, she remained a devoted mother, raising their two daughters, as well as the surviving children borne to him by Fulvia and Cleopatra, and her own three children, fathered by Gaius Claudius Marcellus (whom she had married subsequent to her divorce from Antony). (OCD *s.v.* Octavia [2])

31   A lunatic interrupted a theatrical production by rushing forward to seize and place on his head a crown once belonging to Julius Caesar. The stunned audience members attacked and killed him. (Dio 50.10)

30   Mark Antony and Cleopatra committed suicide in Egypt. Cleopatra's motivation: to escape the inevitable capture by Octavian, who would have compelled her to adorn his triumphal procession in Rome. (Dio 51.10–11)

30   Octavian gave up military exercises such as horseback riding and arms drills, and turned instead to walking or playing various types of nonstrenuous ballgames. (Suetonius *Augustus* 83)

30   Marcus Aemilius Lepidus (son of the triumvir) conspired to assassinate Octavian; Maecenas found out about the plot, and Lepidus was subsequently executed. (OCD *s.v.* Lepidus [4])

30   During the triumphal procession honoring Octavian's victory at Actium, his 12-year-old stepson (and future emperor) Tiberius rode on the back of one of the horses drawing the ceremonial chariot. (Suetonius *Tiberius* 6)

30   After the Battle of Actium, Octavian assigned land and property in Italy to his victorious soldiers, for which he paid the previous owners the sum total of about 600,000,000 sesterces. (Augustus *Res Gestae* 3.16)

29   Octavian presided over a celebration of the *Augurium Salutis*, a ceremony indicating that peace had descended upon the land. (CAH X 130)

28   A census was taken for the first time in 40 years. It revealed a citizen population of 4,063,000. (Augustus *Res Gestae* 1.8)

c.28 The probable founding date of the colony of Nemausus (modern Nimes) in Gaul. Nemausus later became the site of a number of well preserved Roman buildings, including an impressive amphitheater. (OCD *s.v.* Nemausus)

27   A certain Apudius "dedicated himself" to Octavian, in the manner of the Spaniards, *i.e.* should he ever serve in a battle in which Octavian died, he would commit suicide, in the belief that it was wrong for a foot soldier to survive if the leader did not. (Dio 53.20; Valerius Maximus 2.6)

27   Octavian was granted the right to display oak leaves on the door posts of his house, symbolically indicating that he had saved innumerable citizens' lives by bringing the civil wars to a close. (CAH X 129–130)

27   The name of the month Sextilis was changed to Augustus, in honor of Rome's new leader. (CAH X 131)

Appendix A: Chronology of the Second Punic War

Based on The Magistrates of the Roman Republic *and the annotated accounts in* Livy, *particularly the annotated translation of Livy by Aubrey de Selincourt.*

219   Hannibal besieged and captured the Spanish town of Saguntum, a nominal Roman ally.

218   (March.) The Romans declared war on Carthage.

218   Hannibal began marching east; Publius Cornelius Scipio set sail with 60 ships, eventually landing at Massilia, where he established an encampment on the easternmost bank of the Rhone River.

Hannibal crossed the Rhone north of its mouth, thus eluding Scipio's soldiers. (He ferried his reluctant elephants — which refused to swim across the river — by covering rafts with grass and dirt, and transporting the animals on what appeared to them to be dry land.) In the autumn of 218, the Carthaginians made their famous trek over the Alps.

The first encounter between Hannibal and the Romans under Scipio occurred at the Ticinus River. The Carthaginians prevailed. Scipio was severely wounded; his life was saved by the timely intervention of his son, the future Africanus.

2200 Gallic auxiliaries deserted to Hannibal.

Scipio garrisoned his troops on the Trebia River. He was soon reinforced by the other consul, Tiberius Sempronius Longus. Together they attacked the Carthaginians camped nearby. On a cold and sleeting December day, the well-rested Carthaginians won decisively.

171

217   Hannibal was victorious at the Battle of Lake Trasimene, where 15,000 Romans fell; 2500 Carthaginian soldiers also died there. Quintus Fabius Maximus was subsequently chosen dictator, with Marcus Minucius Rufus as master of the horse. The impulsive Minucius enjoyed some military success against Hannibal, but later suffered a severe setback, which would have been worse if not for the timely intervention of Fabius.

216   Hannibal utterly vanquished the Romans at the Battle of Cannae in the summer of this year; it was one of the most crushing defeats for the Romans in their long history. Soon after the battle, Hannibal was hospitably received at the strategically important Campanian town of Capua.

    In Gaul, a Roman force under the command of Lucius Postumius Albinus was trapped and routed by the Boii. Nearly 25,000 Roman soldiers were killed, including Postumius.

215   Hannibal's brother Mago departed from Carthage to Spain with 12,000 infantry and 1500 cavalry, while Hasdrubal went to Sardinia with a like number of troops. Hannibal and King Philip V of Macedonia entered into an alliance. Hannibal besieged Tiberius Sempronius Gracchus at Cumae. The Roman forces overcame their Carthaginian opponents by hurling rocks, spears, and later firebrands, at their siege towers, and so driving them off.

    Titus Manlius Torquatus subjugated the combined Carthaginian and Sardinian forces in Sardinia, in the process capturing Hasdrubal, Hanno and Mago (the most noteworthy feature of the battle, according to Livy). A major battle erupted near the town of Nola, won by the Romans under Marcus Claudius Marcellus. The city of Croton fell to the Carthaginians.

    The Romans recorded a number of successes in Spain, resulting in the capitulation to Rome of most of the Spanish tribes.

214   Near Beneventum, Gracchus defeated a force of Bruttians, Lucanians and Numidians under the leadership of Hanno. The residents of Beneventum treated the victors to a lavish public banquet.

    The strategically important town of Casilinum was captured by a Roman force under the leadership of Fabius and Marcellus.

An initial Roman assault on Syracuse was thwarted in part because of the ingenious defenses devised by Archimedes. Hence, the Roman commander, Marcellus, turned his attention to smaller Sicilian towns, and affected their reduction.

In Spain, the Romans retook Saguntum from the Carthaginians, and also captured Castulo, noted as the birthplace of Hannibal's wife.

213   The Romans under Fabius Maximus besieged and recovered the east central Italian town of Arpi. The engagement was noteworthy in that it was virtually bloodless.

213   The Romans under Lucius Pinarius ruthlessly slaughtered many unarmed citizens of the central Sicilian town of Henna, because of a belief that the town's leaders were about to surrender to Hannibal. Pinarius' plan — making Henna an example to other wavering Sicilian towns — backfired, when most Sicilians, horrified by the butchery, sided with the Carthaginians.

213   Hannibal and the Carthaginians took possession of the important
(or 212)   southern Italian town of Tarentum.

212   The Carthaginian commanders Hanno and Mago led a successful assault on the southern Italian town of Thurii.

The unarmed proconsul Tiberius Sempronius Gracchus was ambushed and killed, probably in Lucania. An undisciplined Roman contingent under the praetor Gnaeus Fulvius Flaccus recklessly engaged Hannibal in battle. Some 16,000 (of 18,000) Roman soldiers lost their lives in the ensuing conflict, which occurred near Herdonea, in south central Italy.

The Romans under Marcus Claudius Marcellus entered Syracuse under cover of darkness and captured it. Marcellus reportedly wept at the sight of the city's devastation, a city that had fallen from the heights of a glorious prominence. A severe plague followed, disastrous alike to Romans, Carthaginians and Syracusans.

The engineer/mathematician Archimedes was killed by a Roman soldier during the capture of Syracuse. Marcellus was greatly upset by the deed, and ordered Archimedes to receive a dignified burial.

In his final battle in Sicily, Marcellus defeated the Carthaginians near Agrigentum.

212   The Scipio brothers — Gnaeus and Publius — were both killed in
(or 211)   battle in Spain.

211   The military priority for the year was the recapture of Capua, for
psychological as well as strategic reasons.

Gnaeus Fulvius Flaccus was charged with military incompetence and treason (because of the disaster near Herdonea in the previous year). Fulvius went into a self-imposed exile before a verdict was rendered.

A battle between Roman and combined Carthaginian and Campanian forces, near the Volturnus River, resulted in a convincing Roman victory.

Hannibal traveled northward from Campania, eventually establishing a military camp a mere three miles from Rome. Soon thereafter, he drew up a battle line near the Anio River; the Romans, under Quintus Fulvius Flaccus, marched out to oppose the Carthaginians, "for a fight in which the prize of victory would be the city of Rome," according to Livy (tr. de Selincourt). However, inclement weather prevented the decisive battle from taking place, and Hannibal soon withdrew.

The fall of Capua to the Romans was accompanied by the severe punishment of its leading citizens. Their property and possessions (including 2070 pounds of gold and 31,200 of silver) were confiscated; all surviving Capuan senators were flogged and beheaded. These measures were proposed and implemented by Quintus Fulvius Flaccus.

Gaius Claudius Nero succeeded the (recently deceased) Scipios as commander in Spain.

210   The Carthaginians defeated the Romans in a naval battle off Tarentum. However, the Romans prevailed in a simultaneous land battle in and around Tarentum.

Marcus Valerius Laevinus (consul in 210) captured Agrigentum. He ordered the town's civic leaders to be flogged and executed, while he sold off the rest of the citizenry into slavery. According to Livy, this action ended the 2nd Punic War in the Sicilian theater.

In Spain, Publius Cornelius Scipio (later Africanus) captured New Carthage. Hannibal was decisively victorious in a battle near Herdonea. Among the fallen: one of the consuls for 211, Gnaeus Fulvius Centumalus.

Hamilcar led a fleet of 40 ships from Africa to Sardinia, where he was successful in raiding the various coastal communities and obtaining war matériel.

209   The Romans under Quintus Fabius Maximus captured the town of Manduria (southeastern Italy) and took 4000 prisoners. Soon thereafter, he seized Tarentum, an act accompanied by great brutality on the part of the Roman legions.

208   Publius Cornelius Scipio defeated Hasdrubal in Spain, at the Battle of Baecula.

The consul Marcus Claudius Marcellus, the "Sword of Rome," was killed near Venusia, in a minor skirmish with some of Hannibal's troops.

Marcus Valerius Laevinus led a fleet of 100 ships from Italy to 83 Carthaginian vessels eventually opposed the Romans, but Laevinus prevailed: 18 enemy ships were captured, and the remainder put to flight.

207   Hasdrubal repeated his brother's feat (of 218) by leading an army across the Alps Mountains. Hasdrubal's trek was considerably easier, however, since he faced less opposition from native tribes, and also because the mountain passes and tracks were better known in 207 than they had been in 218. Soon after the crossing of the Alps, the Carthaginians besieged Placentia.

Hannibal fought two battles against the Romans, led by the consul Gaius Claudius Nero, near Grumentum; both were Roman victories.

The Romans captured four Gauls and two Numidians carrying a message from Hasdrubal to Hannibal, in which Hasdrubal suggested that they combine forces in northern Italy. Armed with this information, Nero marched northward from southern Italy, to join his army with that of the other consul, Marcus Livius Salinator. There, on the banks of the Metaurus River (northeastern Italy), the Romans won their most decisive pre–Zama battle against the Carthaginians. According to Livy, 57,000 enemy troops died, including Hasdrubal, whose severed head Nero later hurled into Hannibal's camp. Nero and Livius later celebrated a joint triumph, although most observers gave greater credit to Nero for the victory.

Marcus Valerius Laevinus led a fleet from Sicily to the coast of Africa, where several successful raids were carried out against Utica, and against Carthage itself.

206   There was no fighting involving Hannibal in this year, as the Romans turned their attention to Spain.

At the Battle of Ilipa in Spain, Scipio's 48,000 Roman troops defeated a Carthaginian army of 50,000. Shortly thereafter, the Carthaginians evacuated Spain, leaving it in Roman hands. The final blow to Carthaginian interests there was the capitulation of Gades to Scipio and his army. (Gades had been Hamilcar Barca's first base of operations in Spain, and its coinage retained Punic lettering until Roman imperial times.)

205   Scipio proposed carrying the war to Africa, a suggestion strongly opposed by Quintus Fabius Maximus. The senate eventually gave grudging approval to Scipio to recruit a force composed of volunteers and soldiers who had fled Cannae and had been sentenced to 12 years of servitude in Sicily.

Gaius Laelius conducted a raid on north Africa, a move which aroused a general panic in Carthage, where it was interpreted as a prelude to a Roman invasion.

The southern Italian town of Locri (which had sided with Carthage) was retaken by Scipio. The propraetor Quintus Pleminius, whom Scipio left in charge of Locri, plundered the town after Scipio's departure to Messana.

204   Locrian ambassadors bitterly described to the senate the atrocities which they suffered at the hands of Pleminius and his men. They successfully obtained restitution.

Scipio assembled and led a huge army from Sicily to Africa. According to Livy, almost 400 transport ships were required to convey the soldiers and their equipment.

203   Scipio attacked and burned a Carthaginian encampment near Utica. The devastation was particularly widespread because most of the buildings in the camp were constructed of wood. Livy states that 40,000 Carthaginians died in the blaze or in the ensuing fighting, and that 5000 more were captured.

The Romans under Scipio defeated Syphax and his Numidians at the Battle of Campi Magni (Great Plains). Scipio was aided by Laelius and by the Numidian king Masinissa; shortly after the battle, Masinissa married Syphax's wife.

Hannibal and his brother Mago were ordered to return to Carthage. For Hannibal, it marked the end of a 16-year stay in Italy. His bitterness at being recalled was reflected in his lament that he had been conquered not by Roman legions, but by the Carthaginian senate. He also second-guessed himself for failing to follow up victories at Trasimene and Cannae with an assault on Rome.

202 Several months after Hannibal returned to Africa, he marched with his army to Zama; Scipio followed. Hannibal took the unusual step of requesting a personal meeting with Scipio, to try to arrange a peace treaty. This effort proved fruitless, and the Battle of Zama followed, the final and decisive engagement of the Second Punic War. Hannibal's army was virtually destroyed; severe terms of peace were imposed upon the Carthaginians, including an indemnity of 10,000 talents, the surrender of all but ten warships, as well as all trained elephants, and the loss of the right to wage war outside Africa, except by permission of Rome.

201 Scipio returned in triumph to Italy. He enriched the treasury by 123,000 pounds of silver, and distributed 400 *asses* apiece to his soldiers.

Appendix B: Chronology of Cicero's Extant Speeches

Date	Latin title	English title
81	Pro Quinctio	On Behalf of Quinctius
80	Pro Sexto Roscio Amerino	On Behalf of Sextus Roscius Amerinus
c.77	Pro Roscio Comoedo	On Behalf of Roscius the Comic Actor
70	In Verrem I–V	Against Verres I–V
69	Pro Tullio	On Behalf of Tullius
69	Pro Fonteio	On Behalf of Fonteius
69	Pro Caecina	On Behalf of Caecina
66	Pro Lege Manilia	On Behalf of the Manilian Law
66	Pro Cluentio	On Behalf of Cluentius
63	Contra Rullum I–III	Against Rullus' [land law] I–III
63	Pro Rabirio	On Behalf of Rabirius
63	In Catilinam I–IV	Against Catiline I–IV
63	Pro Murena	On Behalf of Murena
62	Pro Sulla	On Behalf of Sulla
62	Pro Archia Poeta	On Behalf of Archias the Poet
59	Pro Flacco	On Behalf of Flaccus
57	Post Reditum in Senatu	After His Return [from exile], in the Senate
57	Post Reditum ad Quiritis	After His Return [from exile], to the Citizens
57	De Domo Sua	On His Own House
56	De Haruspicum Responsis	On the Responses of the Soothsayers

56	Pro Sestio	On Behalf of Sestius
56	In Vatinium	Against Vatinius
56	Pro Caelio	On Behalf of Caelius
56	De Provinciis Consularibus	On the Consular Provinces
56	Pro Balbo	On Behalf of Balbus
55	In Pisonem	Against Piso
54	Pro Plancio	On Behalf of Plancius
54	Pro G. Rabirio Postumo	On Behalf of Gaius Rabirius Postumus
54	Pro Scauro	On Behalf of Scaurus
52	Pro Milone	On Behalf of Milo
46	Pro Marcello	On Behalf of Marcellus
46	Pro Ligario	On Behalf of Ligarius
45	Pro Rege Deiotaro	On Behalf of King Deiotarus
44–43	Philippicae	Philippics I–XIV

Appendix C: Chronological Synopsis of Julius Caesar's Life and Career

Based on the annotated biographies by Suetonius and Plutarch, with supplemental information from the Oxford Classical Dictionary *and* The Magistrates of the Roman Republic.

100   Birth. His parents were Gaius Julius Caesar and Aurelia; an uncle was Gaius Marius.

86   The consuls Marius and Cinna nominated him as *flamen Dialis* (priest of Jupiter).

85   Death of his father.

84   Married Cornelia, Cinna's daughter, after having broken his betrothal to a certain Cossutia.

82   Birth of his daughter Julia.

81   Served in Asia, under Marcus Minucius Thermus, governor there at the time.

80   Won the civic crown (awarded for saving the life of a fellow citizen in battle) during an attack on Mytilene.

78   Returned to Rome upon learning of Sulla's death.

77   Unsuccessfully prosecuted Gnaeus Cornelius Dolabella (consul in 81) for provincial maladministration in Macedonia. Also prosecuted (for the same misdeeds, with a similar result) Gaius Antonius (later consul, with Cicero, in 63).

77–   Left Rome for Rhodes, where he studied rhetoric under the noted
74   orator Apollonius Molon (who also instructed Cicero).

77   While en route to Rhodes, he was kidnapped by pirates. After he was ransomed, he pursued his captors and killed them, as he had vowed to do.

71   Elected military tribune, his first elective office.

69   Held the quaestorship. Presented public eulogies for his aunt (Julia) and his wife, both of whom died in this year.

69   Traveled to Spain shortly after delivering the eulogies, to serve on the staff of Gaius Antistius Vetus. (In Gades, he became depressed while viewing a statue of Alexander the Great, for he reflected that by the time that Alexander was his age, he had conquered the known world.)

c.68   Married Pompeia, Sulla's granddaughter.

65   Held the aedileship. Allegedly involved in an abortive plot with Crassus, Publius Cornelius Sulla and Publius Autronius Paetus to murder as many senators as possible and name Crassus as dictator, with Caesar as magister equitum. As aedile, he sponsored banquets, plays and mock beast hunts, as well as a gladiatorial show featuring 320 pairs of combatants.

63   Orchestrated the unsuccessful prosecution of an aged senator, Gaius Rabirius, who 37 years earlier had purportedly been involved in the assassination of the tribune Saturninus.

63   Elected pontifex maximus, over two candidates who would probably have been considered better qualified for the post. At this time, he moved from his house in the Subura (a disreputable section of the city) to the official residence provided for the pontifex maximus.

63   Argued against the death penalty for the captured Catilinarians, instead proposing that they be imprisoned and that their property be confiscated.

62   Held the praetorship. His support of some inflammatory measures offered by the tribune Quintus Caecilius Metellus Nepos resulted in a special decree passed against him by the senate, and his temporary removal from office.

62   Formally accused of complicity in the Catilinarian conspiracy; the accusation came from Lucius Vettius, an informer, and a senator

named Quintus Curius. Caesar successfully defended himself by noting that he warned Cicero of the plot, thus aiding in its collapse.

62   (December.) Publius Clodius infiltrated the (women-only) Bona Dea festival, held at Caesar's house, allegedly because he and Caesar's wife Pompeia were having an affair.

61   Left for Farther Spain, which he had been assigned to govern. He administered the province efficiently, and also won several impressive military victories.

61   Divorced Pompeia, even though it had not been proven that she and Clodius were parties to adultery. Caesar's justification, that members of his household must be above even mere suspicion of wrongdoing, has become famous.

60   Returned to Rome to run for the consulship. His chief opponents: Marcus Calpurnius Bibulus and Lucius Lucceius. Caesar and Bibulus were elected in a contest marred by heavy bribery on all sides.

60   The senate, hoping to limit Caesar's post-consular influence, assigned him a meaningless "province" to govern: woods and mountain pastures. Caesar, outraged at the slight, joined with Pompey and Crassus in the First Triumvirate, a cooperative political alliance of the three (arguably) most powerful Romans of the day.

59   Caesar's consulship, in which he proposed land redistribution and debt alleviation schemes. He so overshadowed Bibulus that the humorists of the time took to referring to the consulship of "Julius and Caesar" (instead of Bibulus and Caesar).

59   Married Calpurnia, daughter of Lucius Calpurnius Piso Caesoninus, consul in 58; his own daughter Julia married Pompey.

59   With the help of Pompey, Piso and Publius Vatinius, he received a five-year command in Gaul.

58–51 Caesar's activities in Gaul, briefly summarized as follows:

    58   Campaigned against the Helvetians and the German king Ariovistus.

    57   Campaigned against the Nervians and the Aduatucians.

56   Campaigns in the Alps and in Aquitania.
55   Invaded Britain for the first time.
54   Invaded Britain a second time.
52   Encounters with the Gallic chieftain Vercingetorix.
51   Final campaigns.

56   (April.) Met with fellow triumvirs Crassus and Pompey at the northern Italian town of Luca, to discuss an extension of his Gallic command for an additional five years, and the candidacy of Pompey and Crassus for the consulship of 55.

54   The deaths of his mother, daughter and granddaughter. The death of his daughter Julia, coupled with the demise of Crassus in the following year, led to the dissolution of the triumvirate.

52   Attempted to renew the marriage ties with Pompey by offering him Octavia, his grandniece (although she was already married to Gaius Claudius Marcellus) and in turn requesting permission to marry Pompey's daughter (although she was already betrothed to Faustus Sulla, son of the dictator). Neither proposed marriage came to pass.

51   The consul Marcus Claudius Marcellus proposed that Caesar be deprived of his Gallic command and recalled to Rome, since Gaul had been pacified. Caesar evaded a recall with the support of the tribunes and the other consul, Servius Sulpicius Rufus.

50   One of the new consuls, Gaius Claudius Marcellus (cousin of Marcus), pressed for Caesar's recall to Rome. Caesar once again enlisted the aid of the tribunes, notably Gaius Scribonius Curio, in resisting. He also offered to give up eight of his ten legions.

50   Left his province for Italy, with his army, when it appeared that all hope of a compromise with the Pompeians was lost.

49   (January 10.) Crossed the Rubicon River, the boundary between Italy and the provinces. This act, Caesar knew, would precipitate a civil war, but there was no turning back: *Jacta alea est*, "The die is cast."

49   Quickly gained control of northern Italy; traveled to Spain, to suppress Pompey's adherents.

48   (January.) Sailed to Greece, to pursue Pompey, who had fled there.

After a nearly disastrous setback at Dyrrhachium, he defeated Pompey's forces at the Battle of Pharsalus, in August. Pompey fled again, this time to Egypt.

48   Granted a one-year dictatorship.

48   Followed Pompey to Egypt, where the latter was murdered. Caesar spent the winter of 48-47 in Egypt.

47   Installed Cleopatra as Egypt's ruler; left for Syria and Pontus in the spring. He routed Pharnaces in a four-hour battle (Zela), the occasion for his famous *veni, vidi, vici* utterance.

46   Early in the year, he traveled to Africa, defeating the last of the Pompeian sympathizers there, at the Battle of Thapsus (April 6).

46   (Summer.) Returned to Rome. He celebrated five triumphs, rewarded his soldiers, and provided shows and banquets for the general populace. Appointed dictator for ten years. In addition, a new office was created for him: *praefectus moribus*, "overseer of morals." Traditionally, the censors assumed this role, but the senate felt that Caesar deserved a title and office more worthy of him than a mere censorship. He was authorized to hold the post for three years.

45   Returned to Spain, where the remnants of Pompey's supporters had mobilized. After defeating them at the Battle of Munda (March 17), he came back to Rome, where he remained until his assassination.

45–   Proposed and or enacted numerous reforms, including: calendar
44   and debt reform; the filling of vacancies in the senate; a reduction of the number of people eligible to receive free grain (from 320,000 to 150,000); travel restrictions on citizens between the ages of 20 and 40; the granting of citizenship to all teachers and physicians in Rome, as an incentive for them to remain there. He also assumed a leading role in the administration of justice and in construction and public works.

44   (February 15.) At the Lupercalian festival (held annually on February 15), Mark Antony attempted to place a crown on Caesar's head. Although Caesar refused it, those who witnessed the event interpreted it as a sign that Caesar had plans to appoint himself

king. This rumor, in turn, was one of the factors which led to his demise.

44   (March 15.) Despite illness and many disquieting omens, he decided to attend a meeting of the senate, where he was assassinated.

Appendix D: Select Chronology of Omens Seen in Rome and Italy

These omens often consisted of bizarre celestial phenomena, unusual behavior by birds and animals, strange births, spontaneous movements by statues, lightning strikes and the like. Priests and prophetic books were generally consulted when omens were observed or reported. The standard remedy seemed to have been a period [often one to three days] of prayer, supplication and sacrificing.

218–
217   A baby, only six months old, exclaimed "Victory!" in a public mar-
        ket place. An ox ascended a staircase in an apartment building,
        and then hurled itself out a window. Phantom ships were seen
        in the heavens. Lightning struck the temple of Hope. All these
        events occurred in Rome. Elsewhere, white-clad images of
        human beings were seen near Amiternum; stones fell from the
        heavens in Picenum; in Gaul, a wolf made off with a sword which
        it had summarily seized from a soldier's sheath. (Livy 21.62)

217   Hannibal's southward march through Italy was accompanied by
        numerous disquieting prodigies: blood emanated from shields;
        at Antium, corn bled when harvested; molten stones fell from
        the sky. In Falerii, inscribed tablets were observed falling from
        the sky. (Plutarch *Fabius Maximus* 2)

216   Mice were occasionally regarded as omen bearers. In 216, during
        the Hannibalic siege of Castilinum, a man who sold a white
        mouse for 200 denarii died of hunger, while the buyer survived.
        (Pliny 8.222)

215   Fire was observed on the sea. At Sinuessa, a cow gave birth to a

colt. At Lanuvium, temple statues bled, while stones fell from the heavens. (Livy 23.31)

214   At Lanuvium, crows built nests in a shrine of Juno. In Apulia, a palm spontaneously combusted. Near Mantua, a swampy area appeared to be tinted with blood. Rainstorms of chalk in Cales and of blood in Rome were observed. An underground river erupted into one of the streets in Rome, and carried away some jars. There were rumors in various places of other unusual phenomena: a spear held by a statue of Mars moving forward by itself; a talking ox in Sicily; an unborn child yelling an exclamation; an altar in the sky. Finally, a swarm of bees was seen in Rome. (Livy 24.10)

213   Lightning struck the walls and gates of Rome, and a temple of Jupiter at Aricia. Phantom warships were observed; blood-colored water was seen in the Tiber, near Amiternum. (Livy 24.44)

208   In Campania, lightning struck several temples and tombs; a similar lightning strike occurred at Ostia, where the town's walls and a gate were affected. In Cumae, gold stored in a temple of Jupiter had been damaged by mice. The forum at Casinum was beset by a swarm of bees, and at Caere, a vulture perched in a temple of Jupiter. The lake near Volsinii displayed blood-tinted water. (Livy 27.23)

190   Lightning struck the roof of the temple of Juno Lucina, damaging the roof and doors. Lightning also hit the city walls and gates at Puteoli, killing two men. At Nursia, storm clouds suddenly appeared in clear weather; two men lost their lives in the ensuing deluge. There were reports of a shower of dirt at Tusculum, and at Raete, a mule gave birth to a colt. (Livy 37.3)

188   An eclipse of the sun occurred and stones rained down on the Aventine Hill. (Livy 38.36)

186   In Picenum, stones fell from the sky for three days, and airborne flames occasionally singed people's clothing. In Rome, lightning struck the temple of Ops. (Livy 39.22)

182   A severe windstorm blew through Rome, knocking down bronze statues on the Capitoline Hill, and also damaging statues in the Circus Maximus. Several temples lost their roofs. A three-footed

mule was born at Raete. Lightning struck a temple of Apollo at Caieta. (Livy 40.2)

181   In the area of the temples of Vulcan and Concord, blood fell from the sky. Spears at the temple of Mars moved. At Lanuvium, the statue of Juno Sospita wept. So many people died in a plague at Libitina that they could not all be buried. A six-month drought was propitiated by a period of prayer. (Livy 40.19)

179   The Ludi Romani were repeated in this year, in response to the following omens: an earthquake; during the celebration of the *lectisternium*, the images of the gods turned their heads of their own accord, and a plate offered to Jupiter tumbled from the table on which it had been placed. Finally, mice were seen nibbling on olives. (Livy 40.59)

177   The consuls decreed sacrifices and a supplication to propitiate the gods, who had demonstrated their displeasure by way of the following omens: a stone plunged from the heavens into a grove of Mars; a limbless boy was born, and someone saw a snake with four legs; in Capua, lightning struck a number of public buildings. A wolf ran wild through the streets of Rome and escaped, although chased by a raucous crowd. Other prodigies observed in 177: in Crustumerium, a bird shattered a sacred stone by pecking at it; in Campania, there were reports of a talking cow; in Syracuse, a stray bull mounted a bronze heifer. (Livy 41.9, 13)

176   The untimely death of one of the newly elected consuls, Gnaeus Cornelius Scipio Hispallus, struck fear into the hearts of many. This sense of dread was increased by the following omens: at Tusculum observers noted a torch in the sky; lightning struck many buildings in towns near Rome, including a temple of Apollo. (Livy 41.16)

174   Numerous omens were observed in this year, possibly in connection with a plague that swept Italy at the time: near Veii, a two-headed boy was born; at Auximum, observers reported the birth of a girl with teeth; in Rome, a rainbow was seen over the Temple of Saturn, although the sky was cloudless, and three suns appeared simultaneously, while during the night several torches flashed across the heavens. In Lanuvium and Caere, a crested

snake with yellow spots was seen. Finally, there were widespread reports of a talking cow in Campania. (Livy 41.21)

173 The war against Perseus, contemplated by the Romans in this year, was heralded by the following omens: at Lanuvium, the specter of a large fleet of ships was seen in the sky; at Privernum, wool sprouted from the ground; near Veii, stones fell from the heavens. The Pomptine region was infested by a swarm of locusts, and in Gaul, fish emerged from clods of earth created by farmers' plows. The appropriate prayers and sacrifices were decreed in response to these signs. (Livy 42.2)

172 Lightning struck and destroyed the Columna Rostrata (a column decorated with the beaks of ships captured in the First Punic War). Showers of blood fell upon the town of Saturnia on three consecutive days; at Calatia, a three-footed mule was born, and a single lightning bolt killed a bull along with five cows. At Auximum, it was reported that dirt rained down from the sky. (Livy 42.20)

169 Portents observed in 169 included the following: at Anagnia, a firebrand was observed in the sky, and there were reports of a talking cow. At about the same time, at Minturnae, the heavens glowed as if on fire. At Raete, the sky rained stones, while at Cumae, a statue of Apollo wept for three days. In Rome, several people saw a crested serpent in the temple of Fortune; a palm sprouted in the courtyard of the temple of Fortuna Primigenia. In response, 40 sacrificial animals were slaughtered, a day of prayer was decreed, and the citizens wore wreaths, the sign of supplication. It was announced that twice toward the end of this year, it rained stones, once in Roman territory, and another time in Veii. (Livy 43.13; 44.18)

167 Several strange phenomena occurred in this year: a temple to the Household Gods was struck by lightning. In the towns of Anagnia, Lanuvium and Calatia, there were reports, respectively, of dirt falling from the sky, a meteor, and blood dripping from the hearth of a Roman citizen, Marcus Valerius. (Livy 45.16)

166 Dirt fell from the skies at many places in Campania, and bloody showers near Praeneste. Wool grew on trees near Veii. Three women, who had carried out religious ceremonies, were killed

in a temple of Minerva at Terracina. Water emanated from the mouth and foot of a bronze statue at the grove of Libitina.

A kite flying over a senate meeting dropped a weasel among the assembled senators. Lightning struck the temple of Safety; the ground produced blood on the Quirinal Hill. At Lanuvium, a shooting star was observed in the night sky. At Cassinum, there were thunderbolts and earthquakes; and the sun was visible nocturnally for several hours. A multi-limbed boy was born at Teanum Sidicinum. (Julius Obsequens *Book of Prodigies* 12)

165   In the temple of the Penates, the doors opened spontaneously one night, and wolves roamed the Esquiline and Quirinal Hills. (Julius Obsequens *Book of Prodigies* 13)

163   The sun was visible at night in Capua. A portion of a flock of sheep was killed by a lightning bolt on the Stellan plain. At Terracina, triplets were born; two suns appeared during the day at Formiae. The sky burned, and a man from Antium was incinerated by the reflection of light from a mirror. At Gabii, it rained milk. A lightning bolt devastated the Palatine Hill. At Forum Aesi, an ox breathed fire from its mouth, but it did not burn itself. Windstorms, lightning strikes, unusual celestial phenomena and strange births also occurred frequently in this year. (Julius Obsequens *Book of Prodigies* 14)

162   A night fire was seen in the sky at Anagnia, and there was a report of a speaking ox at Frusino. A three-footed mule was born at Reate. (Julius Obsequens *Book of Prodigies* 15)

137   As the consul Gaius Hostilius Mancinus was making sacrifices preparatory to sailing to Spain, several sacred chickens escaped from their cages. Mancinus departed despite the unpropitious omen, and was later defeated in Spain by the Numantines. (Livy *Epitome* 54)

133   Tiberius Gracchus' assassination was foreshadowed by numerous omens: sacred birds refused to eat the food offered to them; snakes slithered into one of his battle helmets and laid eggs in it; as he left his house to walk to the forum, he stumbled on the threshold and stubbed his toe so badly that it bled through his footwear; as he proceeded to the forum, several crows were seen fighting on the roof of a house on his left, and one of these

knocked loose a stone which fell at Gracchus' feet. (Plutarch *Tiberius Gracchus* 17)

84   Lightning struck the temples of Luna and of Ceres, thus causing the postponement of elections, and enabling Gaius Papirius Carbo to remain sole consul (his colleague, Lucius Cornelius Cinna having been killed earlier in this year.) (Appian *Civil Wars* 1.78)

67   During the debate in the Tribal Assembly over the granting to Pompey of an extraordinary command against the pirates, a crow flying over the assembly suddenly dropped to the ground; it had been startled by the disapproving noise made by the crowd when one of the tribunes, Lucius Roscius Otho, attempted to dilute the measure by urging the appointment of two men to the command. (Dio 36.30)

65   Thunderbolts and lightning strikes melted several statues on the Capitol, including an image of Jupiter. A statue of the she-wolf that suckled Romulus and Remus fell off its pedestal. The letters in certain public inscriptions became blurry. In response to these signs, sacrifices were decreed, and a larger statue of Jupiter was fabricated. (Dio 37.9)

63   Lightning bolts flashed through the sky on clear days; earthquakes occurred; ghostly forms were seen in numerous places. Traces of fire were observed shooting from the earth into the western sky. (Dio 37.25)

63   At the very time when Cicero was debating inwardly over the course of action to be taken against the Catilinarian conspirators, an unusually bright flame flared up on the altar during a sacrificial ceremony in honor of Vesta. The Vestal Virgins commanded Cicero's wife Terentia — who was present during the ceremony — to hurry home and announce to Cicero that the goddess favored his intentions to order the conspirator's executions. (Plutarch *Cicero* 20)

54   As Marcus Licinius Crassus and his son Publius were leaving a temple of Venus in Syria, Publius tripped and fell, and his father toppled over on top of him, signs that the proposed war against the Parthians would end in disaster. (Plutarch *Crassus* 17)

54   As Crassus transported his army across the Euphrates River, many unfavorable omens greeted them: loud crashes of thunder, accompanied by lightning strikes and high winds. Crassus' intended campsite was hit by lightning. One of his elegantly decked out war-horses galloped wildly into the river and drowned, taking with it the stable boy who was riding it at the time. When food was distributed to the soldiers after the river crossing, lentils and salt were offered first; these items were associated with rites of mourning. Crassus also managed to bungle a ritual sacrifice. (Plutarch *Crassus* 19)

c.49   According to Pliny the Elder (2.91), a comet appeared in the western sky — a potentially bad omen — at the outset of the civil war between Caesar and Pompey. A similar comet was visible in 43, during Octavian's consulship.

48–   Bees invaded the Capitoline Hill and constructed hives near the
47   statue of Hercules. (Dio 42.26)
        Containers filled with human flesh were found in the Temple of Bellona. (Dio 42.26)
        An earthquake occurred, an owl was observed in the city, lightning struck the Temple of Public Fortune. Blood emanated from a bakery and flowed into the Temple of Fortuna Respiciens. Babies were born with their left hands touching their heads. These omens supposedly foretold violent uprisings. (Dio 42.26)

47   When Caesar arrived in Africa to deal with Pompeian supporters there, he slipped and fell as he disembarked from his ship; this would normally have been interpreted as a bad omen. However, the quick-thinking Caesar pretended that he had intentionally fallen, and, grasping and kissing the ground, uttered: "I've got you, Africa!" (Dio 42.58)

46   A wolf was observed in the city, and there was born a pig similar to an elephant except for its feet. (Dio 43.2)

46   On the first day of his triumph in the summer of this year, an axle broke in the chariot in which Julius Caesar was riding; this was particularly ominous since the mishap occurred in front of the Temple of Fortune constructed by Lucius Licinius Lucullus. (Dio 43.21)

44   Caesar's assassination was foretold by numerous signs and omens.

The night before he was killed, his wife dreamt that their house had collapsed, and that she embraced her injured husband to protect him from further harm. On the same night, Caesar had a dream in which he was floating on a cloud and shaking hands with Jupiter. Weapons of the god Mars (stored in his house because of his status as pontifex maximus) rattled during the night, and his bedroom doors opened spontaneously. Despite these and other unfavorable omens, Caesar proceeded to the senate, where he was slain. (Dio 44.17)

43   An epileptic had a seizure during a speech by one of the consuls, Gaius Vibius Pansa. A statue of Pansa in his home rotated of its own accord on the very day when he had planned to leave Rome to campaign against Mark Antony in the Battle of Mutina. A man bringing a palm to Pansa slipped and fell in the blood of sacrificial animals. Other strange events connected with statues: the statue of the Mother of the Gods, which had faced east, spontaneously turned toward the west; a statue of Minerva near Mutina emitted blood and milk. (Dio 46.33)

43   When Octavian gained the consulship at age 19, he observed, on the very day on which he was elected, six vultures, and then 12 — the same omen that foretold to Romulus that he would be the founder of the city of Rome. (Dio 46.46)

43   The Second Triumvirate (like the First) was designed to be a partnership of equals, but various omens indicated to Lepidus and Mark Antony that they would be dominated by Octavian. In Lepidus' case: a snake curled itself around a centurion's sword, and a wolf trotted into his tent while he was eating and upset his table. In Mark Antony's case: milk flowed in trenches near his camp in Gaul, and bizarre chanting noises disturbed him during the night. When the two of them entered Rome, numerous portents were observed: pieces of armor noisily floated into the sky from the ground; bees swarmed in the Temple of Aesculapius; vultures roosted in several temples. (Dio 47.1–2)

42   Portents appearing in connection with the activities of Brutus and Cassius: at Rome, the sun was observed to change its size, from small to very large, and it once appeared at night. An altar of Jupiter was struck by lightning; meteors were seen. Sounds of trumpets and shouting and the crash of armaments shattered the

night air. A dog dragged another dog's dead body to the temple of Ceres, and buried it there. Strange births, of babies and animals, occurred. A ceremonial chariot of Minerva was destroyed, and a statue of Jupiter at the Alban Mount bled from its right hand and shoulder. Some rivers flowed backward.

In Macedonia, a swarm of bees encircled Cassius' camp; ominous irregularities occurred during the subsequent purification ceremony. Vultures and other carrion seeking birds flew over the camp, all the while screeching loudly. (Dio 47.40)

37   A statue of Calypso, or some similar goddess, broke out in a sweat, near Lake Avernus, while a harbor was under construction there. (Dio 48.50)

37   Dolphins fought and killed one another near the African coastal city of Aspis. A rain of blood was seen near Rome, and during the Ludi Romani, no senator sponsored a public banquet, a disquieting departure from tradition. An eagle dropped a white bird into Livia's lap; the bird bore a laurel branch in its mouth. This was taken to mean that Livia would hold the government of Rome in her lap, and in a sense usurp her husband's authority. (Dio 48.52)

36   A fish jumped out of the water near Sicily, and flopped onto the deck of one of Octavian's ships, landing at the feet of Octavian himself. The priests informed him that this omen indicated he would be master of the sea. (Dio 49.5)

32   Many pre–Actium omens were observed in this year and in 31. An ape made its way into the temple of Ceres during a religious ceremony; an owl flew from temple to temple, evading capture at all stops, until it finally perched in the temple of the Genius Populi, and did not leave until nearly the evening. Jupiter's chariot in the Circus Maximus was destroyed. A flaming torch was observed rising over the sea in the direction of Greece. Storms and fires damaged or destroyed many structures, including statues and bridges. In Sicily, a lava flow from Mount Aetna did considerable damage. Perhaps the most bizarre omen of all: a two-headed, 85-foot-long serpent materialized in Etruria. After ravaging the landscape there, it was struck by lightning and killed. And the most disheartening omen for Mark Antony: some Roman children spontaneously organized themselves into two

groups, the Antonians and the Caesarians, and fought a two-day mock battle. The Caesarians won. Finally, a marble statue of Mark Antony was observed oozing blood. (Dio 50.8)

31   A wolf was caught and killed in the temple of Fortune, and during a horse race in the Circus Maximus, a fight between two dogs broke out on the track. (Dio 50.10)

31   A number of pre–Actium omens disturbed Cleopatra: swallows were nesting near her tent; milk commingled with blood dripping from beeswax; statues of her and Antony on the Athenian acropolis were struck by lightning and shaken from their bases. (Dio 50.15)

30   Rome's destined rule over Egypt was foretold by these signs: water and blood fell from the sky in places where it had never before rained; these downpours were accompanied by falling armor. Spontaneous drum, cymbal, flute and trumpet sounds were heard, and a huge, loudly hissing snake suddenly materialized. Comets and ghosts appeared, and statues frowned. (Dio 51.18)

Appendix E: Birth and Death Dates of Noted Individuals

264–27 B.C., with brief biographical information, drawn primarily from the Oxford Classical Dictionary.

Livius Andronicus *c.*284–204: teacher; first writer of Latin comedy

Gnaeus Naevius *c.*270–200: epic poet

Marcus Claudius Marcellus before 268–208: consul (222, 215, 214, 210, 208); called the "Sword of Rome," for his aggressive leadership against Hannibal in the Second Punic War

Titus Maccius Plautus *c.*254–184: writer of comedies, noted in particular for his use of language and dialogue

Hannibal 247–183: the cunning and intractable leader of the Carthaginians during the Second Punic War

King Antiochus III ("the Great") *c.*242–187: conquered much of Armenia, Parthia and Bactria; defeated by the Romans at Thermopylae and Magnesia

Masinissa *c.*240–148: Numidian king, noted for his intelligence, creative diplomacy and physical strength; assisted the Romans at Zama (202)

Quintus Ennius 239–169: "father of Roman poetry"; playwright

King Philip V of Macedon 238–179: leader against Rome in the First Macedonian War

Publius Cornelius Scipio Africanus 236–184: consul (205, 194), a preeminent Roman leader in the Second Punic War, and vanquisher of Hannibal at Zama

Marcus Porcius Cato (Cato the Elder) 234–149: the famed "Censor" (184); consul (195), leading antiphilhellene; statesman, author

Titus Quinctius Flamininus *c.*227–174: consul (198); liberator of Greece; censor (189)

Marcus Pacuvius *c.*220–130: playwright; ranked by Cicero as the greatest Roman tragic poet

Caecilius Statius *c.*223–168: comic dramatist

Publius Terentius Afer (Terence) 194–159: comic playwright

Publius Cornelius Scipio Aemilianus 185–129: consul (147, 134), censor (142), military leader; founder of the Scipionic Circle

Panaetius *c.*185–110: Stoic philosopher who lived in Rome for a number of years

Gaius Lucilius 180–102: satirist; literary innovator

Attalus III of Pergamum *c.*170–133: bequeathed his kingdom to Rome, thus inadvertently triggering the violent events of 133, when Tiberius Gracchus proposed using the windfall to finance his land redistribution plan

Lucius Accius 170–90: literary historian and poet

Tiberius Sempronius Gracchus 163–133: tribune (133); crusading land reformer

Quintus Mucius Scaevola *c.*160–88: consul (117); lawyer, orator; called the "Augur"

Gaius Marius 157–86: military reformer; conqueror of Jugurtha; held seven consulships (107, 104–100, 86)

Manius Acilius Glabrio *c.*155–121: tribune (123), friend and fellow-tribune of G. Gracchus

Gaius Sempronius Gracchus 154–122: tribune (123, 122); proposed numerous reforms, ultimately leading to his violent death

Lucius Aelius Stilo Praeconinus *c.*154–74: scholar, grammarian, author

Lucius Licinius Crassus 140–91: one of the outstanding orators of his day; much praised by Cicero

Lucius Cornelius Sulla 139–78: leading general in the Social and Mithridatic Wars; consul (88, 80); dictator (81–79)

Publius Servilius Vatia 134–44: consul (79); censor (55)

Quintus Sertorius *c.*122–72: established a personal hegemony in Spain for much of the decade of the 70s

King Mithridates VI of Pontus 120–63: longtime Roman nemesis; ultimately defeated by Pompey the Great

Lucius Cornelius Sisenna 119–67: lawyer, historian

Lucius Licinius Lucullus *c.*118–56: consul (74); longtime foe of King Mithridates VI; epicure and patron of the arts

Marcus Terentius Varro 116–27: scholar, prolific author, librarian

Decimus Laberius *c.*115–43: writer of mimes

Marcus Pupius Piso Frugi Calpurnianus *c.*115–60: consul (61); orator, friend of Cicero

Quintus Hortensius 114–50: leading advocate of the early first century, until surpassed by Cicero

Marcus Licinius Crassus 112–53: consul (70, 55); proverbially wealthy

Gaius Marius 110–82: son of the seven-time consul

Titus Pomponius Atticus 110–32: Cicero's close friend, confidant and recipient of much of Cicero's correspondence

Marcus Tullius Cicero 106–43: consul (63); first century Rome's leading orator; prolific author

Gnaeus Pompeius Magnus (Pompey the Great) 106–48: consul (70, 55, 52); most respected and feared politician of his day, save for Caesar

Servius Sulpicius Rufus 105–43: consul (51); jurist, lawyer; Cicero's *Ninth Philippic* honors him

Tiro *c.*103–3: Cicero's trusted scribe and editorial assistant

Quintus Tullius Cicero 102–43: Marcus Cicero's younger brother

Marcus Valerius Messalla Niger c.102–50: consul (61); censor (55); lawyer; friend of Cicero

Gaius Julius Caesar 100–44: conqueror of Gaul; author; statesman; "most noble Roman of them all"

Cornelius Nepos *c.*100–25: first Roman biographical writer

Titus Labienus 100–45: Caesar's primary legate in Gaul

Marcus Valerius Messalla Rufus *c.*100–26: consul (53); author of books (no longer extant) on history and religion

Titus Lucretius Carus *c.*99–55: Epicurean philosopher; author of *De Rerum Natura*

Publius Nigidius Figulus 98–45: grammarian; dabbled in astrology and magic; friend of Cicero

Marcus Porcius Cato Uticensis (Cato the Younger) 95–46: great grandson of Cato the Elder; staunch defender of the Roman republic and an opponent of Caesar

Publius Clodius *c.*92–52: tribune (58) and intractable enemy of Cicero

Publius Ventidius *c.*89–38: military commander; defeated the Parthians in 39 and 38

Marcus Junius Brutus 85–42: most famous of the tyrannicides; author, friend of Cicero

Gaius Valerius Catullus 84–55: celebrated neoteric poet

Julia 83–54: Caesar's daughter

Publius Licinius Crassus *c.*83–53: son of the triumvir

Marcus Antonius (Mark Antony) 82–30: legate of Caesar in Gaul; hater of and hated by Cicero; Cleopatra's paramour

Gaius Licinius Calvus *c.*82–47: orator, poet

Publius Cornelius Dolabella c.80–43: consul (44); Cicero's not-beloved son-in-law

Gnaeus Pompeius 79–45: elder son of Pompey and Mucia Tertia

Tullia 79–45: Cicero's daughter

Gaius Asinius Pollio 75 B.C.–A.D. 4: consul (40); builder of Rome's first public library

Lucius Sempronius Atratinus 73 B.C.–A.D. 7: prosecutor in the Caelius case

Herod the Great c.73–4; king of Judaea

Publius Vergilius Maro (Vergil) 70–19: epic poet, author of *Aeneid* and other poetic works

Cleopatra VII 69–30: Egyptian queen; lover of Caesar and Mark Antony

Gaius Cornelius Gallus 69–26: poet, general, friend of Vergil

Sextus Pompeius c.67–36: son of Pompey the Great

Quintus Tullius Cicero 66–43: the orator's nephew

Quintus Horatius Flaccus (Horace) 65–8: Golden Age poet

Octavia c.64–11: older sister of Augustus

Marcus Valerius Messalla Corvinus 64 B.C.–A.D. 8: author, soldier, literary patron

Gaius Julius Hyginus 64 B.C.–A.D. 17: literary critic; librarian

Octavian (later Augustus) 63 B.C.–A.D. 14; first emperor

Marcus Vipsanius Agrippa 63–12: consul (37, 28, 27); engineered the defeat of Antony at Actium; Augustus' chief subordinate

Titus Livius (Livy) 59 B.C.–A.D. 17: historian; a major source for the Second Punic War

Albius Tibullus c.55–19: author of three books of poetry

Livia Drusilla c.53 B.C.–A.D. 29: wife of Octavian

Gaius Calpurnius Piso 48 B.C.–A.D. 32: consul (15); literary patron

Sextus Propertius c.47–2: author of four books of poetry

Caesarion 47–30: Cleopatra's oldest child; she claimed that Caesar was the father

Publius Ovidius Naso 43 B.C.–A.D. 17: poet; best known work: *Metamorphoses*

Marcus Claudius Marcellus 42–23: for whom Augustus' Theater of Marcellus was named

Julia 39 B.C.–A.D. 14: Augustus' daughter

Nero Claudius Drusus 38–9: Augustus' step-son

Antonia 36 B.C.–A.D. 37: Mark Antony's daughter

Appendix F: Roman Consuls: 264–44 B.C.

1. The following list is based on Broughton's monumental Magistrates of the Roman Republic.

2. An asterisk after a consul's name indicates that he died in office, unless stated otherwise. In all cases, the replacement consul(s) (suffectus, suffect) *is noted.*

3. The list extends only to 44 (instead of 27) due to the general instability that wracked the Republic after Caesar's death. Several years, especially in the 30s, saw multiple consular changes. (The year 33, for example, boasted no fewer than seven different consuls.)

264: Appius Claudius Caudex and Marcus Fulvius Flaccus
263: Manius Valerius Maximus Messalla and Manius Otacilius Crassus
262: Lucius Postumius Megellus and Quintus Mamilius Vitulus
261: Lucius Valerius Flaccus and Titus Otacilius Crassus
260: Gnaeus Cornelius Scipio Asina and Gaius Duilius
259: Lucius Cornelius Scipio and Gaius Aquillius Florus
258: Aulus Atilius Calatinus and Gaius Sulpicius Paterculus
257: Gaius Atilius Regulus and Gnaeus Cornelius Blasio
256: Lucius Manlius Vulso Longus and Quintus Caedicius*
     Suffect: Marcus Atilius Regulus
255: Servius Fulvius Paetinus Nobilior and Marcus Aemilius Paullus
254: Gnaeus Cornelius Scipio Asina and Aulus Atilius Calatinus
253: Gnaeus Servilius Caepio and Gaius Sempronius Blaesus
252: Gaius Aurelius Cotta and Publius Servilius Geminus
251: Lucius Caecilius Metellus and Gaius Furius Pacilus
250: Gaius Atilius Regulus and Lucius Manlius Vulso Longus
249: Publius Claudius Pulcher and Lucius Junius Pullus
248: Gaius Aurelius Cotta and Publius Servilius Geminus

247: Lucius Caecilius Metellus and Numerius Fabius Buteo
246: Manius Otacilius Crassus and Marcus Fabius Licinus
245: Marcus Fabius Buteo and Gaius Atilius Bulbus
244: Aulus Manlius Torquatus Atticus and Gaius Sempronius Blaesus
243: Gaius Fundanius Fundulus and Gaius Sulpicius Galus
242: Gaius Lutatius Catulus and Aulus Postumius Albinus
241: Aulus Manlius Torquatus Atticus and Quintus Lutatius Cerco
240: Gaius Claudius Centho and Marcus Sempronius Tuditanus
239: Gaius Mamilius Turrinus and Quintus Valerius Falto
238: Tiberius Sempronius Gracchus and Publius Valerius Falto
237: Lucius Cornelius Lentulus Caudinus and Quintus Fulvius Flaccus
236: Publius Cornelius Lentulus Caudinus and Gaius Licinius Varus
235: Titus Manlius Torquatus and Gaius Atilius Bulbus
234: Lucius Postumius Albinus and Spurius Carvilius Maximus
233: Quintus Fabius Maximus Cunctator and Manius Pomponius
        Matho
232: Marcus Aemilius Lepidus and Marcus Publicius Malleolus
231: Marcus Pomponius Matho and Gaius Papirius Maso
230: Marcus Aemilius Barbula and Marcus Junius Pera
229: Lucius Postumius Albinus and Gnaeus Fulvius Centumalus
228: Spurius Carvilius Maximus and Quintus Fabius Maximus
        Cunctator
227: Publius Valerius Flaccus and Marcus Atilius Regulus
226: Marcus Valerius Messalla and Lucius Apustius Fullo
225: Lucius Aemilius Papus and Gaius Atilius Regulus
224: Titus Manlius Torquatus and Quintus Fulvius Flaccus
223: Gaius Flaminius and Publius Furius Philus
222: Marcus Claudius Marcellus and Gnaeus Cornelius Scipio Calvus
221: Publius Cornelius Scipio Asina and Marcus Minucius Rufus
220: Marcus Valerius Laevinus and Quintus Mucius Scaevola
219: Lucius Aemilius Paullus and Marcus Livius Salinator
218: Publius Cornelius Scipio and Tiberius Sempronius Longus
217: Gnaeus Servilius Geminus and Gaius Flaminius*
        Suffect: Marcus Atilius Regulus
216: Gaius Terentius Varro and Lucius Aemilius Paullus
215: Lucius Postumius Albinus* and Tiberius Sempronius Gracchus
        Suffects: Marcus Claudius Marcellus (resigned); Quintus Fabius
        Maximus Cunctator
214: Quintus Fabius Maximus Cunctator and Marcus Claudius
        Marcellus

213: Quintus Fabius Maximus Cunctator and Tiberius Sempronius Gracchus

212: Quintus Fulvius Flaccus and Appius Claudius Pulcher

211: Gnaeus Fulvius Centumalus Maximus and Publius Sulpicius Galba Maximus

210: Marcus Claudius Marcellus and Marcus Valerius Laevinus

209: Quintus Fabius Maximus Cunctator and Quintus Fulvius Flaccus

208: Marcus Claudius Marcellus* and Titus Quinctius Crispinus*
Both consuls replaced by a dictator: Titus Manlius Torquatus

207: Gaius Claudius Nero and Marcus Livius Salinator

206: Lucius Veturius Philo and Quintus Caecilius Metellus

205: Publius Cornelius Scipio and Publius Licinius Crassus Dives

204: Marcus Cornelius Cethegus and Publius Sempronius Tuditanus

203: Gnaeus Servilius Caepio and Gaius Servilius Geminus

202: Marcus Servilius Pulex Geminus and Tiberius Claudius Nero

201: Gnaeus Cornelius Lentulus and Publius Aelius Paetus

200: Publius Sulpicius Galba Maximus and Gaius Aurelius Cotta

199: Lucius Cornelius Lentulus and Publius Villius Tappulus

198: Sextus Aelius Paetus Catus and Titus Quinctius Flamininus

197: Gaius Cornelius Cethegus and Quintus Minucius Rufus

196: Lucius Furius Purpurio and Marcus Claudius Marcellus

195: Lucius Valerius Flaccus and Marcus Porcius Cato

194: Publius Cornelius Scipio Africanus and Tiberius Sempronius Longus

193: Lucius Cornelius Merula and Quintus Minucius Thermus

192: Lucius Quinctius Flamininus and Gnaeus Domitius Ahenobarbus

191: Publius Cornelius Scipio Nasica and Manius Acilius Glabrio

190: Lucius Cornelius Scipio Asiagenus and Gaius Laelius

189: Marcus Fulvius Nobilior and Gnaeus Manlius Vulso

188: Marcus Valerius Messalla and Gaius Livius Salinator

187: Marcus Aemilius Lepidus and Gaius Flaminius

186: Spurius Postumius Albinus and Quintus Marcius Philippus

185: Appius Claudius Pulcher and Marcus Sempronius Tuditanus

184: Publius Claudius Pulcher and Lucius Porcius Licinus

183: Marcus Claudius Marcellus and Quintus Fabius Labeo

182: Gnaeus Baebius Tamphilus and Lucius Aemilius Paullus

181: Publius Cornelius Cethegus and Marcus Baebius Tamphilus

180: Aulus Postumius Albinus and Gaius Calpurnius Piso*
Suffect: Quintus Fulvius Flaccus

179: Quintus Fulvius Flaccus and Lucius Manlius Acidinus Fulvianus

178: Marcus Junius Brutus and Aulus Manlius Vulso
177: Gaius Claudius Pulcher and Tiberius Sempronius Gracchus
176: Gnaeus Cornelius Scipio Hispallus* and Quintus Petillius
    Spurinus
    Suffect: Gaius Valerius Laevinus
175: Publius Mucius Scaevola and Marcus Aemilius Lepidus
174: Spurius Postumius Albinus Paullulus and Quintus Mucius
    Scaevola
173: Lucius Postumius Albinus and Marcus Popillius Laenas
172: Gaius Popillius Laenas and Publius Aelius Ligus
171: Publius Licinius Crassus and Gaius Cassius Longinus
170: Aulus Hostilius Mancinus and Aulus Atilius Serranus
169: Quintus Marcius Philippus and Gnaeus Servilius Caepio
168: Lucius Aemilius Paullus and Gaius Licinius Crassus
167: Quintus Aelius Paetus and Marcus Junius Pennus
166: Marcus Claudius Marcellus and Gaius Sulpicius Gallus
165: Titus Manlius Torquatus and Gnaeus Octavius
164: Aulus Manlius Torquatus and Quintus Cassius Longinus
163: Tiberius Sempronius Gracchus and Manius Juventius Thalna
162: Publius Cornelius Scipio Nasica* and Gaius Marcius Figulus*
    Both consuls resigned; suffects: Publius Cornelius Lentulus and
    Gnaeus Domitius Ahenobarbus
161: Marcus Valerius Messalla and Gaius Fannius Strabo
160: Lucius Anicius Gallus and Marcus Cornelius Cethegus
159: Gnaeus Cornelius Dolabella and Marcus Fulvius Nobilior
158: Marcus Aemilius Lepidus and Gaius Popillius Laenas
157: Sextus Julius Caesar and Lucius Aurelius Orestes
156: Lucius Cornelius Lentulus Lupus and Gaius Marcius Figulus
155: Publius Cornelius Scipio Nasica and Marcus Claudius Marcellus
154: Quintus Opimius and Lucius Postumius Albinus*
    Suffect: Manius Acilius Glabrio
153: Quintus Fulvius Nobilior and Titus Annius Luscus
152: Marcus Claudius Marcellus and Lucius Valerius Flaccus
151: Lucius Licinius Lucullus and Aulus Postumius Albinus
150: Titus Quinctius Flamininus and Manius Acilius Balbus
149: Lucius Marcius Censorinus and Manius Manilius
148: Spurius Postumius Albinus Magnus and Lucius Calpurnius Piso
    Caesoninus
147: Publius Cornelius Scipio Aemilianus and Gaius Livius Drusus
146: Gnaeus Cornelius Lentulus and Lucius Mummius Achaicus

145: Quintus Fabius Maximus Aemilianus and Lucius Hostilius
   Mancinus
144: Servius Sulpicius Galba and Lucius Aurelius Cotta
143: Appius Claudius Pulcher and Quintus Caecilius Metellus
   Macedonicus
142: Lucius Caecilius Metellus Calvus and Quintus Fabius Maximus
   Servilianus
141: Gnaeus Servilius Caepio and Quintus Pompeius
140: Gaius Laelius and Quintus Servilius Caepio
139: Gnaeus Calpurnius Piso and Marcus Popillius Laenas
138: Publius Cornelius Scipio Nasica Serapio and Decimus Junius
   Brutus
137: Marcus Aemilius Lepidus Porcina and Gaius Hostilius Mancinus
136: Lucius Furius Philus and Sextus Atilius Serranus
135: Servius Fulvius Flaccus and Quintus Calpurnius Piso
134: Publius Cornelius Scipio Aemilianus and Gaius Fulvius Flaccus
133: Publius Mucius Scaevola and Lucius Calpurnius Piso Frugi
132: Publius Popillius Laenas and Publius Rupilius
131: Publius Licinius Dives Crassus Mucianus and Lucius Valerius
   Flaccus
130: Lucius Cornelius Lentulus* and Marcus Perperna
   Suffect: Appius Claudius Pulcher
129: Gaius Sempronius Tuditanus and Manius Aquillius
128: Gnaeus Octavius and Titus Annius Rufus
127: Lucius Cassius Longinus Ravilla and Lucius Cornelius Cinna
126: Marcus Aemilius Lepidus and Lucius Aurelius Orestes
125: Marcus Plautius Hypsaeus and Marcus Fulvius Flaccus
124: Gaius Cassius Longinus and Gaius Sextius Calvinus
123: Quintus Caecilius Metellus Baliaricus and Titus Quinctius
   Flamininus
122: Gnaeus Domitius Ahenobarbus and Gaius Fannius
121: Lucius Opimius and Quintus Fabius Maximus Allobrogicus
120: Publius Manilius and Gaius Papirius Carbo
119: Lucius Caecilius Metellus Delmaticus and Lucius Aurelius Cotta
118: Marcus Porcius Cato and Quintus Marcius Rex
117: Lucius Caecilius Metellus Diadematus and Quintus Mucius Scaevola
116: Gaius Licinius Geta and Quintus Fabius Maximus Eburnus
115: Marcus Aemilius Scaurus and Marcus Caecilius Metellus
114: Manius Acilius Balbus and Gaius Porcius Cato
113: Gaius Caecilius Metellus Caprarius and Gnaeus Papirius Carbo

112: Marcus Livius Drusus and Lucius Calpurnius Piso Caesoninus
111: Publius Cornelius Scipio Nasica Serapio* and Lucius Calpurnius
     Bestia
     No suffect listed in MRR
110: Marcus Minucius Rufus and Spurius Postumius Albinus
109: Quintus Caecilius Metellus Numidicus and Marcus Junius
     Silanus
108: Servius Sulpicius Galba and Lucius (or Quintus?) Hortensius*
     Suffect: Marcus Aurelius Scaurus
107: Lucius Cassius Longinus and Gaius Marius
106: Quintus Servilius Caepio and Gaius Atilius Serranus
105: Publius Rutilius Rufus and Gnaeus Mallius Maximus
104: Gaius Marius and Gaius Flavius Fimbria
103: Gaius Marius and Lucius Aurelius Orestes*
     No suffect listed
102: Gaius Marius and Quintus Lutatius Catulus
101: Gaius Marius and Manius Aquillius
100: Gaius Marius and Lucius Valerius Flaccus
 99: Marcus Antonius and Aulus Postumius Albinus
 98: Quintus Caecilius Metellus Nepos and Titus Didius
 97: Gnaeus Cornelius Lentulus and Publius Licinius Crassus
 96: Gnaeus Domitius Ahenobarbus and Gaius Cassius Longinus
 95: Lucius Licinius Crassus and Quintus Mucius Scaevola
 94: Gaius Coelius Caldus and Lucius Domitius Ahenobarbus
 93: Gaius Valerius Flaccus and Marcus Herennius
 92: Gaius Claudius Pulcher and Marcus Perperna
 91: Lucius Marcius Philippus and Sextus Julius Caesar
 90: Lucius Julius Caesar and Publius Rutilius Lupus*
     No suffect listed
 89: Gnaeus Pompeius Strabo and Lucius Porcius Cato*
     No suffect listed
 88: Lucius Cornelius Sulla and Quintus Pompeius Rufus
 87: Gnaeus Octavius* and Lucius Cornelius Cinna*
     Cinna expelled; Octavius killed. One suffect was chosen:
     Lucius Cornelius Merula
 86: Lucius Cornelius Cinna and Gaius Marius*
     Suffect: Lucius Valerius Flaccus
 85: Lucius Cornelius Cinna and Gnaeus Papirius Carbo
 84: Lucius Cornelius Cinna* and Gnaeus Papirius Carbo
     No suffect listed

83: Lucius Cornelius Scipio Asiagenus and Gaius Norbanus
82: Gaius Marius* and Gnaeus Papirius Carbo*
    Gaius Marius was the son of the seven-time consul; a dictator
    served in place of suffects: Lucius Cornelius Sulla
81: Marcus Tullius Decula and Gnaeus Cornelius Dolabella
80: Lucius Cornelius Sulla and Quintus Caecilius Metellus Pius
79: Publius Servilius Vatia Isauricus and Appius Claudius Pulcher
78: Marcus Aemilius Lepidus and Quintus Lutatius Catulus
77: Decimus Junius Brutus and Mam. Aemilius Lepidus Livianus
76: Gnaeus Octavius and Gaius Scribonius Curio
75: Lucius Octavius and Gaius Aurelius Cotta
74: Lucius Licinius Lucullus and Marcus Aurelius Cotta
73: Marcus Terentius Varro Lucullus and Gaius Cassius Longinus
72: Lucius Gellius Publicola and Gnaeus Cornelius Lentulus Clodianus
71: Publius Cornelius Lentulus Sura and Gnaeus Aufidius Orestes
70: Marcus Licinius Crassus and Gnaeus Pompeius Magnus (Pompey the
    Great)
69: Quintus Hortensius Hortalus and Quintus Caecilius Metellus
    Creticus
68: Lucius Caecilius Metellus* and Quintus Marcius Rex
    A certain Vatia became suffect, but he also died during the year;
    therefore, Marcius completed the year as sole consul.
67: Gaius Calpurnius Piso and Manius Acilius Glabrio
66: Manius Aemilius Lepidus and Lucius Volcatius Tullus
65: Lucius Aurelius Cotta and Lucius Manlius Torquatus
64: Lucius Julius Caesar and Gaius Marcius Figulus
63: Marcus Tullius Cicero and Gaius Antonius Hybrida
62: Decimus Junius Silanus and Lucius Licinius Murena
61: Marcus Pupius Piso Frugi Calpurnianus and Marcus Valerius
    Messalla Niger
60: Quintus Caecilius Metellus Celer and Lucius Afranius
59: Gaius Julius Caesar and Marcus Calpurnius Bibulus
58: Lucius Calpurnius Piso Caesoninus and Aulus Gabinius
57: Publius Cornelius Lentulus Spinther and Quintus Caecilius
    Metellus Nepos
56: Gnaeus Cornelius Lentulus Marcellinus and Lucius Marcius
    Philippus
55: Marcus Licinius Crassus and Gnaeus Pompeius Magnus (Pompey the
    Great)
54: Lucius Domitius Ahenobarbus and Appius Claudius Pulcher

53: Gnaeus Domitius Calvinus and Marcus Valerius Messalla Rufus
52: Gnaeus Pompeius Magnus (Pompey the Great) and Quintus Caecil-
     ius Metellus Pius
     Scipio (who held office for the last few months of the year only)
51: Servius Sulpicius Rufus and Marcus Claudius Marcellus
50: Lucius Aemilius Lepidus Paullus and Gaius Claudius Marcellus
49: Gaius Claudius Marcellus and Lucius Cornelius Lentulus Crus
48: Gaius Julius Caesar and Publius Servilius Isauricus
47: Quintus Fufius Calenus and Publius Vatinius
46: Gaius Julius Caesar and Marcus Aemilius Lepidus
45: Gaius Julius Caesar, the sole consul until resigning in October
     Suffects: Quintus Fabius Maximus* and Gaius Trebonius; Gaius
       Caninius Rebilus replaced Fabius Maximus
44: Gaius Julius Caesar* and Mark Antony
     Suffect: Publius Cornelius Dolabella

Bibliography of
Modern Sources

Austin, R.G. (ed.). *M. Tulli Ciceronis: Pro M. Caelio Oratio*, 3d ed., Oxford, 1960.

Balsdon, J.P.V.D. *Life and Leisure in Ancient Rome*. New York, 1969.

Bennett, C.E. *Horace: The Odes and Epodes*. New York, 1914.

Bieber, Margarete. *The History of the Greek and Roman Theater*. Princeton, 1961.

Boren, Henry C. *Roman Society*, 2d ed. Lexington, Mass., 1992.

Bowder, Diana (ed.). *Who Was Who in the Roman World 753 B.C.–A.D. 476*. Ithaca, N.Y., 1980.

Broughton, T.R.S. *The Magistrates of the Roman Republic* (Volumes I and II). New York, 1951–1952.

Cambridge Ancient History (Volume VIII): Rome and the Mediterranean 218–133 B.C., 2nd ed. Cambridge, England, 1954.

Cambridge Ancient History (Volume IX): The Roman Republic 133–44 B.C., 2nd ed. Cambridge, England, 1951.

Cambridge Ancient History (Volume X): The Augustan Empire 44 B.C.–A.D. 70, 2nd ed. Cambridge, England, 1952.

Cary, Earnest [sic], and Foster, Herbert Baldwin (trs.). *Dio's Roman History*. Cambridge, Mass., 1916.

_____ (tr.). *The Roman Antiquities of Dionysius of Halicarnassus*. Cambridge, Mass., 1937.

Cary, M. *History of Rome*, 2d ed. New York, 1954.

Cowell, F.R. *Cicero and the Roman Republic*. London, 1948.

Duff, J.W. *A Literary History of Rome from the Origins to the Close of the Golden Age*, 3d ed. New York, 1953.

Feder, Lillian. *Apollo Handbook of Classical Literature*. New York, 1964.

Gardner, R. *Cicero: Pro Caelio, De Provinciis Consularibus, Pro Balbo*. Cambridge, Mass., 1958.

_____ (tr.). *Cicero, the Speeches: Pro Sestio and In Vatinium*. Cambridge, Mass., 1958.

Grant, Michael. *Greek and Latin Authors: 800 B.C.–A.D. 1000*. New York, 1980.

Gruen, Erich. *The Last Generation of the Roman Republic*. Berkeley, 1974.

Harper's Dictionary of Classical Literature and Antiquities. New York, 1962.

Hendrickson, G. L. (tr.). *Cicero Brutus*. Cambridge, Mass., 1939.

Ker, Walter (tr.). *Cicero Phillipics.* Cambridge, Mass., 1926.

MacDonald, C. (tr.). *In Catilinam I–IV; Pro Murena; Pro Sulla; Pro Flacco.* Cambridge, Mass., 1977.

McKay, A.G. *Houses, Villas and Palaces in the Roman World.* Southampton, England, 1975.

MacKendrick, Paul. *The Mute Stones Speak.* New York, 1960.

Oxford Classical Dictionary, 2nd ed. Oxford, 1970.

Payne, Robert. *The Horizon Book of Ancient Rome.* New York, [no date].

_____. *The Roman Triumph.* New York, 1962.

Perrin, Bernadotte (tr.). *Plutarch's Lives.* Cambridge, Mass., 1984.

Rackham, H. *Pliny: Natural History.* Cambridge, Mass., 1940.

Rolfe, J.C. (tr.). *The Attic Nights of Aulus Gellius.* Cambridge, Mass., 1927.

_____ (tr.). *Cornelius Nepos.* Cambridge, Mass., 1929.

_____ (tr.). *Sallust.* Cambridge, Mass., 1921.

_____ (tr.). *Suetonius.* Cambridge, Mass., 1913.

Sabben-Clare, James. *Caesar and Roman Politics 60–50 B.C.* London, 1971.

Schlesinger, Alfred, and Evan Sage (trs.). *Livy.* Cambridge, Mass., 1951.

Scullard, H.H. *From the Gracchi to Nero.* London, 1963.

_____. *A History of the Roman World 753–146 B.C.,* 3d ed. New York, 1961.

Shipley, Frederick (tr.). *Velleius Paterculus: Compendium of Roman History.* Cambridge, Mass., 1924.

Stockton, David. *The Gracchi.* Oxford, 1979.

Talbert, Richard (ed.). *Atlas of Classical History.* New York, 1985.

Thornton, J.C., and M.J. Thornton. *Ovid's Selected Works.* New York, 1939.

Ward-Perkins, John. *Roman Architecture.* New York, 1977.

Warner, Rex. *Fall of the Roman Republic: Six Lives by Plutarch.* New York, 1958.

Watts, N.H. (tr.). *Cicero, the Speeches: Pro Archia Poeta; Post Reditum in Senatu; Post Reditum ad Quirites; De Domo Sua; De Haruspicum Responsis; Pro Plancio.* Cambridge, Mass., 1923.

Way, A.G. (tr.). *Caesar: Alexandrian African and Spanish Wars.* Cambridge, Mass., 1955.

Wheeler, Arthur (tr.). *Ovid: Tristia; Ex Ponto.* Cambridge, Mass., 1975.

White, Horace (tr.). *Appian's Roman History.* Cambridge, Mass., 1913.

Wiedemann, Thomas. *Emperors and Gladiators.* New York, 1992.

Williams, W. Glynn et al. (trs.). *Cicero: The Letters to His Brother Quintus.* Cambridge, Mass., 1954.

_____. *Letters to His Friends.* Cambridge, Mass., 1929.

Winstedt, E.O. (tr.). *Cicero: Letters to Atticus.* Cambridge, Mass., 1912.

Yavetz, Zwi. *Julius Caesar and His Public Image.* London, 1983.

Bibliography of Ancient Sources

Appian. *Civil Wars; Punic Wars; Spanish Wars.*
Augustus. *Res Gestae.*
Cicero, Marcus. *Brutus; De Divinatione; De Haruspicum Responsis; De Officiis; De Provinciis Consularibus; In Catilinan; In Verrem; Letters to Atticus; Letters to His Brother Quintus; Letters to His Friends; Philippics; Pro Archia; Pro Caelio; Pro Flacco; Pro Murena; Pro Sestio.*
Cicero, Quintus [?]. *A Handbook of Electioneering.*
Cornelius Nepos. *Lives of: Atticus; Hannibal.*
Dio Cassius. *History of Rome.*
Diodorus Siculus. *World History.*
Dionysius of Halicarnassus. *Roman Antiquities.*
Frontinus. *Stratagems.*
Gellius, Aulus. *Attic Nights.*
Horace. *Satires.*
Julius Obsequens. *Book of Prodigies.*
Livy. *From the City's Founding: A History of Rome.*
Pliny the Elder. *Natural History.*
Plutarch. *Lives of: Aemilius Paullus; Antony; Caesar; Cato the Younger; Cicero; Crassus; Gaius Gracchus; Tiberius Gracchus; Lucullus; Marius; Pompey; Sulla; Sertorius.*
Sallust. *Histories; War with Catiline.*
Seneca. *De Beneficiis.*
Strabo. *Geography.*
Suetonius. *Lives of: Augustus; Julius Caesar; Tiberius. Illustrious Men.*
Valleius Paterculus. *Compendium of Roman History.*

Index

This is primarily an index of names, although wars, battles and laws have also been included. Classicists and ancient historians have, curiously, never standardized a method for indexing tripartite Roman names; hence, Gaius Julius Caesar (for example) will appear under "J" (or "I") in some indices or reference books and under "C" in others.

In this index, most individuals bearing three names will be listed according to their cognomen (the third name). Examples are Gaius Julius Caesar, whose name, inverted, appears under "C," Marcus Fulvius Nobilior, entered under "N," and Gnaeus Domitius Ahenobarbus, under "A."

Exceptions: authors who are more widely known by their second name (nomen) than by the cognomen; hence, Quintus Horatius Flaccus (anglicized to "Horace") appears under "H.'" Other exceptions: Marcus Caelius Rufus (best known as "Caelius") is entered under "C"; all Fabii Maximi are under "F"; Aulus Cluentius Habitus is under "C"; Quintus Hortentius Hortalus is under "Hortensius."

Individuals with multiple cognomina are listed according to the first cognomen: Publius Cornelius Scipio Africanus, for example, is to be found under the letter "S." The entry appears thus: Scipio Africanus, Publius Cornelius.

In some cases, the same name is held by more than one person. (No fewer than five different consuls, for example, went by the name Marcus Claudius Marcellus.) In a few cases, it is difficult, perhaps impossible, to differentiate these individuals. Fortunately, most are distinguishable; to facilitate the identification process, the year(s) in which the individual held the consulship is provided with his name: Marcellus, Marcus Claudius (cos 222, 215, 214, 210, 208); Marcellus, Marcus Claudius (cos 50) etc.

T.R.S. Broughton's *The Magistrates of the Roman Republic* is indispensable in an indexing undertaking such as this, and it is to that superlative reference work that the compiler of an index must turn frequently for the final word on any questions pertaining to the identity or chronology of office holders in republican Rome.

The following abbreviations have been employed: cos (for consul); cos suff (consul suffectus); pm (pontifex maximus); qu (quaestor); pr (praetor); tr (tribune).